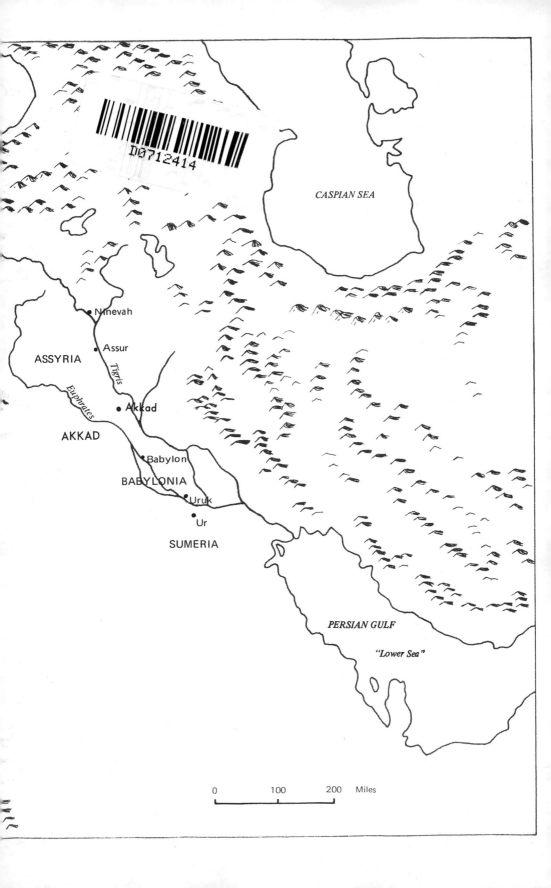

CASPIAN SEA

Ninevah

Assur

ASSYRIA

Tigris

Euphrates

Akkad

AKKAD

Babylon

BABYLONIA

Uruk

Ur

SUMERIA

PERSIAN GULF

"Lower Sea"

0   100   200   Miles

The Drunkenness of Noah

RABBI H. HIRSCH COHEN

A brilliant exegesis, whose insights derive from psychoanalysis, philology, and geology. The author relates both Noah's nakedness and drunkenness to the Lord's commandment to replenish the earth, and shows that both these aspects form an integral aftermath to the Flood story. The Flood, in turn, he relates to the eruption of Thera in the Mediterranean.

The scholarship is additionally innovative in that it leads to a repudiation of the documentary theory, once a prime test of most biblical scholars. Cohen's studies in Genesis reveal only one literary strand, not the three previously alleged. The closely related antediluvian and postdiluvian events manifest a hitherto unsuspected consistency that could have been achieved only by a single author using the historico-philological method of interpretation, Cohen educes this consistency and discovers the simple meaning of the text.

"The author makes a valuable contribution not only to Biblical studies but also to our understanding of the ancient Near East"—Rabbi Leon J. Weinberger.

The Drunkenness of Noah

by

H. Hirsch Cohen

THE UNIVERSITY OF ALABAMA PRESS

University, Alabama

Copyright © 1974 by
THE UNIVERSITY OF ALABAMA PRESS
ISBN 0–8173–6702–0
Library of Congress Catalog Card Number 73–54
All rights reserved
Judaic series jacket designed by Lee Bain

COPYRIGHT ACKNOWLEDGMENTS

For the use of selections from copyrighted material grateful acknowledgment is made to the following:

Atheneum Publishers and Longmans for quotations from *Two By Two* by D. Garnett, copyright © 1964 by Atheneum Publishers and Longmans. Used by permission of Atheneum Publishers, U.S.A. and The Longman Group, England.

Cambridge University Press for quotations from *The Origin of European Thought* by R. B. Onians, copyright © 1951 by The Syndics of the Cambridge University Press. Used by permission.

Doubleday and Co., Inc. for quotations from *Genesis,* Anchor Bible, vol. 1, by E. A. Speiser, copyright © 1964 by Doubleday and Co., Inc. Used by permission. For quotations from *Psalms I, 1–50,* Anchor Bible, vol. 16, by Mitchell Dahood, copyright © 1966 by Doubleday and Co., Inc. Used by permission.

Robert Gordis for quotations from *The Song of Songs* (New York, 1954, 1961, 1973), copyright © 1954 by Robert Gordis. Used by permission.

Harvard University Press for quotations from *Eumenides* by Aeschylus, copyright © 1930 by the President and Fellows of Harvard College. Used by permission. For the quotation from *Letters From The Earth* by Mark Twain, edited by Bernard DeVoto, copyright © 1962 by the President and Fellows of Harvard College. Used by permission.

The Jewish Publication Society of America for quotations from *The Jewish Publication Society Bible—The Holy Scriptures,* edited by M. L. Margolis et al., copyright © 1917 by The Jewish Publication Society of America. Used by permission. For quotations from *The Legends Of The Jews* by L. Ginzberg, copyright © 1909 by The Jewish Publication Society of America. Used by permission. For quotations from *The New Jewish Publication Society Bible—The Torah,* edited by H. M. Orlinsky et al., copyright © 1962 by The Jewish Publication Society of America. Used by Permission.

The Johns Hopkins Press for the quotation from *Archeology And The Religion Of Israel* by W. F. Albright, copyright © 1942 by The Johns Hopkins Press. Used by permission.

McGraw-Hill Book Co. for the quotation from *Lost Atlantis* by J. V. Luce, copyright © 1969 by McGraw-Hill Book Co., U.S.A., and Thames and Hudson Ltd., England. Used by permission.

National Council of the Churches of Christ in the U.S.A. for verses marked (RSV) from the *Revised Standard Version Bible,* Old Testament, copyright © 1952 by the Division of Christian Education, National Council of the Churches of Christ in the U.S.A. Used by permission.

The Pontifical Biblical Institute for quotations from "Traces of Assyrian Treaty Formulae in Deuteronomy" by M. Weinfeld, copyright © 1965 by *Biblica.* Used by permission.

Princeton University Press for selections from "Ugaritic Myths, Epics and Legends," translator H. Ginsberg; "Akkadian Myths and Epics," translator E. A. Speiser; and "Babylonian and Assyrian Historical Texts," translator A. Leo Oppenheim, in James B. Pritchard, *Ancient Near Eastern Texts Relating to the Old Testament,* third revised edition with

For Claudia, Debby, and Douglas

CONTENTS

PREFACE

The genesis of this book may be traced to a chance reading of Gaston Bachelard's *The Psychoanalysis of Fire*, a book that caught my attention with its intriguing title. Bachelard's analysis of the interaction between fire and alcohol on the psychic level acted as that "tiniest drop of the right kind" that Joseph Conrad, in his author's note to *The Secret Agent*, describes as precipitating the process of crystallization. What crystallized for me was the conviction that I had stumbled upon the one clue that eventually would lead to an explanation of Noah's drunkenness. The interpretations of the biblical scholars, which I presented to the students in my introductory Bible course, were inadequate because they never explained to my satisfaction why a man worthy enough to be saved from the waters of the Flood should be portrayed later as lying naked in a drunken stupor.

In the process of expanding upon this insight derived from Bachelard's book, I discovered that Noah's nakedness was directly related to his drunkenness; that both his drunkenness and his nakedness formed an integral aftermath of the Flood story; and that their full significance could be appreciated only by probing into the conditions that precipitated the Flood. I knew by then that I had uncovered considerably more than the proverbial tip of the iceberg—to follow these leads would mean not a paper for some journal on biblical studies but a book.

The realization that I had embarked upon writing a book on the Noah story filled me with no little trepidation. Not being a professional biblical scholar, I was entering an area that is generally off-limits to the amateur, even the well-read amateur. Even more alarming at the time, I knew that I had to repudiate the documentary theory, once a prime tenet of most biblical scholars. This hypothesis perceives evidence of more than one author of the Pentateuch. In Genesis it distinguishes three different literary strands: the Priestly source (P), the Yahwist (J), and the Elohist (E); these strands were woven together by a redactor, who evidently made no great effort to harmonize differences in fact or style between these three traditions. My studies in Genesis, even though limited to a relatively small portion of the book, reveal only one literary strand: the closely interrelated antediluvian and postdiluvian events manifest a hitherto unsuspected consistency of cause and effect that could be achieved only by a single author. In this respect I agree wholeheartedly with the late Professor Umberto Cassuto of the Hebrew University, Jerusalem that the book of Genesis is a single, unified composition, created according to plan from a multiplicity of traditions extant in ancient Israel.

My arguments, if cogent, could be most unsettling for those scholars who still subscribe to the documentary hypothesis. They will have to re-assay the criteria used to identify the strands of P, J, and E throughout the rest of the Pentateuch; for having erred in these few chapters of Genesis, they most likely repeated the same mistakes elsewhere. However, for many other scholars my repudiation of the documentary hypothesis most likely will spark no sharp reaction, because it will be viewed as one more argument in a lengthening series discrediting what was once, but is no longer, the foundation stone of most biblical exegesis.

I have used what may appear to be an excess of notes, if only to forestall any questions as to how I arrived at my conclusions. Where I make no acknowledgment, it is to be understood (unless I am guilty of an over-sight) that I am the originator of that statement or idea. I also inserted in a few notes recently published material that could not be incorporated easily into the body of the text. Though hardly complete, my bibliography will show that I have tried to cover most of the germane material published in English; I realize, however, that the information explosion has made it vir-tually impossible to keep up with all the reading produced in one's limited field, no matter what that field is. And the problem of finding enough hours in the day to do a proper job of researching—always a hopeless task—is compounded when one adopts, as I have, an interdisciplinary approach.

My debt to the scholarly community is incalculable. I have availed my-self of the results of the prodigious labors expended upon biblical studies, particularly by the philologists, whose work provided the basis for most of my novel translations in the Genesis stories. I am especially grateful to Umberto Cassuto and Richard Onians, emeritus Professor of Latin at the University of London. Cassuto's word-by-word commentary on the first thirteen chapters of Genesis is the most discerning I have come across—our differing interpretations notwithstanding. Not only did Cassuto explain away many of the so-called contradictions in fact and differences in style by disclosing an inner logic to Genesis, but, more importantly perhaps, he demonstrated by the historic-philological method of interpretation how to arrive at the simple meaning of the text. Others have used this approach but not with quite the same effectiveness. Onians, in his masterful presenta-tion of the system of beliefs about life, death, mind, soul, and body pre-vailing in the Greek and Roman worlds and the backgrounds of thought from which these beliefs developed, provided the key to an understanding of a number of biblical conceptions regarding cognition and the soul.

These insights have enabled me to utilize what E. H. Carr, the British historian, has called "imaginative understanding," which enables the historian to penetrate the thoughts behind the acts of the people with whom he is dealing. By means of this imaginative understanding, I have tried to put myself in the place of the narrator, given his particular apprehension of the world, and reason as he would have reasoned, realizing full well that as a product of my age I can view the past and achieve an understanding of the past only through the eyes of the present.

Except for the chapter where I show that the biblical description of the Flood accords with what happened historically in the Aegean Sea, nowhere else in the Noah story do I designate what should be regarded as having historical precedent; my primary purpose is not to differentiate in the context of the twentieth century between fact and myth. Rather, I am concerned solely with imaginatively reconstructing the reasoning that lay behind the biblical record, and for that reason I can accept without captiousness the details of the Genesis stories as statement of fact. For example, in my statement, "Noah was then six hundred years old," I accept the narrative fact regarding Noah's age as stated. Only then can I show that Noah's being six hundred years old was an integral factor in the narrator's reconstruction of the background to the Flood. Or, to cite another instance, when I write that Moses needed a glow, I infer this need from statements already accepted as fact in the narrative. In short, I have tried to illuminate and make intelligible the narrator's reasoning so that his story can be understood as he would have wanted it understood.

Perhaps my attempt at reconstructing these events in Genesis, as refracted through the mind of the narrator, amounts to no more than stringing cobwebs of theory over chasms of deplorably fragmentary data, to use the figure of speech of Professor Moshe Greenberg of the Hebrew University, but the effort had to be made; despite all the advances, "no insider," to quote Professor Greenberg, "need be told how far we are from understanding many of the most familiar passages of Hebrew narrative, not to speak of prophecy and poetry." Only after researching the Noah story did I realize just how far away an accurate translation of a number of familiar passages was. The different editions of the Bible give little or no hint of the uncertainty and surmise underlying their translations. Only in my comparison of translations from a representative selection of various editions available at the time does the uncertainty become obvious. And so, I have attempted to make some sense out of those passages in the Noah story that scholars have acknowledged as being too obscure or paradoxical—if only to bridge the gaps of data with a few more tenuous cobwebs of theory.

My book is relatively free of scholarly jousting—and deliberately so. I tried to stay clear of any systematic attempt to examine and rebut other interpretations because I was determined to address myself not only to the scholar, who certainly is conversant with argument and counterargument, but also to the educated layman who seeks to comprehend the totality of human endeavor. With culture rapidly becoming lost to us because knowledge has been fractioned into specialized fields accessible only to the expert, I wanted my book to extend beyond the narrow circle of the specialist to the nonprofessional, who, hopefully, would share my esteem for the genius of the biblical narrator. But to respond to the power and the magnificence of the narrator's stories, he would have to have a book that would sustain his interest and be easily understood. To introduce Genesis on a level where it would serve as this source of enlightenment to the knowledgeable layman carried a risk: I might so popularize my book that scholars could criticize it for lack of detailed explanation or documentation. In effect, my resolve to address myself to the nonprofessional meant that I had to walk a tightrope: on one hand I had to present sufficient evidence to satisfy the rigorous demands of scholarship, while on the other I had to avoid the technical language and professional jousting that could vitiate the interest of the layman. This balancing act could not be sustained. Try as I might, I often lost my footing on that fine dividing line due to the particular nature of my approach. My hypotheses rest primarily upon the new word meanings I have unearthed while following the weaving, twisting trail of related words. A step-by-step analysis of how I arrived at my definitions does not make for fast, easy reading, no matter how involved the reader may become in this exercise of philological sleuthing. And so, to offset this likely impediment, I excised a considerable amount of material from the main body of the text and put it in the notes; but even with this literary surgery a measure of perseverance still is required of the reader.

For those scholars and laymen who seek from the Bible a theological underpinning for their ecology campaign, the Noah story holds greater promise than any other section: a forceful case for the development of a theology of ecology can be made from the very conditions that precipitated the Flood. Furthermore, the biblically oriented theologians who accept my interpretations will have to change their opinion of the Hebrew God as depicted in the Flood story. The God of Genesis appears as a redeeming deity, more concerned with deliverance than punishment. Once the narrator's description of the physical, as well as moral, deterioration of the world is accepted, God is seen as intent upon preserving life on earth—paradoxical as this must sound to those who have been taught that God brought on the Deluge to punish man for his wickedness.

In my interpretation of the Noah story, I had no need to refer to the construction of the ark, the selection of wildlife, or the means used by Noah to measure the abatement of the waters; my hypotheses are complete as they stand. The reader who desires an in-depth treatment of these topics should read Cassuto, vol. 2, 55–114.

I have cited in my notes the Jewish source material in English translation, available in most synagogue or public libraries, to facilitate consultation for the reader without a background in Hebrew. The transliterated Hebrew words are enclosed in single quotes, their English meanings in double quotes.

ACKNOWLEDGMENTS

I wish to express my gratitude to Professor William Rosen of the University of Connecticut, Professor James A. Sanders of the Union Theological Seminary, and Dr. James W. Mavor, Jr., of the Woods Hole Oceanographic Institution, all of whom, while not being in complete agreement with all of my conclusions, encouraged me in my undertaking and graciously offered their suggestions.

I want to thank the librarians of the University of Connecticut and the Hartford Seminary Foundation for the use of their facilities. In particular I would like to express my appreciation to the staff of the Reference Department of the University of Connecticut Library for the courteous and efficient manner with which they handled my numerous requests for interlibrary loans and photocopies of articles.

Finally, I must mention the debt I owe my family. It is not enough to say that I am deeply grateful for the sacrifices they had to make so that I could have the time to write; the many hours of family activities that I could not share with them can never be restored. To say, then, that I am immeasurably grateful to my wife Claudia and to my children Debby and Douglas for their patient acceptance of adjustments that had to be made in our family routine, for their faith in the worthwhileness of my ideas, and for their encouragement is to attempt, inadequately at best, to find the words that will convey how profoundly indebted I am to them.

STORRS, CONNECTICUT   H. HIRSCH COHEN
1974

xi

KEY TO ABBREVIATIONS

ANET   Pritchard, J., ed. *Ancient Near Eastern Texts Relating to the Old Testament*

BASOR   *Bulletin of the American Schools of Oriental Research*

BDB   Brown, F.; Driver, S. R.; and Briggs, C. *A Hebrew and English Lexicon of the Old Testament*

BZ   *Biblische Zeitschrift*

Chicago   *The Complete Bible—An American Translation.* The University of Chicago Press

HUCA   *Hebrew Union College Annual*

JAOS   *Journal of the American Oriental Society*

Jastrow   Jastrow, M. *A Dictionary of the Targumim, the Talmud Babli and Yerushalmi, and the Midrashic Literature*

JBL   *Journal of Biblical Literature*

JJS   *Journal of Jewish Studies*

JNES   *Journal of Near Eastern Studies*

JPS   *The Holy Scriptures.* Jewish Publication Society of America, 1917

JSS   *Journal of Semitic Studies*

JTS   *Journal of Theological Studies*

NEB   *The New English Bible,* 1970

NJPS   *The New Jewish Publication Society Bible—The Torah,* 1962

PEQ   *Palestine Exploration Quarterly*

RSV   *The Revised Standard Version,* 1953

VT   *Vetus Testamentum*

TRANSLITERATION OF HEBREW

Hebrew Consonants

Character	Transliteration	Pronunciation	Character	Transliteration	Pronunciation
א	ʾ	(silent)	מ, final ם	m	m
בּ	bb	b	נ, final ן	n	n
	b (at beginning of word)	b	ס	s	s
ב	b	v	ע	ʿ	(silent)
ג	g	g	פּ	pp	p
ד	d	d		p (at beginning of word)	
ה	h	h (silent at end of word)	פ, final ף	p	f
ו	w	v	צ, final ץ	ṣ	ts
ז	z	z	ק	q	k
ח	ḥ	ḵ (guttural)	ר	r	r
ט	ṭ	t	שׂ	ś	s
י	y	y	שׁ	š	sh
כּ, final ך	kk	k	תּ	tt	t
כ, final ך	k	ḵ (guttural)		t (at beginning of word)	
ל	l	l	ת	t	t

Except for those consonants noted above, consonants with a dot (dagesh forte) are written double but retain the same pronunciation as when written single.

Hebrew Vowels (preceded by ג, g)

Character	Transliteration	Pronunciation	Character	Transliteration	Pronunciation
גָ	gā	gä	גֵ	gē	gā
גָּה	gâ	gä	גֵי	gê	gā
גֳ	gŏ	gä	גִ	gi	gi
גַ	ga	gä	גִי	gî	gē
גֲ	gă	gä	גֻ	gu	gü
גֶ	ge	ge	גוּ	gû	gü
גֱ	gĕ	ge	גֹ	gō	gō
גֶי	gè	ge	גוֹ	gô	gō
גְ	gᵉ	g			

These pronunciation symbols are found in the *Merriam-Webster Collegiate Dictionary.*

1

THE DRUNKENNESS OF NOAH

Noah, the tiller of the soil, was the
first to plant a vineyard. He drank
of the wine and became drunk. . . .

Exoneration and Condemnation

The arresting contrast between the antediluvian Noah, rescued from death
by his goodness, and the postdiluvian Noah, sprawled out in drunken disar-
ray, has provoked a running controversy over the centuries between the
apologists, who try to salvage Noah's reputation as the man "blameless in
his age," and the more kindly critics, who regard him as perhaps the best of
a degenerate lot.

In Noah's defense some rabbinic sages, possibly to exonerate God of any
charge of misjudgment of character, pictured Noah as an innocent dupe
ensnared by Satan's strategem to revenge himself upon God for having
exiled him to the earth below. Satan happened to come along when Noah
was planting the slip of vine. He proposed that they become partners in the
planting of a vineyard, and Noah agreed. Then Satan slaughtered in succession a lamb, a lion, a pig, and an ape; and with the blood of each he
manured the vines so that Noah, meek as a lamb when sober, would begin
boasting after a few drinks of a lion's strength, and after a few more would
lurch about like an ape, all the while exhibiting the slovenly habits of a pig.[1]

The *Zohar,* the medieval source book of Jewish mysticism, perceived
Noah as having been driven into a drunken stupor by his idealism. He
planted the vine, which was believed to have come from the Garden of
Eden, to better understand the sin of Adam so that he then could forewarn
the world of its effect.[2] The Church Fathers, Origen and Chrysostam,
also excused Noah for not knowing the full strength of wine.[3] In more
modern terms this portion of the Noah story is called an "inventor-saga,"
in which Noah, the first to learn the mystery of his new discovery, was com-
pletely-overwhelmed in the process by its unsuspected power.[4]

In his fresco in the Sistine Chapel, Michelangelo sympathetically depicted the drunkenness of Noah as the tragic confrontation between youth
and old age. The listless and aging body of the reclining Noah symbolized
the infirmity and weakness of age, while the athletic bodies of his sons were
the incarnations of youth in its prime.[5]

1

Not all, however, sought to exonerate Noah. In a talmudic discussion on the meaning of the biblical verse describing Noah as a "just man and perfect in his generations," one rabbinic sage interpreted the phrase, "in *his* generations," to mean that Noah could be described as righteous only when compared to the men of his wicked generation; in a more righteous age, he would not have been superior to the average person. Supporting this opinion, another rabbi compared Noah to a barrel of wine, which stored in a vault of acid would be fragrant by comparison with the acid; however, the same wine in another place would not be fragrant.[6]

Noah fared as poorly with Rashi, a renowned medieval rabbinical exegete, who evidently pondered the question as to why Noah, with all the varieties of plant life at his disposal, should have chosen to plant a vine supplying intoxicating drink. Unable to come up with a satisfactory defense of Noah's action, he concluded that Noah degraded himself by not planting something else.[7]

The most scathing criticism of Noah is to be found in the modern novel *Two By Two—A Story Of Survival,* a work originally conceived as a frivolous gloss on the Noah story and only later becoming a parable for our hydrogen-bomb world. In this book one of the twin stowaways on the ark had this to say about Noah:

> An obscure drunkard in a hick town in Palestine whom everyone laughed at, has his revenge on his neighbours, and becomes the sole progenitor of the world to be. You can't beat that.[8]

Later, her sister also condemned Noah:

> It's all Noah's doing. Even if God planned it, Noah could have refused to commit such an appalling crime. As it is, the flood has made him. No one would have heard of him without the flood. He was a quite unremarkable old man with bad habits: by drowning everyone else he has become the most important person in existence.[9]

This theme of Noah's notoriety is found much earlier in Mark Twain's *Letters From the Earth.* Far from depicting Noah as a fiend, who wanted the Flood so as to revenge himself upon his neighbors and achieve the fame heretofore denied him, Mark Twain concluded that fame came as a natural consequence of the Flood:

> The Ark is such a wonder to all the nations around that it has raised Father from obscurity to world-wide fame and Methuselah is jealous of that. At first, people used to say, "Noah?—pray who is Noah?"—but now they come miles to get his autograph. It makes Methuselah tired.[10]

Modern Exegetical Opinion

Though far removed from any theological obligation to safeguard God's reputation or Noah's, many contemporary biblical scholars, nevertheless, absolve God of any possible misjudgment of character and Noah of misbehavior simply by attributing the drunkenness to someone other than the noble patriarch. There is the righteous Noah, and there is the drunken Noah—two entirely different people who bear not the slightest relationship to one another. They simply come from two disparate traditions where the only thing they have in common is their name.[11]

This hypothesis hardly resolves the problem, for to say that the drunken Noah came from a tradition different from that of the righteous Noah raises the question of why in the first place the hero of the Flood ever became identified with the father of viniculture. What in the folk mind linked these two traditions together? If Noah is presumed to be the Hebrew adaptation of the hero of the Babylonian flood epic,[12] why would tradition have given him the same name as the inventor of viniculture? Simply to assert that two different traditions existed regarding the same man is to beg the question.

Since no convincing answers to these questions have been produced, I will proceed on the assumption that one (not two) tradition existed—that the story of Noah is a unity. On this premise, the text will be examined for evidence to explain why the righteous Noah lay drunk in his tent. The primary clue that hopefully will resolve this seemingly insoluble problem is found in the causative agent for Noah's impropriety—wine.

Wine and Sexuality in the East Mediterranean World

In the ancient East Mediterranean world wine was something more than a beverage gladdening the heart. For the Greeks wine, fire, and phallus formed a triad denoting sexuality. This association appears on a Grecian vase where on one side Dionysus stands, cantharus in hand, holding a vine of grapes, and on the other side sits Hephaestus on an ithyphallic ass. A wine pitcher hangs down from the ass's phallus. In other representations of the ass, either Hephaestus rides the ass, which has a wine pitcher on its phallus; or a naked woman, presumably a maenad, rides an ass with a wine pitcher on its phallus.[13]

Such scenes on the Grecian vases suggest "that the wine pitcher is where it is because the artist is indicating that in the symbolism wine and phallus are identical.... Wine, sex, and fire are one."[14] Even when these elements were reversed, the same relationship persisted. Thus, in another picture Dionysus, who is wine, rides upon the ithyphallic ass, from whose phallus hangs fire in the form of a lantern. Again, wine, sex, and fire are one.[15] In another, less detailed artifact the ithyphallic satyrs pluck and press the grapes and store the wine, while above them maenads and satyrs dance before Dionysus, who holds a drinking horn. The phalli point toward the grapes or the wine, signifying the phallicism and wine symbolism are complementary, if not identical.[16]

The Egyptians depicted iconographically the connection between sex and fire (light). In the tombs of Ramses VI (middle of the twelfth century B.C.E.) a large central figure with an erect phallus stands with his body and head in the heavens. A series of dotted lines runs from his body to the heavenly bodies and to twelve little figures holding out their hands to receive little red balls along these dotted lines. One of the dotted lines leads from the end of the phallus to a figure catching a red ball of light. The stream in this design represents at the same time fire and life, in the sense of birth.[17] This theme is repeated with the god Amon-Khem, who, with an erect phallus, grants life to the king, who bears a flaming censer. "The phallic nature of the sun-stream in the sense of a stream of fire is here produced in the notion of the seminal power of fire."[18] This symbolic equation between fire and phallicism led the Egyptians to picture the god Min as one who permeated the world with the torrential fire of his phallus.[19] Though wine is absent from these examples of Egyptian iconography, it was so closely connected with Greek representations of fire and sex that the Greeks assumed Osiris to be the Egyptian name for their wine god, Dionysus.[20]

The biblical *Song of Songs* reveals this same interrelation of wine, fire, and sex. In this poem extolling the physical basis of love, the lover compared his chosen one to a palm tree and declared his intention to climb its branches and enjoy its delights:

> How fair and how pleasant art thou, love,
>   with its delights!
> Thy form is like a palm tree,
> Thy breasts, like clusters of grapes.
> I said: "I will climb up into my palm tree,
> And take hold of its branches.
> Let thy breasts be as clusters of the vine,
> And the fragrance of thy face like apples,
> For thy kiss is like the finest wine
> That gives power to lovers,
> And stirs the lips of the sleepers with desire." (Song of Songs 7:7–10)[21]

Wine gave power to lovers, heightening their desire and enhancing their vigor for lovemaking. This idea then appeared in the reverie of the maiden, who wished her lover were her foster-brother:

> Would thou wert indeed my brother,
> Who had suckled at my mother's breasts!
> If I found thee outside, I could kiss thee;
> Yet no one would despise me.
> I would bring thee to my mother's house
> Who had taught me,
> I would give thee spiced wine to drink,
> The juice of pomegranates.
> His left hand would be beneath my head,
> And his right hand would embrace me.
> I would exclaim,
> "I adjure you, O daughters of Jerusalem:

> Why should you disturb or interrupt our love
> Until it is satiated?" (Song of Songs 8:1–4)[22]

In her fantasy the maiden would have brought her lover to her home, there to make love. As a prelude, she would have served him a spiced wine made from the juice of pomegranates, after which the lover would begin his lovemaking. This sequence of events seems to illustrate how wine's unique chemistry stirred the lover to make his passionate advances.

The imagery of fire emerges in the maiden's climactic avowal of love—a declaration so passionate that she described it as the "flame of God," a literary expression equivalent to "a mighty flame."[23] Unable to bear any separation from her lover, she pleaded to be as close to him as his seal, worn either as a ring or necklace:

> Set me as a seal upon thy heart,
> As a seal upon thine arm,
> For love is strong as death,
> Passion is unyielding as the grave.
> Its flashes are flashes of fire,
> A flame of God.
> Many waters can not extinguish love,
> Nor can the floods sweep it away.
> If a man gave all the wealth of his house
> In exchange for love,
> He would be laughed to scorn. (Song of Songs 8:6–7)[24]

Though far more restrained than the symbolism of Grecian or Egyptian art, the verbal imagery in the *Song of Songs* contained the elements of the triad—wine, fire, and sex.

This interrelationship between wine and sexuality also appears in the Hebrew word זְמוֹרָה, 'z^emôrāh,' "branch, twig."[25] But this was no ordinary branch, for in the book of Numbers it was specifically designated a branch of the vine by the cluster of grapes it bore:

> They reached the Valley of Eshcol, and there they cut down a branch with a single cluster of grapes. . . . (Num. 13:23, NJPS)

This vine branch, the symbol of wine, introduces the element of sexuality by the part it played in a fertility ritual connected with the Naʿaman (or Adonis) cult:

> . . . therefore you plant slips of Naʿaman and you sow it (with) the z^emora of a strange (god). In the day of your planting you hedge it in, and in the morning you make your seed to blossom; but the branches are consumed by fire in the day of destruction. (Isa. 17:10–11)[26]

The function of זְמוֹרָה, 'z^emôrāh,' in this fertility ritual is revealed in its postbiblical meaning of "phallus"[27] (a meaning also found in the cognate Arabic),[28] thereby supporting the hypothesis that the זְמוֹרָה,

'z⁺môrāh,' "vine branch," was used in the Naʿaman fertility ritual as a phallus.[29] This vine branch, combining the components of wine and sex, supports the evidence in the *Song of Songs* that wine in biblical thought was associated with sexuality.

The Seminal Power of Fire

The reason why wine, fire, and sex were symbolically interrelated in Greek, Egyptian, and Hebrew thought is found in primitive man's discovery of how to make fire. The usual rationalist explanation of how ancient man got the idea of producing fire by rubbing together two pieces of dry wood is to say that he must have observed how a forest fire was started with the rubbing together of branches. But this explanation must be rejected on the grounds that nothing in the phenomena of nature ever suggested to primitive man that fire could be created by this method. Not only had he never seen a forest fire start by the rubbing together of two branches, but he probably wandered for untold periods of time before seeing fire, whether in the form of an erupting volcano or a forest set afire by lightning. And even if he had seen fire in these forms, why should it be supposed that this creature, hardened against the rigors of the seasons, would have run forward to warm himself? More likely, he took flight, as frightened as most animals are at the sight of fire.[30] Accordingly, since the stimulus for primitive man's sustained rubbing of two pieces of dry wood did not come from the outside—from nature—it had to come from the inside— from his physiological and psychological responses to his own acts of rubbing. "The *objective* attempt to produce fire by rubbing is suggested by entirely intimate experiences. In any case, it is in this direction that the circuit between the phenomenon of fire and its reproduction is the shortest. The love act is the first scientific hypothesis about the objective reproduction of fire."[31] In the sexual act rubbing produced a pleasurable glow in primitive man. Externalizing this experience, he eventually reproduced the same glow by gently pushing a wooden stick through a groove till it ignited.[32] This procedure must have taken time and patience, but in the resultant fire he saw a manifestation of the glow he experienced in sexual release.

The belief that the blazing warmth of this fire compared with the warmth that accompanied a state of sexual excitation led primitive man to feel that he must have a similar fire within himself capable of producing this comparable glow.[33] At least, this seems to be the point of an Australian and a South American myth. In the Australian myth a man killed a totemic animal, believed to carry fire within its body. Examining the body to see how the animal made fire, or where it came from, the man pulled out the male organ of generation, cut it open, and found that it contained very red fire.[34] In the South American myth the hero pursued a woman to get fire. Seizing her, he forced her to reveal the secret of fire. After several evasions, she sat flat on the floor with legs wide apart; and taking hold of the upper part of her abdomen, she gave it such a shake that a ball of fire rolled out of the genital canal onto the floor.[35]

These myths reveal primitive man's belief that the glow he experienced in a sexual encounter, so similar to the warmth he felt before a fire, must have come from an identical fiery substance located in the male or female genital tract, the part of the anatomy where the warmth was felt most intensely. Here is seen the same idea as was experienced in the relatively sophisticated ancient Egyptian portrayal of little red balls as seminal fire, following along the dotted lines that led from the erect phallus of a god, and in the Grecian vase where the fire of a lantern hung on the phallus of the ithyphallic ass. The belief that fire was located in the genital tract was even shared by an eighteenth-century French physician whose theory of human fertilization based on fire as a generating force designated spermatic fluid as a "fiery substance."[36]

Since this seminal fire alone engendered life, it can be postulated that prescientific man would have sought to insure himself against its loss in the act of procreation. The problem of replenishing the fire that left the body through the genital tract was solved when in the course of time prehistoric man discovered a fiery substance that he could drink, thereby incorporating within his system the seminal fire he lost through intercourse.[37] That drink was alcohol. Prescientific man observed that alcohol quickly radiated heat from the pit of the stomach through the entire person; and, like the power contained in a spark or seed, it held great power within a small volume.[38] What is more, in the case of brandy, man witnessed how this "fire-water," which burned the tongue, could flame up before his eyes when ignited by a spark.[39] That ancient man attributed the special property of making "seminal fire" to a fiery drink can be inferred from the scene on the Grecian vase, in which the wine pitcher, symbolizing all alcoholic beverages, was substituted for the lantern on the ass's phallus. Here, the connection between the fiery drink and the genital tract is obvious.

Replenishment of the Earth's Population

The special powers ascribed to wine and other intoxicants require a drastic revision in popular opinion of Noah: in all likelihood his intoxication did not stem from any deficiency of character but from his wholehearted attempt to execute the command he received from God upon disembarking from the ark.

The narrator said that when Noah left the ark with his family and all the living creatures, he built an altar and there burned an offering. In acknowledging this act, God promised never again to destroy all life on earth. Then He blessed Noah and his sons with what must be regarded as more of a command than a blessing:

Be fertile and increase, and fill the earth. (Gen. 9:1, NJPS)

God was explicit: He wanted Noah and his sons to begin the job of replenishing the earth with the human species. The responsibility God placed
upon them was tremendous. They had to start repopulating a decimated
earth. But God's order was carried out only partially:

> These three were the sons of Noah, and
> from these the whole world branched out. (Gen. 9:19, NJPS)

This sentence, directly preceding the section dealing with the drunkenness
of Noah, should be regarded as a kind of paragraph heading to describe the
results of what would transpire in the verses to follow. In effect, it introduced
the subject of procreation with a summary of the results. Significantly,
Noah's name was missing. It said that the whole world branched out from
the three sons of Noah, not from *Noah* and his three sons. Noah failed
to carry out God's wish, even though the command to repopulate was given
to all four.

That Noah failed does not mean that he did not try to comply with God's
command. To the contrary, he made a stupendous effort. Perhaps he felt
that the effort was necessary because of his age—he was then six hundred
years old, and Sarah dismissed the idea of ever bearing a child due to her
advanced years and those of her husband Abraham.[40] Whether or not
Noah's advanced age did weigh upon his mind, he most likely approached
his task with one resolve: to be sure that his procreative ability was at its
maximum strength. To make certain, he would need wine—lots of it. Consequently, he planted a vineyard to produce that fiery substance so necessary
to increase his supply of seminal fire and thereby enhance his generative
capacity. What followed is learned from the text:

> . . . and he drank of the wine, and became
> drunk, and lay uncovered in his tent. (Gen. 9:21, RSV)

His determination to maintain his procreative ability at full strength resulted
in drinking himself into a state of helpless intoxication.

A rabbinic homily intuited Noah's objective to be that of having sexual
intercourse with his wife in its understanding of the word אָהֳלֹה, ''āhŏlōh,'
"in his tent." Because אָהֳלֹה, ''āhŏlōh,' has the consonantal ending
generally denoting the feminine gender, the rabbinic interpreter understood
the word as meaning "her tent," namely the tent of Noah's wife[41]—Noah
went to his wife's tent to cohabit with her.

The Drunkenness of Lot

Far more corroborative evidence for this explanation of Noah's drunkenness comes from the Bible itself, in the circumstances leading to the drunkenness of Lot and Uriah, the Hittite.

The drunkenness of Lot must be viewed against the background of the
destruction of Sodom and Gomorrah by sulphurous fire from the heavens.
Only four people escaped: Lot, his wife, and his two daughters. Fleeing

Sodom just before the holocaust, Lot and his family reached the town of Zoar, where Lot's wife was turned into a pillar of salt because she ignored the prohibition against gazing upon the scene of destruction.[42] Fearful that Zoar offered no safety, Lot and his daughters headed for the hill country and finally found refuge in a cave.

The theory may be postulated, in agreement with the rabbinic sages,[43] that Lot's older daughter, perhaps after surveying the vast, smoking scene of horror in the valley below, was convinced that the whole world had gone up in flames. The thought that she, her father, and her sister were the sole survivors in the entire world moved her to propose to her younger sister a desperate plan to save the human species from extinction:

> Our father is old, and there is not a man on earth to consort with us in the way of all the world. Come, let us make our father drink wine, and let us lie with him, that we may maintain life through our father. (Gen. 19:31–32, NJPS)

Espousing this plan of action, the daughters plied their father with wine until he drank himself into such a stupor that he was oblivious of the cohabitation that occurred between himself and his older daughter. The following night saw a repetition of the previous night's performance: Lot drank so much wine that he also was unaware of his sexual involvement with his younger daughter.

Lot's experience duplicated Noah's in a number of significant details. First, he too survived a disaster believed to be of cataclysmic proportions, with the result that he believed that he and his daughters were the sole survivors on earth. Second, he too was considered to be an old man at the time of his escape from the sulphurous fire. His age differed from Noah's in years, but not in degree. Third, he too became intoxicated to the point of stupefaction. Such close similarity of detail suggests that the factors resulting in Noah's drunkenness were the same that caused Lot's intoxication.

The Vindication of Lot and his Daughters

Branding Lot or his daughters as lustful, shameless creatures has been a reaction of both ancient and modern commentators to this episode of incest, although one of the talmudic sages sought to excuse Lot on the grounds that he was only partially conscious of his acts. Subtly arguing from the basis of the vocalization of the Hebrew word for "and when she arose," a rabbinic sage asserted that Lot, while unaware when his older daughter lay down with him, certainly knew when she arose. Yet, even this more lenient view was disputed when another sage contended that Lot, while unable to undo what had transpired with his older daughter, could have prevented a similar occurrence with his younger daughter by remaining sober. That he did nothing to prevent this from happening a second time exposes him to the charge of complicity.[44]

Another rabbinic commentator even accused Lot of lust when he observed that "whoever is aflame with adulterous desire is eventually fed with his own flesh."[45] In other words, he commits incest. Since Lot did commit incest, he indicated thereby how consuming must have been his adulterous desire to have been driven to such extremes. And two other sages, on the basis of their interpretation of a verse from Proverbs—"He that separateth himself seeketh desire" (8:1)—also concluded that Lot must have lusted after his daughters.[46]

Rashi, the renowned medieval exegete, held Lot's older daughter responsible for what transpired, reasoning that Scripture wanted to gloss over the sin of the younger daughter by simply saying that "she lay with *him*,"[47] and not that she lay with her *father*. This logic led to the conclusion that Scripture singled out the older daughter for condemnation as the initiator of the forbidden act by mentioning explicitly that "she lay with her *father*."[48]

Complete exoneration of Lot and his daughters is the compassionate judgment of a modern exegete: "The young women were concerned with the future of the race, and they were resolute enough to adopt the only desperate measure that appeared available. The father, moreover, was not a conscious party to the scheme. All of this adds up to praise rather than blame."[49] I concur in this appraisal, except that there was no scheme. It would seem, considering the power the ancients attributed to wine, that Lot was a conscious and cooperative party to his daughters' plan to perpetuate the race. Even if initially he was unaware of their "scheme," Lot would have known sooner or later that something was afoot once he became aware that his daughters were plying him with more wine than he was accustomed to drink. Certainly, he would have known that plying him with wine was not to celebrate the end of all human life on earth. That Lot, once alerted, did not refuse his daughters' requests that he drink more wine suggests that he knew very well why his daughters were plying him with alcohol: wine not only would increase his capacity to procreate—now so woefully diminished by his advanced years—but would at the same time arouse within him the desire to consummate the sexual act with his daughters. Equally concerned with the future of humanity as were his daughters, Lot seems to have acquiesced completely in their plan to provide him with sufficient stimulus and the seminal fire for impregnation. Quite possibly, his drunkenness attests to the difficulties he and his daughters believed they would encounter in bringing him up to peak condition for procreation.

Uriah—the Unaccommodating Husband

The story of David's hospitality toward Uriah, the husband of Bathsheba, corroborates the explanation of Lot's and Noah's drunkenness. After David learned from Bathsheba that he had impregnated her, he devised a plan to save her from the charge of adultery and the subsequent death penalty. He arranged to have Uriah recalled from the siege of Rabbah so that he would have intercourse with his wife while home on leave. Then, everyone would assume that Bathsheba had become pregnant during her husband's leave from the fighting front.

Unfortunately for Uriah, the scheme did not turn out quite as David had planned. When Uriah presented himself before his king, he was welcomed by David with these words:

> Go down to thy house, and wash thy feet. (II Sam. 11:8, JPS)

"Washing one's feet" in this context was a euphemism for having sexual intercourse. To David's surprise and chagrin, Uriah failed to heed his monarch's advice; instead, he stayed at the palace and slept that night among the servants.

Not to be thwarted, David pressed Uriah to tell him why he preferred to sleep among the royal servants instead of with his wife. Uriah replied that his military code of ethics forbade his going home and enjoying the pleasures of the marriage bed:

> The ark, and Israel, and Judah, abide in booths; and my lord Joab, and the servants of my lord, are encamped in the open field; shall I then go into my house, to eat and to drink, and to lie with my wife? as thou livest, and as thy soul liveth, I will not do this thing. (II Sam. 11:11, JPS)

His inflexibility on this point should have convinced David that all efforts to bring Uriah together with Bathsheba would be doomed to failure. But David persisted, for he still had not used the ultimate "persuader"—wine.

On the night before Uriah's departure for the battlefield, David plied him with wine to the point of intoxication. If David regarded wine as nothing more than a beverage to induce merriment and perhaps intoxication, he would have had little reason for pushing wine upon Uriah, for why should David care what Uriah ate or drank, once he realized that he rigidly opposed sleeping with his wife? In fact, David should have been so crushed with disappointment that he would have avoided this man, whose obstinacy wrecked his plan to save Bathsheba, instead of urging him on to greater merriment and intoxication. David's behavior becomes intelligible, however, once granted that he believed wine to be capable of stimulating a man's sexual desires as well as increasing his capacity for procreation. By plying Uriah with wine, he probably tried to quicken Uriah's desire for his wife to such a degree that he would repudiate his earlier resolve to stay away from her. David also might have wanted to push Uriah to the point of intoxication for another reason: his seminal potency would have been so great that people would have thought nothing unusual if Bathsheba had become pregnant after only one night's intercourse with her husband.

David's plan did not work out as he anticipated. Uriah, though drunk, evidently had not imbibed enough wine to suppress his inhibitions against committing the forbidden act. David might have plied him with more wine but perhaps refrained for fear that Uriah, like Noah, would fall asleep on the spot or might have been so out of touch with his surroundings that he would not have found his way to Bathsheba. Whatever the considerations for not pushing more wine upon Uriah, David's stratagem seemingly reveals the popular belief that wine could excite sexual desire and generate seminal capacity.[50]

The conditions leading to the drunkenness of Lot and Uriah corroborate the theory that Noah's intoxication resulted from his need to increase his procreative power and not from a weakness for alcohol or from any ignorance of the effects of alcohol. How ironic that he who hastened to obey the divine command calling for a replenishment of the earth's population should have to suffer the opprobrium attached to drunkenness. Noah deserves not censure but acclaim for having played so well the role of God's devoted servant.

2

THE NAKEDNESS OF NOAH

Inside the Tent

Speculation by biblical exegetes as to what happened to the drunken, naked Noah inside the tent has been whetted by the enigmatic statement that Noah, upon awakening from his stupor, "knew what his youngest son had done unto him" (Gen. 9:24, JPS). Apparently, more than Ham's voyeurism is involved, but precisely what is not amplified by the narrator. This paucity of information as to what occurred in the tent stimulated the ancient Jewish commentators to enlarge upon the story with the lurid details allegedly omitted by the narrator.

The rabbinic sages of the Midrash and Talmud generally agreed that Noah was castrated in the tent. In reconstructing the incident, some rabbis pictured Canaan, Ham's little son, entering the tent, looping a cord around his grandfather's exposed testicles, and castrating him by drawing it tight. Relating this gruesome deed to Shem and Japheth, Ham treated his father's castration as if it were a big joke.[1] Other rabbis maintained that Ham, not Canaan, unmanned his father, thereby causing Noah to cry out: "Now I cannot beget the fourth son whose children I would have ordered to serve you and your brothers! Therefore it must be Canaan, your first-born, whom they enslave."[2] But some sages denied that Ham was guilty of such foul play. Instead, they accused a lion of castrating Noah. As Noah disembarked from the ark, a sick lion struck his genitals with a swipe of his paw so that he never again could perform the marital act.[3]

Far from ridiculing these rabbinic commentaries as mere imaginative exercises, some modern scholars concur that much of the original story has been omitted and that the gap in the carelessly edited narrative may be filled by the midrashic account of his castration.[4] In fact, this episode has been related to the castration of Uranus by his son Cronos. Mother Earth, seeking revenge against Uranus for banishing the Cyclops to the Underworld, persuaded Cronos and his brother Titans to attack their father. Armed by Mother Earth with a flint sickle, Cronos surprised Uranus as he slept and castrated him.[5] The editors of Genesis, however,

13

were so horrified that a son could behave in this unfilial manner that "they suppressed Ham's castration of Noah altogether as the Greeks suppressed the myth of Cronos's castration until Christian times."[6]

Many modern scholars agree that the story of Noah and Ham bears the unmistakable signs of the biblical editor and would regard the episode of Noah's falling into a drunken stupor and his cursing Canaan as a connecting passage, linking the Yahwist (J) account of the Flood with his Table of Nations in chapter ten of Genesis.[7] This story then becomes a splinter from a more lengthy narrative, in which the roles of Ham and Canaan had to be "telescoped,"[8] and is apt to be puzzling precisely because it has to be laconic to bridge a gap.[9]

The questions modern scholarship has addressed itself to do reflect puzzlement. If Ham was guilty of some vile deed against his father, why did Noah direct his curse against Canaan? Why did the narrator speak of Ham as the youngest son, when the word order of the sons of Noah, which to most scholars seems to indicate their order of birth,[10] made Ham the second-born?

To these questions modern scholarship offers two possible answers. The view of many critics is that the passage derives from a different tradition, one in which either Ham or Canaan was cited as the third son of Noah.[11] The second theory is that the statement refers not to Noah's youngest son, but to Ham's, who is Canaan.[12] In such a case the loss or suppression of the details of what actually transpired between Ham and Canaan has resulted in this "disturbed" text. Clearly, the problem remains unsolved, with both views leaving much to be desired.[13]

Despite the apparent failure of ancient and modern exegetes to answer satisfactorily all the questions that have been raised, the problem seems capable of solution. To solve it, however, the assumption must be made that nothing has been suppressed or lost in its present form and that the narrator presented all the details necessary for a full understanding of the episode.

The Taboo of Looking

After hearing Ham relate that he had seen his father's nakedness, Shem and Japheth took a garment, walked backward into the tent to avoid gazing upon their father in his nakedness, and covered him.

> Their faces were turned away, and they
> did not see their father's nakedness. (Gen. 9:23, RSV)

Judging from what the text actually states, Ham's sin consisted solely of gazing upon the nakedness of his father. Shem and Japhet corroborate this conclusion by the measures they took. Had Ham castrated his father, as suggested by the rabbinic sages, the brothers most likely would have doctored their mutilated father rather than simply draping a garment over him. Yet, by mentioning that the sons did nothing more than cover their father, the narrator seems to imply that this measure was of sufficient assistance to Noah. That Shem and Japheth approached their father with their faces averted, perhaps to avoid repeating their brother's sin, strengthens the probability that Ham's offense lay in gazing upon his father's nakedness.

Looking was not the simple act for biblical man that it is today. It contained the potential of danger, as for example: God refusing the request of Moses to let him behold His Presence with the warning that "man may not see me and live" (Ex. 33:20, JPS); Manoah, father of Samson, after viewing the angel of the Lord, crying to his wife: "We shall surely die, because we have seen God" (Judg. 13:22, JPS); Elijah avoiding the sight of God by covering his face with his mantle;[14] Lot's wife turning into a pillar of salt upon viewing the destruction of Sodom and Gomorrah.[15]

From its study of the unconscious, psychoanalysis appreciably adds to an understanding of why biblical man regarded the act of looking as so perilous by asserting that looking implies identification. "If a man looks upon God face to face, something of the glory of God passes into him. It is this impious act, the likening of oneself to God, which is forbidden when man is forbidden to look at God."[16] As shall be seen later in this chapter, Lot and his company were forbidden to look upon the destruction of Sodom and Gomorrah for a reason closely akin to identification.

Though the ancients never heard of "identification," they intuited, judging from even these few examples, that there was something in the act of looking that closely resembled the psychoanalytic concept of identification; that is, by looking at someone, one could acquire his characteristics. In short, looking became an act of acquisition.

The Hebrew language itself reflects the concept that looking can be a means of acquisition in the number of words for "see, look" that are identical with or closely related to the words for "fence" or "wall." The fence, of course, symbolizes ownership; everyone recognizes that the enclosed object has been acquired at some time in the past and is owned by the person who has erected the fence. Biblical man went one step further: by relating the word for "looking" to the word for "fence," he acknowledged that something could be encompassed even without the visible signs of enclosure—the eye of the beholder could encompass everything within his radius of vision.[17] Accordingly, the words:

שׁוּר, 'šûr,' "look, behold, see"[18]
שׁוּר, 'šûr,' "wall"[19]

שׂוּךְ, 'śûk,' possibly related to שׂכה, 'śkh'; Syriac סכא, 'sk',' "see"[20]
שׂוּךְ, 'śûk,' "hedge in, fence in"[21]

לָקַח, 'lāqah,' "seize with the eye, ear, or mind"[22]
לָקַח, 'lāqah,' "take"[23]

Thus, the Hebrew language expresses the idea that looking can result in acquiring that which is viewed. It also occurs in English in the words "hold" and "behold."

Incidents involving Abraham and Moses offer further proof of the interrelationship between looking and acquiring. After God led Abraham to the land of Canaan, He instructed him to do the following:

> Raise your eyes and look out from where you are, to the north and south, to the east and west, for I give all the land you see to you and your offspring forever. (Gen. 13:14-15, NJPS)

Abraham, following these instructions, could claim ownership of Canaan; the land became his after he performed the ceremony of *looking* around in all four directions.[24]

God instructed Moses to do the same thing, even though under slightly different circumstances. When God refused Moses permission to "cross over and see the good land on the other side of the Jordan, that good hill country, and the Lebanon" (Deut. 3:25, NJPS), He nevertheless added:

> Go up to the summit of Pisgah and gaze about, to the west, the north, the south and the east. Look at it well, for you shall not go across yonder Jordan. (Deut. 3:27, NJPS)

Such precise instruction to look in all *four* directions ordinarily would seem odd if God simply were allowing Moses to survey the land that now was barred to him, but it becomes intelligible if the act of looking in all four directions is regarded as a formal act of acquisition. If God wanted merely to satisfy Moses' curiosity, He could have told him to look to the west, to the northwest, and to the southwest. But to require Moses to turn to the *east*, where the land of Canaan was *not*, signified a ritual of possession, whereby the leader of the Israelites lay claim to the land west of the Jordan. Corroboration of this theory may be found in the narrator's observation that when Moses died, his eyes were undimmed.[25] He mentioned the condition of Moses' eyesight possibly to anticipate the objection that since Moses could neither see clearly nor far-off, the claim of the Israelites to the land of Canaan should not be recognized.

Ham's Claim to Potency

Once the act of looking is acknowledged as a means of acquiring that which one sees, the reason why Ham came outside the tent to tell his brothers that he saw his father's nakedness is easily understood. Far from engaging in a deliberate attempt to besmirch his father's honor by making him the butt of his dirty mouthings, as some commentators contend, Ham seemingly was intent upon establishing a claim. He was telling his brothers that by looking upon his nude father, he thereby had acquired his father's potency!

To claim his father's potency would have to mean that Ham caught Noah in the act of procreation. The text, however, says nothing about Noah engaging in intercourse, only that Noah was drunk and naked inside his tent. Yet, from the information given, Noah evidently did have intercourse or intended having it.

This inference is based upon the description of Noah as אִישׁ הָאֲדָמָה, "'îš hā'ǎdāmāh,'[26] generally understood as "a tiller of the soil." This phrase, however, may be translated differently and, in this context, made to yield more sense. First, עוֹבֵד, "'ôbēd,' "worker, tiller," and not אִישׁ, "'îš,' "man," generally accompanies אֲדָמָה, "'ǎdāmāh,' "earth, soil," to convey the sense of tilling the soil. Second, אֲדָמָה, "'ǎdāmāh,' while used as "cultivated ground" also may mean "earth," in the sense of "world, globe."[27] Furthermore, granted the assumption that a qualifying word or phrase must be of sufficient importance to the story to merit its inclusion, what new element does the phrase "a man of the soil" convey about Noah? That he was a farmer, eminently successful in cultivating his vineyard, is learned in the next few words. That he was not the first farmer is known from the Garden of Eden story, where Adam already had achieved that distinction. This leaves, therefore, the more plausible translation: "the man of the earth."[28] Interpreted in this light, the phrase does introduce something new to the story. Since it can not imply that Noah was the *sole* survivor of the Flood, it must imply that he emerged from the ark as "the master of the earth."[29] After all, as master of the one family to escape the Deluge, Noah certainly qualified as "the master of the earth."

The narrator thereby established Noah's position as sovereign head of the earth for what follows in the sentence:

> Noah, the master of the earth,
> was the first to plant a vineyard. (Gen. 9:20)

Far from describing Noah as the first man to introduce the technique of viniculture, the narrator appears more concerned to explain that Noah, by virtue of the leadership and sovereignty implied in his title of "the master of the earth," exercised his prerogative in planting a vineyard *first*—ahead of his sons. Noah's designation as "master of the earth" determined his precedence in planting and later in drinking the wine of his harvest, the source of his seminal power. Therefore, Noah's title of "the master of the earth" established his right to be the first to begin the job of replenishing the earth.

The Significance of the Garment

With this background, the question raised by the exegetes can begin to be answered. Noah's nudity most likely had no direct connection with his being drunk; he neither uncovered himself because he was incapable of controlling his actions nor disrobed because he was hot from drinking so much wine. Rather, Noah's actions should be viewed as preliminary to sexual intercourse. First, he drank the wine to obtain the seminal potency necessary for the prodigious task of repopulating the earth. Once sufficiently "fortified," Noah uncovered himself before having sexual relations. At this point, the narrator seems to be averse to furnishing further details, since he does not proceed further along this subject. Though the text does not state that Ham caught his father in the act of intercourse, he must have been present throughout the act—until Noah fell asleep—peering from his hiding place to assimilate thereby his father's strength in his gloating stare.[30] Possessing part or all of his father's strength, he would become thereby the most powerful of the sons and consequently would stand to inherit the mantle of leadership on Noah's death.

In this story some likeness to the theme of the Kronos myth, but without the savagery of castration, is discernable in the light of analytic psychology. According to one interpretation, Uranus, the father of Kronos, sensing that the ascendency of his sons would effect his decline and displacement, clung to his generative powers and refused to impart them to his sons. Kronos, intent upon procuring these generative powers, castrated his father in a desperate act to attain manhood.[31] In the biblical drama, however, the means of seizing potency and power was not by a physical attack upon the father but by a look. From what can be inferred about the narrator's attitude toward those blessed by God, it is unthinkable that the narrator would want to give the impression that such savagery was perpetrated upon the one deemed worthy by God to survive the Flood. Consequently, Ham had to tell his brothers what he saw so that they in turn would acknowledge and legitimate his claim to power and leadership. But with such a prize at stake, what if Shem and Japheth refused to believe a brother who had dared to intrude upon the prohibited? If he had no shame, might he not also have lied to achieve his goal? These considerations might well have flashed through Ham's mind, for he then furnished uncontestable proof to make his claim to leadership creditable and binding upon them.

In two other incidents in Genesis irrefutable proof was required to supplement the verbal report. In the first, Joseph's brothers had to present tangible proof of his tragic end to convince their father that he was dead and to prevent their being held responsible for his death.[32] Otherwise, Jacob could have charged them with negligence of the brother he entrusted to their care. Mindful of this possibility, the brothers produced Joseph's "blood-stained" garment, proof that Joseph was devoured by a wild beast, so that they could not be charged with negligence on the basis of the law in Exodus:

> If it [the animal] was torn by beasts, he shall bring it as evidence; he need not replace what has been torn by beasts. (Ex. 22:12, NJPS)

As "shepherds" for their brother, they proved by his torn, blood-soaked garment that he fell victim to a wild beast through no fault of their own. Obviously, in so grave a matter as the death of a brother, they realized that any verbal protestation of innocence would not be enough. They would have to produce the kind of proof that would wring from Jacob an admission that they were not liable for penalties.

The other celebrated case requiring evidence to substantiate oral testimony involved Joseph and Potiphar's wife. Evidently, this woman had to show Joseph's garment (his undergarment?) to her servants and later to her husband to verify her charge that Joseph attempted to rape her.[33] Had not Joseph so ingratiated himself with her husband, she might not have had to produce the circumstantial evidence supporting her accusation.

In light of these two incidents, oral testimony had to be supported with hard proof; it seems reasonable to infer that Ham had to do something more than tell his brothers what he saw—he had to prove it. But how? With a piece of evidence that no one could controvert: the one item of clothing that Noah had to take off preliminary to intercourse. That Ham produced this garment is shown in the following verse:

> Then Shem and Japeth took a garment, laid it upon both their shoulders, and walked backward and covered their father's nakedness. . . . (Gen. 9:23)[34]

This translation is rendered satisfactorily except for one word—the *key* word: instead of "*a* garment," read "*the* garment," for the definite article, ה, 'ha,' "the," is prefixed to "garment." Though in some instances in the Bible the definite article expresses a general definition, the definite article in this case designates, as it usually does, something specific—in this instance, a particular item of clothing. That specific garment could have belonged to no other than Noah. Reconstructing the scene, Ham must have skirted the sleeping, naked Noah, picked up his father's garment that had been cast aside, and stepped outside to show "*the* garment" to his brothers.

Protection against the Infection of Weakness

The theory that the garment with which Shem and Japheth covered their father was really Noah's is supported by the reaction of Shem and Japheth to Ham's announcement. They believed it immediately and completely. Nowhere is found a hint of doubt. Had they the slightest reservation, they might have questioned Ham in much the same manner Isaac questioned Jacob when he disguised himself as Esau. Or they might have peered inside the tent to verify Ham's report. Instead, there were no probing questions and no peeking—just immediate acquiescence. Belief in Ham's report, particularly when the role of leader was at stake, only could have been caused by the shock they received when Ham produced their father's garment as proof of what he saw. The brothers acknowledged the veracity of Ham's report by taking the garment from him, walking backwards, and covering their father.

The brothers have been praised for the respect they paid their father by walking backward with the garment on their shoulders. No matter that Ham looked upon his father's nakedness; Shem and Japheth scrupulously avoided doing so. In view of what has been said about the consequence of looking, is it so certain that respect for their father was the sole consideration for walking backwards into the tent? The actions of some characters in a Hittite myth suggest that Shem and Japheth acted more out of fear than respect. They probably feared being "infected" by their father's debility.

In the Hittite myth[35] the Dragon fought the weather god and vanquished him; whereupon the goddess Inaras asked the mortal Hupasiyas to subdue the Dragon. Hupasiyas consented on the condition that he have intercourse with her. Inaras fulfilled his request and afterwards concealed him in her house. Then Inaras, clad in all her finery, invited the Dragon to a banquet in his honor. Up from his hole came the Dragon with his crew to attend the banquet. So gluttonously did they eat that when they finished, they discovered they could not get back into their hole. At this point Hupasiyas stepped out of his place of concealment, bound the Dragon with a rope, and presented him to the weather god to be slain. Even though the Dragon was now dead, Inaras did not allow the mortal Hupasiyas to return to his family; instead, she settled him in a house she built on a crag. Before leaving the house, Inaras instructed Hupasiyas not to look out of the window, lest he see his wife and children. On the twentieth day of his internment Hupasiyas disobeyed instructions: gazing out of the window he caught sight of his wife and children. When Inaras finally returned from her excursions, Hupasiyas greeted her by whining for permission to return to his home. Surmising that his request was prompted by what he saw from the window, Inaras demolished the house and Hupasiyas with it.

The interrelationship between the stipulation of Hupasiyas that he sleep with the goddess and the order prohibiting Hupasiyas from looking out of the window, lest he see his family, is impressive. Hupasiyas's insistence that he first have intercourse with the goddess was not to gratify any sexual desire but to acquire through this magical means the necessary superhuman strength to combat the Dragon. Among primitive peoples the widespread belief exists that personal characteristics can be transmitted and acquired through sexual intercourse.[36] The prohibition forbidding Hupasiyas from looking upon his wife and children developed as a corollary to the belief that superhuman strength was acquired from copulation with the goddess; for, just as contact with the strong confers strength upon the weaker, so contact with the weak confers weakness upon the strong.[37] Uriah's refusal to sleep with his wife might well have stemmed from his belief that a warrior's physical contact with a woman could drain away his strength.[38] Further—now the reason for the prohibition—not only physical contact but the very *sight* of a woman could cause debility.[39] Hence, Hupasiyas was incarcerated on an inaccessible cliff and prohibited from seeing his wife to prevent impairment or transmission to mortals of the divine "essence" that he received through intercourse with the goddess Inaras.[40]

That the sight of someone or something impaired or spoiled can affect adversely a witness to the injury or impairment would explain why Lot and his family were instructed not to turn around and gaze upon the destruction of Sodom and Gomorrah. Seemingly, the narrator believed that were they to do so, they would be stricken by the sight of the supernatural destructive power at work just as surely as though they were back in Sodom, in the midst of the holocaust. Presumably, then, the warning to Lot and his family was given to protect them from the deadly peril of exposing themselves to an annihilating force, particularly when it came from God. Consequently, Lot's wife was not turned into a pillar of salt because she disobeyed the order not to turn around and look at the burning plain, but because she visually absorbed into her body the lethal force of the sulphurous fire, which rained down from the heavens.

The concept contained in the Hittite myth and in the story of the death of Lot's wife presents the behavior of Shem and Japheth toward their father from an entirely different aspect. Instead of showing respect for Noah, the brothers, by regarding their father as irreparably weakened, evidently sought to protect themselves against possible "infection" by walking backwards to avoid looking at him. Evidently the narrator regarded this matter of possible infection as highly significant, for he stressed the fact that Shem and Japheth could not possibly have seen their father's "weakness":

> . . . their faces were turned the other way, so that they did not see their father's nakedness. (Gen. 9:23, NJPS)

Perhaps Noah's "weakness" was the reason why he failed to beget any more children, despite the seminal fire he absorbed from the wine: his generative power, once having been appropriated by Ham's voyeurism, was too weakened thereafter to function.

Perception in Greek Thought

And now the denouement:

> And Noah awoke from his wine, and knew what his youngest son had done unto him. (Gen. 9:24, JPS)[41]

The text says nothing about Shem and Japheth informing their father of what happened to him while he lay in his stupor. They did not do so because there was no need to tell him. He already knew—without being informed by anyone! Such a phenomenon becomes credible once the ancients' conceptions regarding sense perception are understood. To gain this enlightenment, examples from ancient Greek literature illustrate how the Greeks understood the functional details of perception.

The Greeks located the seat of consciousness in the 'phrenes,' "lungs," and in the 'thymos,'[42] "the vital principle that thinks and feels and prompts to action."[43] The 'thymos' itself was the breath, vaporous and occasionally visible,[44] that moved about in the passage of the lungs and was conditioned by them. The Homeric Greeks had a richer concept of "breath" than that which is regarded as the inhaled and exhaled outer air.[45] To them breath was warm and moist from the body's water-vapor, which visibly condenses upon meeting a bright surface or cooler air.[46] The vapor came from the blood, which in turn was thought of as a hot liquid concentrated in the heart and in the lungs.[47] "This 'thymos' is not the blood-soul as opposed to the breath-soul nor indeed mere breath but breath related to blood, not mere air but something vaporous within, blending and interacting with the air without, something which diminishes if the body is ill nourished, but is increased when the body is well nourished."[48]

Consciousness was identified with breath because (1) being conscious was to have breath, and (2) breathing and blood flow were affected by any emotional upheaval. The Homeric Greeks considered the 'thymos' as the "spirit," the breath that was consciousness, variable, dynamic, changing as feeling and thought change.[49] Thought and feeling were as inextricably linked together then as they are today, except that the Greeks believed feeling and thought to be the work of the lungs.[50] Thus, Euripides wrote of "to breathe big breaths" as a way of expressing to be high-spirited, to have high thoughts.[51] And Homer could have the gods "breathe" thoughts into man, since he thought and felt with his breath-soul and lungs.[52] Man, in turn, could breathe thoughts out as well as absorb them from the gods.[53] His speeches came forth with the breath of intelligence in them; the listener breathed them into his 'thymos,' thus adding to his store of knowledge.[54] With thoughts as words and words as breath, the Greeks concluded that the organs of breath, the lungs, were the organs of the mind.[55]

Notwithstanding the location of the eyes and ears in the head, Homer believed that words were perceived and received by the lungs.[56] Anatomically, this relationship between perception and the lungs is not as far-fetched as it may appear, for within the head there is a passage where the outer air passes through the ear to the pharynx to the lungs.[57]

But what is more, Homer believed that the lungs were capable of seeing: one "sees in one's 'phrenes' or 'lungs.'"[58] Seeing delighted the lungs and was the work of the 'thymos' or breath.[59] Quite possibly in this construct, what was received through the eyes was breathed from the objects seen.[60] In the Homeric hymn to Demeter, beauty was breathed around the goddess, suggesting that beauty was breathed in through the eyes from objects.[61] This phenomenon would explain why in Aeolic "to breathe at" means "to look at."[62]

Finally, the 'thymos' received perceptions from the skin,[63] meaning that it was not confined to the chest and the passages to the eyes, ears, nose, and mouth. Homer speaks of the 'thymos' leaving the "limbs, members" of a dead body, indicating that the arteries, which after death were found empty and dilated, were believed to contain this "breath" and that the pores in the skin were "passages" inwards.[64]

Against this background of cognition, sleep was thought to be a liquid, mist, or moist vapor poured upon the eyelids and 'phrenes,' "lungs."[65]

Wine was believed to subdue and possibly damage a person's 'phrenes,' "lungs," causing them to become inefficient when moist with wine or sleep.[66] Dryness, accordingly, was the equivalent of alertness and sobriety.[67] For Diogenes, intelligence and understanding were the work of dry and pure air;[68] and for Ennuis, awakening from sleep to normal consciousness was a "drying" process.[69]

Most significant for this investigation was the belief that consciousness could recede under the influence of sleep or wine, yet never be extinguished; for, paradoxically, wine was thought to have a stimulating effect upon the cognitive process. Since any liquid went to the lungs and since 'thymos' was vapor from liquid, prophetic inspiration was sought by drinking blood, water, honey, or wine or by inhaling its vapor.[70] And even when the passages of the senses were closed in sleep, the mind still retained consciousness of its environment through the breath.[71] Thus, in *Eumenides* Aeschylus declared that the recipient consciousness had knowledge upon waking:

> Ghost of Clytaemnestra:
>   "Mark ye these gashes in my heart, whence
>   they come!
> For the mind asleep hath clear vision,
>   but in daytime
> the fate of mortal men cannot be foreseen."[72]

Belief in the "evil Eye" was based on the conception that breath bore perception to the seat of consciousness. Accordingly, Calasiris wrote:

This air which surrounds us penetrates through eyes and nostrils and mouth and the other passages into the depths of the body and takes with it its qualities from outside, and it sows in those who receive it "pathos" of the quality with which it flows in. Accordingly, when anyone looks with envy at what is noble, he fills the surrounding atmosphere with a quality of hate and blows the breath from himself full of bitterness into him that is near.[73]

Because the 'thymos' could carry either the noxious or beneficial qualities of the outside in breath to the 'phrenes' (the seat of consciousness) of a person asleep or intoxicated, Homer concluded that one "sees in one's 'phrenes' or lungs."

This brief résumé of what the Homeric Greeks believed about sense perceptions and consciousness provides the key to an understanding of how Noah could have declared upon awakening from his drunken stupor that he *knew* what Ham had done. Using the above concepts of cognition, the hypothesis can be made that Noah was made aware of what was happening by his 'thymos' even though his 'phrenes,' "lungs," were wet with sleep and wine. Noah's consciousness had not receded to the point where it was totally extinguished; his breathing carried to his 'phrenes' this "clear vision" of what Aeschylus knew to be possessed by the mind asleep. Further, Ham exuded his evil design, permeating the atmosphere and penetrating Noah's orifices, where it was brought by his 'thymos' to his 'phrenes,' the seat of consciousness and cognition. When Noah awoke from his wine, he accordingly knew precisely what his youngest son had done to him and why.

Lest this explanation be rejected on the grounds that the Homeric Greek concepts of 'thymos' and 'phrenes' were foreign to biblical thought, another episode in Genesis shows the Hebrew נֶפֶשׁ, 'nepeš,' to be the equivalent of the Greek 'thymos.'

The Concept of נֶפֶשׁ, 'nepeš,' in the Isaac-Jacob Stories

In the episode where Jacob disguised himself as Esau to secure the blessing of his blind and aged father, Isaac told Esau, his older son, to go into the fields and hunt venison:

> . . . and make me savoury food, such as I love, and bring it to me, that I may eat; that my soul may bless thee before I die. (Gen. 27:4, JPS)[74]

Isaac's request to Esau to hunt venison and prepare a festive dish to his liking has occasioned the superficial judgment that Isaac thought only of his stomach,[75] even to the end of his days. But was Isaac really so gastronomically centered that he had to eat of the delicacies that tickled his palate in his younger days before he would even consider the more serious business of making a death-bed deposition of his possessions?

The answer to this question lies in the Greek concept of the 'thymos.' The Greeks regarded a person wasting away physically or in spirit as melting, dissolving, or wasting away his 'thymos,' or eating it by consuming "the vapour that is the final product of food and is the stuff of consciousness, spirit."[76] Circe asked why Odysseus sat like a dumb one, eating his 'thymos' instead of eating his food and drink. Elsewhere in the Iliad, the heart or the lungs, which contained the 'thymos,' were said to be "eaten" or "wasted" (diminished).[77] Homer believed that the 'thymos,' this stuff of consciousness, actually diminished in a body that was undernourished. Finally, the Greeks believed that the dying imparted the 'thymos' to the next of kin by a kiss.[78] With the last breath the agent that produced breath departed the body; if there was no one to receive it, it was likely to perish.

These characteristics of the 'thymos,' when applied to the Isaac-Jacob episode, elucidate details that hitherto have escaped notice or have been misconstrued. In all likelihood, Isaac, aware that his days were fast drawing to a close, decided to impart the essence of his נֶפֶשׁ, 'nepeš,' to his older son. But his frail and weakened state denoted a 'nepeš' that had wasted or diminished in some respect. Consequently, to ensure imparting a strong 'nepeš' to Esau, he asked his son to hunt venison and then prepare a savory dish so that he might strengthen and replenish his wasted and diminished 'nepeš.'

Isaac's request for wild game was not unusual, having been made many times before:

> Now Isaac loved Esau, because
> he did eat of his vension. (Gen. 25:28, JPS)

Isaac's need for venison evidently stemmed from a belief that wild game possessed special properties essential to the well-being of his 'nepeš,' properties not to be found in the dishes made from domesticated animals. If Isaac simply wanted venison because of its gamy flavor, he need not have asked Esau to go to the bother of hunting for it; he had only to ask his wife to prepare the meat of a domesticated animal in such a way as to duplicate the taste of venison—an easy thing for her to do, since she assured Jacob that she could prepare such a dish without Isaac ever telling the difference. Since Rebecca would have had no reason to keep this talent secret from Isaac down through the years, he presumably knew his wife could prepare a dish to taste like venison. That Isaac continued to request venison of Esau throughout this period of time indicates that Isaac desired the food not for its particular taste but for the special qualities found in wild, energy-abounding animals, properties that were absent in dishes made from the meat of lambs or kids—properties that nourished his 'nepeš.' Now, at the end of his days, Isaac's request for the same kind of food seems to indicate that without this special nourishment he feared that he would be imparting to Esau a 'nepeš' as wasted as he.

With Esau out hunting for game, Rebecca urged Jacob to gain his father's blessing by disguising himself as Esau. He complied by changing into Esau's garments, but he could not assume Esau's voice. Jacob's voice aroused Isaac's suspicions, and so he asked how it was that he found game so quickly. Evidently, Jacob's answer did not relieve his father's disquietude, for Isaac then replied:

> Come near, I pray thee, that I may feel thee, my son, whether thou be my very son Esau or not. (Gen. 27:21, JPS)

Jacob did as instructed. Isaac felt his arms, but the disguise worked.

> "The voice is the voice of Jacob, but the hands are the hands of Esau." And he discerned him not, because his hands were hairy as his brother Esau's hands: so he blessed him. (Gen. 27:22-23, JPS)

What follows in the next verse has been completely misunderstood by translators and commentators. The biblical translations generally portray Isaac as so uncertain about the man before him that he tried to resolve his doubts with yet another question:

> As he prepared to bless him, he asked,
> "Are you really my son Esau?" (Gen. 27:24, NJPS)[79]

This reading contravenes the clear and definite statement of the narrator in the preceding sentence that Isaac "recognized him not." The test by touch had convinced Isaac that the person before him was Esau. Consequently, his question to Jacob was not meant to probe further. This becomes apparent when the function of the word זֶה, 'zeh,' "this," rendered as "really" in "Are you really my son Esau?" is appreciated. The key to understanding the purpose of 'zeh' lies in three other instances where the question included 'zeh' in a similar construction.

After the forces of Ishbosheth broke under the onslaught of Joab's troops, Abner, their commander, fled, hotly pursued by Asahel, the brother of Joab. Looking behind him, Abner said: "Is it thou, Asahel?" (II Sam. 2:20, JPS). Though 'zeh' was used in the same way as in the Jacob story, it was not translated as: "Is is *really* you, Asahel?" The translator knew that Abner was not asking a question at all. Abner knew who his pursuer was, otherwise he never would have used his name vocatively. Note that he did not ask: "Are you Asahel?"

Similarly, when Obadiah, King Ahab's overseer, met the prophet Elijah while searching the countryside for fodder for the starving beasts of the king's stable, he too asked a question:

> And as Obadiah was in the way, behold, Elijah met him; and he knew him, and fell on his face, and said: "Is it thou, my lord Elijah?" (I Kings 18:7, JPS)

The words אַתָּה זֶה, ''atāh zeh,' were the same Isaac addressed to Jacob. Yet, Obadiah had to know that the man whom he paid obeisance to and addressed by name was Eliah; otherwise, as King Ahab's overseer, he never would have had to accord him such respect. Obviously, Obadiah's question was not to ascertain Elijah's identity.

The third example of Isaac's question again occurred in the Elijah story. This time Ahab himself met Elijah and accosted him with the words: "Is it thou, thou troubler of Israel?" (I Kings 18:17, JPS). That Ahab called Elijah "troubler of Israel" indicates that he knew the person he was addressing. Hence, his words were not intended to ascertain Elijah's identity.

In all three instances where 'zeh' was used, the question contained the information it supposedly was seeking: the identity of the addressee was known. Accordingly, then, the question is really not a question at all. Rather, it appears to be a formal salutation or acknowledgment of one's presence, molded into this form by the distinctiveness of Hebrew expression.

Isaac's question to Jacob, therefore was a formal acknowledgement of his presence or identity, a convention befitting the solemnity of a death-bed deposition. Having taken formal cognizance of his son, Isaac then partook of the food to strengthen his 'nepeš' prior to blessing him. When he finished, Isaac bid Jacob to step closer to receive his kiss. Placing his mouth upon the mouth of his father, Jacob breathed in the breath, the 'nepeš,'[80] the vital stuff of consciousness, of his father. In such close contact, Isaac smelled on Esau's garments the unmistakable odor of the fields, and so must have been moved to begin the first part of his benediction with reference to the fields:

> So God give thee of the dew of heaven,
> And of the fat places of the earth,
> And plenty of corn and wine. (Gen. 27:28, JPS)

After bestowing upon him the blessing of God's natural bounty, Isaac concluded his benediction by delineating the character of his son's future relationship to those both near and far:

> Let peoples serve thee,
> And nations bow down to thee.
> Be lord over thy brethren,
> And let thy mother's sons bow down to thee,
> Cursed be every one that curseth thee,
> And blessed be every one that blesseth thee. (Gen. 27:29, JPS)

Had his blessing consisted entirely of words, Isaac might have assuaged Esau's anguish at discovering his brother's deceit and theft by redressing the wrong with another benediction. But the blessing was two-fold, the first part of which consisted of the physical transfer of Isaac's 'nepeš.' For this reason Isaac could not comply with Esau's request, lamenting:

> Thy brother came with guile,
> and hath taken away thy blessing. (Gen. 27:35, JPS)

Under these circumstances presumably all Isaac could do to still Esau's pain was to prophesy that at some future time he would fling off his brother's yoke of servitude.

Jacob's blessing of Joseph and his two sons paralleled in a number of important details the above episode of the stolen blessing. First, there was the self-nurturing of the one giving the blessing. When Jacob learned that Joseph was approaching, he inferred that his son was coming to receive the parental blessing; and so he "strengthened himself" (Gen. 48:2). Jacob must have eaten something to strengthen his נֶפֶשׁ, 'nepeš,' sufficiently for that moment of transference. Second, there was the ceremonial question. Jacob, as Isaac before him, formally asked the identity of the persons standing before him.[81] Ordinarily, this question might be regarded as superfluous, for the text stated that Jacob received word that Joseph was coming, presumably with his sons. That Jacob, preliminary to the formal transfer of the 'nepeš' went into detail over the disposition of his lands and spoke of "adopting" Joseph's two sons as his own indicates that he must have known that all three were standing before him. Consequently, Jacob's question to Joseph regarding the identity of those present was not to elicit information but to initiate the ritual culminating in the physical part of the blessing. Joseph responded with equal formality:

> They are my sons, whom God
> hath given me here. (Gen. 48:9, JPS)

Third, there was the actual transference of the 'nepeš.' Jacob kissed Joseph and his sons, transferring his 'nepeš' to them in the same manner Isaac imparted his blessing to him. The one added feature of this episode was the contact the recipient of the blessing had with Jacob's knees—a detail that throws further light upon the close relationship between Hebraic and Greek concepts.

The Greeks also believed the knee to be the seat of paternity, of life, of generative power, for in the joint cavity of the knee was a liquefiable substance that contributed to the seed.[82] By touching the knee, the recipient of the blessing thereby received the life fluid. Here again, this same concept is found first in the Hebrew language, where the root of the Hebrew word for "knee," בֶּרֶךְ, 'berek,' is the same as the root for "bless,"בָּרַךְ, 'bārak.'[83] It is also found in the act where Joseph's sons, far from being so young as to be fondled on their grandfather's knees, were brought into contact with his knees presumably to receive Jacob's life fluid. Evidently, this belief that the knee was the seat of generative power prompted the barren Rachel to offer her maid Bilhah to Jacob:

> Consort with her that she may bear on my knees and that through her I too may have children. (Gen. 30:3, NJPS)[84]

Additional evidence demonstrating the close relationship between Hebraic and Greek thought is found in the words חָזָה, 'ḥāzāh,' "see, perceive, behold,"[85] and חָזֶה, 'ḥāzeh,' "breast (of animals)."[86] In these identical words (except for their vowels) is seen what was found among the Greeks, namely that perception was linked to the breast or chest (lung area).[87]

These word relationships and the Isaac-Jacob story would seem to confirm the hypothesis that the Hebrew 'nepeš' at times was the equivalent of the Greek 'thymos' and that the narrator, sharing the same concept of perception as the Greeks, conceived of Noah as being conscious of all that transpired in the tent through portions of the human anatomy other than those now associated with sense perception. Though asleep, Noah "breathed in" through the passages of his ears, nose, mouth, and the pores of his skin Ham's noxious subterfuge, which permeated the atmosphere in the tent. Thus, without any emendations to the text, a rational explanation emerges of how Noah could have known of what had happened while he was in his drunken stupor.

This reliance upon Greek concepts to illuminate the meanings of some biblical words or episodes derives from the thesis that "Greek and Hebrew civilizations are parallel structures built upon the same East Mediterranean foundation."[88] Crete and Canaan by the second millenium B.C.E. were formed into a single cultural entity by such channels of cultural interchange as military conquest, transplanted commercial or military enclaves, the interpenetration of commercial empires, the importation of mercenaries, the mobility of craftsmen and religious personnel, and the international attraction of religious centers. The Hebrews in Canaan thereby were exposed to the epic literature of the East Mediterranean world through the highly polished literary medium of the Canaanites. It is only natural that their ideas regarding perception should have come from the same sources that later gave rise to the corresponding Greek theories on this subject.

Noah's Cursing of Canaan

There remains to be explained the reason why Noah vented his wrath upon the innocent Canaan when Ham was the affronting party:

> And Noah awoke from his wine, and knew
> what his youngest son had done unto him. (Gen. 9:24, JPS)
> And he said:
>> "Cursed be Canaan;
>> The lowest of slaves
>> Shall he be to his brothers." (Gen. 9:25, NJPS)[89]

Assuming that this is not a "disturbed" text reflecting two different traditions, Noah's act of relegating Canaan to the class of the lowest of slaves was not as unjust as it might seem when what Noah could *not* do is considered. He was prevented from retaliating against Ham, no matter how much he might have wanted to, by the same factors that precluded Isaac from cursing Jacob after discovering the fraud perpetrated upon him. Had his plot not worked according to plan, Jacob knew that his father would have cursed him, for he mentioned this likelihood as a counterargument to his mother's scheme. That Isaac did not imprecate Jacob once the theft of the blessing was exposed implies that Isaac could not curse one who was empowered with the strength of his blessing. Jacob, protected by Isaac's 'nepeš' and verbal blessing, was safe from retaliation. Just as a blessing could neutralize a curse,[90] so a curse could not be vented once a blessing had been pronounced upon the same person.[91]

Ham presumably knew that once he possessed the potency, the generative power of his father, he would be protected against any malediction, as indeed he was. He would then be in a position to pass along this potency of leadership to Canaan and his progeny. To thwart Ham's scheme, Noah —if this hypothesis is correct—would have had to curse Ham's son, Canaan, who was not shielded by any such generative power.

Noah's imprecation, his only words in the entire flood story and its aftermath, seems to have been a "death-bed" bequest, possibly precipitated by Ham's theft of his potency. Though the next line in the text states that Noah lived three hundred and fifty years after the Flood, his words are still to be considered a death-bed bequest, for this added information is simply part of the narrative formula of recording length of life before the following and conclusive statement:

> And all the days of Noah were
> nine hundred and fifty years; and he died. (Gen. 9:29, JPS)

To ascertain what Noah meant by "cursing" Canaan, the story of Joshua and the wily Gibeonites provides a possible answer, for here too the identical nature of the punishment matched a similar case of deception.

Joshua's conquest of Jericho and Ai terrorized the inhabitants of Gibeon, who anticipated the same fate for living in the path of the invading Israelites. To avert their certain annihilation, a party of Gibeonites disguised themselves as travel-weary emissaries, who had come from a distant land to conclude a covenant of peace with the victorious Israelites. The ruse worked. Convinced by their appearance that they indeed had journeyed from afar, the Israelites pledged "to let them live" (Josh. 9:15, JPS). Shortly thereafter, the Israelites discovered that they had been tricked by the Gibeonites, for now their covenant rendered Gibeah inviolable. Joshua indeed did spare the lives of the Gibeonites, but he exacted his revenge nevertheless:

> Wherefore have ye beguiled us, saying: We are very far from you, when ye dwell among us? Now therefore ye are cursed, and there shall never fail to be of you bondmen, both hewers of wood and drawers of water for the house of my God. (Josh. 9:22–23, JPS)

The Gibeonites, having been judged guilty of trickery, were banned by this decree from mingling or becoming assimilated with the Israelites; as outcasts, they were destined from birth to perform all the menial functions associated with the Israelite sacrificial cult.

In light of Joshua's "cursing" of the Gibeonites, Noah's "cursing" of Canaan should be viewed more as a judgment than as a malediction. Like the future generations of Gibeonites, the children of Canaan were condemned to lasting servitude:

> The lowest of slaves
> Shall he be to his brothers.

Far from acting out of vengeance, Noah seemingly degraded the future generations of Canaan to frustrate Ham's design of transferring his newly acquired special strength and power to Canaan and his progeny. Noah's decree had to be pronounced before Ham could transfer the force of Noah's נֶפֶשׁ, 'nepeš,' to his son, thereby rendering him invulnerable. With Ham no longer able to threaten the position and status of Shem and Japheth and their progeny, Noah assured the safe succession of leadership.

3

THE LIBERTINE
GENERATION OF THE FLOOD

The Human Side of the Disaster

What manner of man was Noah really? Noah, "the righteous man," the sole survivor of the cataclysm, spoke but once during the entire Flood episode, and then only after he was affected personally. His angry response to Ham's attempt to usurp his power indicates that he could respond with a sense of outrage. But had he no feelings for the condemned inhabitants of the world? Had he no remorse for the drowning masses, who must have tried to reach the ark in a desperate effort to save themselves from the cresting waters? Or was Noah utterly callous to their cries for help? Michaelangelo must have been preoccupied with such questions when he made the dying sinners the focal point of his fresco in the Sistine Chapel and made the ark a matter of secondary interest.[1] The doomed hold the attention, not the survivors. In humanizing the Flood story, Michaelangelo expressed the rationalist view that the fearful death of the unfavored was "a greater and more important fact than that a patriarch and his children were saved."[2] For Michaelangelo the story of the ark may have been legend, but as a story of human suffering it was true.

So inconceivable to Clifford Odets was the thought that the righteous Noah could be oblivious to the soul-shattering shrieks of the dying that the dramatist had to alter the Flood story to fit in with his concept of how Noah, the human being—not the legendary character—must have acted and felt. In his play "The Flowering Peach," Odets portrayed Noah as a person overcome by the magnitude of the catastrophe that was about to be visited upon the earth's inhabitants—a portrayal presumably formed by the playwright's reaction to the devastation wrought in World War II. Noah was so shaken by the dream-vision of the impending disaster that he had to bolster himself with liquor before he could confide the horrifying revelation to his wife.

The reconstructed drinking scene depicted a deeply compassionate Noah, who neither rejoiced in the justice to be meted out to the wicked nor reveled in his own deliverance. So stricken was he by what would happen to "old lady Kamens, a grandmother nineteen times" and "to thousands and thousands of others"[3] that he entreated God up to the beginning of the Deluge to relent: "For the last time, O Lord, must it be . . . ?"[4]

Odets focused upon the response of a decent human being overwhelmed by the enormity of death. Through his characterization of Noah, he asserted—with the terrible certainty of having lived through a period of history that claimed the lives of over thirty-eight million men, women, and children—that no person of any sensibility could escape the pain and suffering that accompanied the widespread destruction of life. Further, he showed through the diluvian setting of his play, that this heartache was not unique to any one era; it was as acute for the age of the cloudburst as it is for the age of the atomic burst.

That people responded with suffering and compassion was evident in another account of the Deluge—the Babylonian. In the principal Babylonian flood story, the author described the feelings of Utnapishtim, the sole survivor, after the storm had abated and the sea grown quiet:

> I opened a window, and light fell upon
> my face.
> I looked upon the sea, (all) was silence,
> And all mankind had turned to clay;
> The . . . was as level as a (flat) roof.
> I bowed, sat down, and wept,
> The tears running down over my face.[5]

Considering how false the gods were to one another and to man and how they gathered over the sacrificer like a swarm of hungry flies, it is remarkable that such compassion for the dead ever was expressed in the first place, never mind being voiced with such eloquence. This response from an epic in which "the moral and ethical motive is almost completely absent"[6] makes Noah's silence incomprehensible to the modern mind.

A number of rabbinic sages, however, were not surprised at Noah's seeming callousness, for they never regarded him as particularly praiseworthy. According to a rabbinic legend, Noah did speak. More correctly, he harangued. When the Flood finally broke loose, seven hundred thousand men, women, and children surrounded the ark, imploring Noah to let them in. His refusal revealed a total lack of compassion:

> Are ye not those who were rebellious toward God, saying, "There is no God?" Therefore He has brought ruin upon you, to annihilate you and destroy you from the face of the earth. Have I not been prophesying this unto you these hundred and twenty years, and you would not give heed unto the voice of God? Yet now you desire to be kept alive! . . . Therefore God will not hearken unto you and give you ear; naught will you accomplish![7]

Some rabbinic sages would have commended Noah for his attitude toward the generation of the Flood, for they were disgusted with what they believed to be mankind's crime: gross sexual immorality. The 'Bene

Elohim,' interpreted by the rabbis to be either the sons of nobles or the sons of God, cohabited with virgins, married women, men, and beasts.[8] The generation of the Flood composed nuptial songs in honor of pederasty and bestiality and drew up marriage contracts to legalize the union between men and beasts.[9] Condemnation of such depravity forbade their putting into Noah's mouth any plea for a stay of execution. God was long-suffering with everything but sexual depravity.[10]

Most modern commentators, like these rabbinic sages, evidently find nothing unusual in Noah's silence, for they never raise the question. They disagree with the rabbis of old, however, as to the nature of mankind's crime, claiming that wickedness,[11] lawlessness,[12] and arbitrary oppression[13] precipitated the Flood. "The culpability of the generation of the flood lies strictly in the socio-moral sphere."[14]

Such an assessment of the moral state of the antediluvian world has created more problems than it has solved. Widespread injustice and social unrighteousness would have created the oppressed, the victimized. In such a situation the narrator, so sensitive to the demands of justice, hardly would have portrayed God as destroying the victims along with their cruel oppressors. And to assume that the world was filled wholly with unregenerates, the oppressed having been annihilated, is not warranted because the text said nothing about any widespread slaughter of the innocent. The only killings recorded prior to the Flood were those perpetrated by Cain and Lamech. Surely, if more murders had been committed, they likewise would have been noted by the narrator. The crime of the generation of the Flood must have been something other than "lawlessness," "social unrighteousness," or "arbitrary oppression." Accordingly, an examination of the indictment begins to determine the nature of humanity's horrendous sin.

The Sexual Denotation of "Evil"

The Lord saw how great was man's wickedness on earth, and how every plan devised by his mind was nothing but evil all the time. (Gen. 6:5, NJPS)

The charge against humanity was רָעָה, 'rā'āh,' "wickedness": man's plans were רַע, 'ra',' "evil." Both words come from the same Hebrew root, רעע, 'r'.'[15] Ordinarily "evil" and "wickedness" would presuppose a universally accepted code of ethics. While God creating man without a moral sense is inconceivable, in these first six chapters of Genesis only the prohibition against killing and taking blood-revenge were emphasized.[16] Note, however, that the narrator refrained from using 'ra',' "evil," or its derivatives to condemn the deeds of Cain and Lamech; yet he used this word in the preceding episode of Adam and the tree of good and evil. A correct understanding of the exact sense of 'ra',' "evil," as used in the Adam and Eve story might well provide a lead in determining its meaning in the Noah narrative.

The tree of knowing good and evil, according to one interpretation, represented sexual consciousness. The phrase הַדַּעַת טוֹב וָרָע, 'hadda'at

ṭôb wārāʿ,' "knowing good and evil," is interpreted as meaning
sexual knowledge and experience, since הַדַּעַת, 'haddaʿat,' is derived from
יָדַע, 'yādaʿ,' "to know," an almost universal euphemism for sexual
relations.[17] The phrase "good and evil" is regarded as having originated in
the two aspects of sexual experience: טוֹב, 'ṭôb,' "the good," the manifestation of the sexual drive regarded as normal by biblical society; and רַע,
'raʿ,' "the evil," the deviant expression.[18]

This theory is supported by two biblical episodes in which a form of
יָדַע, 'yādaʿ,' was used to connote this deviance.[19] When the two angels visited Lot in Sodom, they were besieged by the townspeople, shouting:

> Where are the men that came in to thee this night? Bring them out to us, that
> we may know them. (Gen. 19:5, JPS)

Clearly, וְנֵדְעָה אֹתָם, 'weēdʿāh ʾōtām,' "that we may know them,"
expressed a lust for mob homosexuality. The theme of homosexual rape
was also present in the story of the Levite and his concubine, whose lodging
in Gibeah was surrounded by its inhabitants crying:

> Bring forth the man that came into thy house, that we may know him. (Judg.
> 19:22, JPS)

Instead, the concubine was pushed out of the house, to be so abused sexually
that by morning she lay dead at the door of the house. Here, וְנֵדָעֶנּוּ,
'weēdāʿennû,' "that we may know him," a form of the same word
in the Garden of Eden story, likewise conveyed sexual intimacy.

In the Sodom and Gibeah episodes, those intent upon homosexual rape
were implored אַל . . . תָּרֵעוּ, 'ʾal . . . tārēʿû,' "do not do wickedly,"[20] before being offered a woman to satisfy their lust. Obviously, "do not do
wickedly," far from referring to cohabitation between the sexes, referred
to what the Bible condemned as unnatural sexual practices. Such being the
case, the inference is made that in respect to that tree in the Garden of
Eden רַע, 'raʿ,' "evil," referred to deviant sexual practices while טוֹב,
'ṭôb,' "good," referred to the natural. The phrase "knowing good and
evil" thus becomes a stereotyped idiom encompassing the entire range of
sexual experience.[21]

The theory that this tree in the Garden of Eden represented sex has not
gone unchallenged; yet even in the argument attempting to disprove this
thesis, the presence of the sexual element is acknowledged: when Adam ate
the fruit of the tree of good and evil, he acquired a knowledge of evil that
may have included these censured sexual acts;[22] and when Adam and Eve
experienced shame over their nudity after eating the forbidden fruit, they
revealed quite clearly the sexual connotation attached to this fruit.[23]

Such acknowledgment permits the hypothesis that רַע, 'raʿ,' and רָעָה,
'rāʿāh,' in the Noah story contained the same idea of deviant sex that
was found in the stories of Adam and Eve in the Garden of Eden, Lot in
Sodom, and the Levite in Gibeah: what has been translated heretofore as

"evil" and "wickedness" should be understood as denoting sexual perversion—a phenomenon so well-known in the ancient world that a Ugaritic myth attested to its presence among the gods.

Baal, the fertility god, stood up in the midst of the gods, carousing at a banquet, and spat in disgust at the lewdness of the handmaids:

> C[ome]s Puissant Baal,
>   *Advances* the Rider of the Clouds.
> Lo, he takes his stand and *cries defiance,*
>   He stands erect and spits
>   In the midst of the *as[sem]bly* of the
>   divine beings:
> "*Ab[omination]* has been placed upon my
>   table,
>   Filth in the cup I drink.
> For two [kinds of] banquets Baal hates,
>   Three the Rider of the Clouds:
> A banquet of shamefulness,
>   A banquet [banquet] of baseness,
>   And a banquet of handmaids' *lewdness.*
> Yet herein is flagrant shamefulness,
>   And herein is handmaids' *lewdness.*"[24]

This expression of disgust from a god accustomed to all types of sexual extravagances by his worshippers to promote fertility testifies to the gross immorality that doubtlessly prevailed in certain Canaanite quarters. It may be assumed that the biblical narrator either knew of this tale or was aware of the human situation that occasioned this picture of depravity among the gods.

Man's Evil "Imagination"

One word in the indictment of the generation of the Flood eludes definitive translation—יֵצֶר, 'yēṣer,' "imagination":

> And the Lord saw that the wickedness of man was great in the earth, and that every imagination of the thoughts of his heart was only evil continually. (Gen. 6:5, JPS)

This translation fails, however, to convey any sharp distinction between "imagination" and "thought." As "imagination," 'yēṣer' adds nothing to the sense of the sentence that is not conveyed by "thoughts." Omitting 'yēṣer,' the sense of the sentence, as rendered in the above translation, remains intact: the Lord saw . . . that the thoughts of his heart were evil continually.

One rendition did try to draw a distinction between 'yēṣer,' "imagination," and מַחְשְׁבֹת, 'maḥšᵉbōt,' "thoughts":

> The Lord saw how great was man's wickedness on earth, and how every plan devised by his mind was nothing but evil all the time. (Gen. 6:5, NJPS)

And in another version:

> When the Lord saw that the wickedness of man on the earth was great, and that the whole bent of his thinking was never anything but evil. . . . (Gen. 6:5, Chicago)[25]

While these renditions have capsuled the "imagination of the thoughts" into "plan" or "the whole bent of thinking," they exhibit more interpretation than a straight, literal translation of the text.

Probably, the narrator had in mind for 'yēṣer,' "imagination," a meaning quite distinct from "thoughts." Accordingly, a translation must be sought that preserves this distinction without sacrificing the literalness of the text. Such a translation is possible if 'yēṣer' is defined as "form" or "that which is given form." Then 'yēṣer' is not only "imagination" but also the *concretization* of such imagining: "imagery or 'imaging' corresponds, in a conceptual world which is simpler but more powerful than ours, to our 'imagination'—not the power of imagination, but its products."[26] If 'yēṣer' means the finished product of man's thoughts and not merely the imaging, it changes the idea behind the text markedly. Man was not condemned for *thinking* acts of depravity but for their fulfillment, for the concretization of their imagining. Now the passage reads with the new definitions of the words in question:

> And the Lord saw that the sexual abnormality of man was great on the earth and that every concretization of the thoughts of his heart was perverse all the day.

The Putrescence of a "Corrupt" Earth

Supporting the above rendition of the Hebrew text is the description of how the earth itself was contaminated by these forms of sexual perversion, a description that becomes apparent once the meaning of some of the Hebrew words is probed. The usual translation does not even allude to sexual excesses:

> The earth became corrupt before God; the earth was filled with injustice. When God saw how corrupt the earth was, for all flesh had corrupted its ways on earth, God said to Noah, "I have decided to put an end to all flesh, for the earth is filled with lawlessness because of them: I am about to destroy them with the earth." (Gen. 6:11–13, NJPS)

By using תִּשָּׁחֵת, 'tiśśāḥēt,' "became corrupt," with the word "injustice" or "lawlessness,"[27] the narrator seems to have been implying that the earth—the human race—had become morally debased. But was "earth" in this passage a personification of mankind? Evidently not, for if "earth" was such a personification of humanity, why would the narrator have God saying that He was about to destroy man *with the earth?* Would it not have been sufficient just to say that He was going to destroy the "earth," meaning thereby all its people? It must be concluded, therefore, that when the narrator spoke of the earth becoming corrupt, he was describing its *physical* state and not the degradation of its inhabitants.

In this case the root שָׁחַת, 'šāḥat,' "be spoiled, marred, corrupt,"[28] must have referred to the physical ruination of the earth: the narrator seemingly was describing the earth as rotten and putrefied.

This idea of putrescence is strengthened by the possible relationship of the root שָׁחַת, 'šāḥat,' in the preceding passage to יֶשַׁח, 'yešaḥ,' and שַׁחַת, 'šaḥat.'[29] The close relationship of 'yešaḥ' to its Arabic cognate, meaning "dirt, filth, soil," leads to the belief that 'yešaḥ' means "fecal matter."[30] The other word, 'šaḥat,' was used in the book of Job either as a storage pit for manure composed of straw and dung (usually in a state of watery putrescence) or as an outdoor silo where fodder fermented.[31] In either case a highly offensive odor was associated with 'šaḥat,' "pit." If indeed the root 'šaḥat' in the Genesis narrative is associated with the malodorous smell of fecal matter, sour silage, or watery putrescence, it would vividly convey the idea of the physical putrefication of the earth; for the narrator would be saying, in effect, that the earth stank with the same kind of odor emitted by the watery putrescence of a manure pit or sour fermentation of fodder.

Parallel to שַׁחַת, 'šaḥat,' in verse eleven is חָמָס, 'ḥāmās,' generally translated as "violence,"[32] "lawlessness,"[33] "injustice."[34] However, there is reason to believe that his generalized term is derived from an older descriptive term for physical deterioration; as such it would aptly parallel the narrator's description of the earth in the first half of the verse.

To substantiate this hypothesis, in the mishnaic Hebrew, 'ḥāmās' can mean, among other things, "to be heated, passionate."[35] Also connected with heat is חָמֵץ, 'ḥāmēṣ,' "to ferment, be sour,"[36] a word closely related etymologically to 'ḥāmās';[37] its relationship to "heat" is seen in the fact that fermentation cannot begin without heat.

This connection between 'ḥāmās,' "violence," and 'ḥāmēṣ,' "fermentation," most likely prevails between אָלַח, 'ālaḥ,' "to be corrupt morally, be tainted," and its Arabic cognate "to turn sour (milk),"[38] and between בָּאַשׁ, 'bā'aš,' "to stink,"[39] and its Aramaic equivalent בְּאִשׁ, 'bi'yš,'[40] or בִּישׁ, 'bîš,'[41] "evil, wickedness." These two examples seem to indicate that the more generalized terms for "unrighteousness" and "evil" derive from the more concrete and sensible "stench."[42] If such is the case, 'ḥāmās' contains not only the more generalized definition of "violence, lawlessness, unrighteousness" but also an earlier, more physically descriptive meaning of "malodorous pollution." Such a reading of 'ḥāmās' radically changes the sense of the passage:

> The earth had become stinkingly rotten before God, and the earth [meaning also its atmosphere] was filled with a malodorous pollution.

The Crime of Bestiality

To validate the argument for rejecting 'ḥāmās' as "unrighteousness, lawlessness," attention is directed to the word "flesh" in the verse that described those responsible for this calamitous state of the world:

... The end of all flesh is come before Me; for the earth is filled with violence
through them; and, behold, I will destroy them with the earth. (Gen. 6:13, JPS)

As used in Genesis 6:17, 19, and 7:15, בָּשָׂר, 'bāśār,' "flesh," referred to
all life on earth—animal and human alike. Since the text neither stated nor
intimated that animals were created with a sense of moral discrimination,
the narrator could scarcely have been speaking of the injustice or lawlessness of animals. Nor does the spirit of justice in the Torah permit the
thought that God would destroy animals as a punishment for a sin they
could not possibly have committed. To retain "violence" as the translation of 'ḥāmās' would be saying, therefore, that the animals acted in
accordance with the violent instincts they were born with—hardly an evil
for which they must be held responsible. However, the difficulty vanishes
once 'ḥāmās' is rendered as "malodorous pollution," for when applied
to animals it means that a stench resulted from the sexual perversions
people practiced with animals.

That bestiality was practiced in the ancient world is known from Hittite
and biblical law and Mesopotamian potency incantations.[43] In the
Hittite law code a man could be killed or spared by the king for copulating
with a head of cattle,[44] a sheep,[45] or a pig.[46] However, "if a man
does evil with a horse or mule, there shall be no punishment."[47] Biblical
law, in sharp contrast, was categorical in its condemnation of bestiality.
Unconditional death was to be meted out to the offender, even to the extent
of putting the animal to death:

> If a man has carnal relations with a beast, he shall be put to death; and you
> shall kill the beast. If a woman approaches any beast to mate with it, you shall
> kill the woman and the beast; they shall be put to death—their bloodguilt is upon
> them. (Lev. 20:15–16, NJPS)

If 'ḥāmās' has been rendered correctly as "malodorous pollution,"
the consummate skill of the narrator is striking here. The Flood episode
had to be integrated into the narrator's theological reconstruction of man
and the universe; for, to ignore what was so celebrated in Sumerian,
Akkadian, and Babylonian mythology would have marked his story as
incomplete and even theologically suspect in the eyes of his contemporaries.
Consequently, he had to work out a rationale for the Flood that harmonized
with his concept of God's justice and mercy. This he did by charging man
with bestiality—an act that physically polluted the earth and its atmosphere.

That bestiality polluted the soil is learned from Leviticus 18, at the conclusion of the precepts dealing with sexual relationships among the members of the larger family circle:

> Do not defile yourselves in any of those ways, for it is by such that the nations
> which I am casting out before you defiled themselves. Thus the land became
> defiled.... (Lev. 18:24–25a, NJPS)

But then the Bible, according to the English translations, added that the land too must be considered guilty—and punished:

> ... and I called it to account for its iniquity, and the land spewed out its inhabitants. (Lev. 18:25b, NJPS)

A singular judgment indeed, if defilement of the land resulted from defiled sinners walking upon the soil:[48] with such frequent references to "sin," "iniquity," "wickedness," "guilt," "evil," "transgression," and "folly" in the Bible, one would think that there would be frequent mention of the earth's pollution and ensuing punishment for the countless sins committed upon it by the earth's inhabitants. But such is not the case at all. Only in Leviticus 18 was it said that the land too had to bear the full consequences of the sinful acts performed upon it. The fact that such a punishment seems so incongruous with the narrator's concept of justice and the fact that nowhere else did the Bible call the earth to account for the iniquity of others suggest the possibility that this was a special category of sinful behavior and that the expression פָּקַד עָוֹן, 'pāqad 'āwôn,' usually translated as "visit iniquity," had a totally different signification in this particular instance.

When separated from עָוֹן, "āwôn,' the word פָּקַד, 'pāqad,' can mean "attend to"[49] or "take care of."[50] From the root "be crooked,"[51] עָוָה, "āwôn,'[52] initially connoted the kind of "crookedness" that issued from a twisted or perverted nature; psychologically, the association "crooked, wry, twisted" leads naturally into "iniquity, sin, wickedness."[53] Whether as guilt or as the "crooked action" issuing from a perverted nature, the psalmist conceived of "āwôn,' as a deep dyed stain from which he implored God to cleanse him.[54] The third word in this key phrase, עָלֶיהָ, "ālèhā,' can, of course, be translated "upon it (her)."

Incorporating these definitions into the reconstruction of verse twenty-five, a strikingly changed mood on the part of God is perceived—solicitude, rather than vengeance:

> ... and I have attended to the abnormality
> (that was)[55] upon it. ...

Or, applying the psalmist's understanding of "āwôn':

> ... and I have attended to the deep stain
> of perversion (that was) upon it. ...

Exactly how God took care of this abnormality afflicting the land is revealed in further scrutiny of פָּקַד, 'pāqad,' which corresponds in form to the mishnaic בָּדַק, 'bādaq,' when the identical second and third consonants are transposed[56] and the פ, 'p,' and ב, 'b,' are interchanged.[57] Assuming that correspondence in form in this particular case reflects a correspondence in meaning,[58] one of the definitions of 'bādaq'—"to cure the body by means of a purgative"—is so germane to this verse that the mishnaic 'bādaq' appears to have preserved an unrecognized meaning for 'pāqad.' Proceeding on this assumption, these verses are seen to describe an explicit cause and effect sequence:

1. God sees that the land has become polluted by bestiality and other forms of sexual perversions.
2. God cleanses the earth with a purgative.
   The purgative works so effectively that the earth vomits out the polluting inhabitants.

Since this purgative would have had to have been taken internally, עָלֶיהָ, "ālèhā," "upon it," is better translated as "because of it, for its sake"[59] or "from it."[60] The text now reads:

> ... and I have cleansed with a purgative
> the pervertedness from it. . . .

Or:

> ... and I have cleansed with a purgative
> the pervertedness for its sake. . . .

No matter which reading of Leviticus 18:25a is followed, each one of these portrays God as responsible for purging the victimized earth of its pollution.

Thus, in the flood story, when the bestiality of man transformed the earth from that which was "good" to that which was foul smelling, what was needed was not punishment[61] but something to cleanse the earth, a purgative to bring it back to its former state of goodness. For a merciful god, only water with its marvelous cleansing properties could be used. What had been regarded heretofore as the waters of destruction has become the waters of healing, cleansing the earth's sores and washing the atmosphere to make it a fit place for life to flourish once again. Unfortunately, the contamination of the earth seems to have been so widespread that no refuge could be found for wildlife, with the result that animals and birds perished for lack of available space on the ark—the unfortunate victims of man's depravity.

The Wantonness of the Banished Divine Beings

Mankind's fall into sexual depravity must have had its origin in the acts of divine beings, who were so drawn by the feminine allure of the daughters of men that "they took as their wives any of them they liked."

This mention of divine beings cohabiting with mortals is for some scholars an "isolated fragment" of "undisguised mythology."[62] Its presence testifies to a transmutation of a Canaanite tradition to an acceptable Hebrew one. In Canaanite literature the term "sons of god" indicated the gods collectively—an assembly of gods.[63] In biblical doctrine the attributes of the various pagan deities became concentrated in the Lord or in His messengers, depending on their suitablility.[64] With angels sub-

stituted for Canaanite deities, the terms that formerly denoted the col-
lectivity of the gods came to designate in the Bible the angelic congregation.
However, not all angels enjoyed the same status; they were divided into
higher and lower ranks.[65] Since the usual term **מַלְאָכִים**, 'mal'ākîm,'
"angels," was not used, the angels in this paragraph must be the degraded
ones, who were cast into divine disfavor.[66]

This inference is confirmed by their manner of taking wives. The text
related that these divine beings, captivated by the beauty of the daughters
of men, "took as wives any they liked" (Gen. 6:2, NJPS). Their behavior
appears respectable enough until the standards these angels used to
choose their wives from among the physically attractive daughters are
examined. Did they allow for a sufficient period of time to get acquainted
with these mortal women, or were they so taken by their feminine charms
that they dispensed with such amenities? The answer to these questions
is found in the word **בָּחֲרוּ**, 'bāḥārû,' "they chose."

The root **בָּחַר**, 'bāḥar,' "choose,"[67] also means "test, try."[68] The
use of this word indicates that the angels chose by testing, by a kind of trying out. The only possible test would be that of sexual intercourse: the
angels took as wives those who satisfied them sexually. Indeed, the idea of
cohabitation in 'bāḥar' is found also in its Arabic cognate: 'baḥara,'
"to cleave or till the ground."[69] If there is one universally acclaimed
symbol of womanhood, it is the earth, as expressed in "mother earth" or
"the bosom of the earth." Accordingly, anyone penetrating or cleaving
"mother earth" with a plough is engaged in an activity symbolically associated with sexual union. Thus, Samson, enraged that the Philistines
had learned the answers to his riddle by pressuring his fiancée, charged
them with the kind of misconduct that would be associated ordinarily with
sexual impropriety:

> If you had not plowed with my heifer, you would not have found out my riddle.
> (Judg. 14:18, RSV)

This same concept is depicted on a Grecian vase showing six naked men
carrying a phallic plough.[70] The contemporary expression, "to sow
one's wild oats," also equates sowing and tilling with sexual union. These
varied examples strengthen the assumption that the divine beings employed
the same criterion in choosing their wives as did King Ahasuerus—that of
"trying out" each candidate to determine the most sexually compatible
spouse.[71] That the narrator recorded no protest from the fathers or
the daughters seems to signify their complete acquiescence in these prenup-
tial trials.

Nor did the narrator have to state that the sexual union between "demoted" angels and mortal women was abominable. It was taken for granted
that these marriages would stand condemned because they violated the
prohibition against the "mixing" of different species.

The Bible strictly forbade the mixing of different forms of life. Animals of one species were not permitted to copulate with those of another.[72] To maintain this separation of the species, the Bible went to such extremes as forbidding the hitching together of an ox and an ass to a plough.[73] Further, the prohibition against "mixing" applied with equal force to plant life and to the inanimate. For example, two kinds of seed could not be sown in the same field;[74] and wool and linen, once associated with a living object, could not be used together in the manufacture of a garment.[75] The knowledge of these laws probably rendered unnecessary any explicit condemnation of the angels by the narrator; the opprobrium attached to this act would be felt by anyone familiar with the story.

The Connection between Genesis 3 and 6

That these degraded angels behaved so shamelessly should occasion no surprise, for the narrator prepared for their wantonness by characterizing them in Genesis 3:5 of the Garden of Eden story as:

אֱלֹהִים יֹדְעֵי טוֹב וָרָע

'ĕlōhîm yōdʿê ṭôb wārāʿ

(. . . you will be like) gods knowing
both good and evil. (NEB)

In the more recent NJPS and NEB editions of the Bible, the alternate readings have reflected the division of opinion over whether אֱלֹהִים, ''ĕlōhîm,' should be translated as "God" or "divine beings," the two definitions of this word. However, if the phrase יֹדְעֵי טוֹב וָרָע, 'yōdʿê ṭôb wārāʿ,' "knowing good and evil," is understood to be restrictive and not parenthetical, the problem is eliminated; for then the narrator, far from adding just another bit of information, used the phrase to designate a specific group of divine beings: those who knew good and evil, or—according to the hypothesis previously developed—those who were sexually conscious. Only *these,* the sexually conscious of all the members of the heavenly congregation, would Eve resemble in character, once she ate the forbidden fruit.

Having interpreted טוֹב וָרָע, 'ṭôb wārāʿ,' "good and evil," as descriptive of sexuality, translating ''ĕlōhîm,' as "God" is, of course, ruled out; for to characterize God as a sexual being would be contrary to accepted understanding of biblical cosmology; nowhere has creation been described as a sexual process. Unlike the pagan myths, the idea of material emanation from the creator was foreign to the Bible. Baal might be a sexual being, not so the God of the Hebrews.

Granted the possibility of interpreting ''ĕlōhîm' as "divine beings" and 'ṭôb wārāʿ,' "good and evil," as sexuality, how then is Genesis 3:22 to be explained, where, on the basis of this hypothesis, God seemingly was depicted as a sexual being? The text reads:

וַיֹּאמֶר יְהֹוָה אֱלֹהִים הֵן הָאָדָם
הָיָה כְּאַחַד מִמֶּנּוּ לָדַעַת טוֹב וָרָע

> Wayyōʼmer Yahweh ʼĕlōhîm hēn hāʼādām
> hāyāh kᵉʼaḥad mimmennû lādaʿat ṭôb wārāʿ
> And the Lord God said, "Behold the man
> is become as one of us, to know good and
> evil. . . .' (JPS)

According to this, the more literal JPS translation, God included Himself with the other divine beings as knowing "good and evil" or, in the terminology of this interpretation, as "being conscious of sexuality." Obviously something is wrong here: either the hypothesis precluding God from being counted among the sexually conscious divine beings is invalid, or the key word מִמֶּנּוּ , 'mimmennû,' "of us," has been mistranslated in this particular instance.

Proceeding on the assumption that 'mimmennû,' may have another meaning, it is found that in its alternate form as the third person, masculine, singular, this is so: Instead of meaning "of him" or "from him," 'mimmennû' on occasion has been translated as the third person, masculine, plural—"*of them*"—as in the following:

(1)　...וְנָפַל מִמֶּנּוּ רָב
　...wᵉnāpal mimmennû rāb
(The Lord said to Moses, "Go down,
warn the people not to break through
to the Lord to gaze,) lest many
of them perish." (Ex. 19:21, NJPS)

(2)　....לֹא־נָפַל מִמֶּנּוּ דָּבָר אֶחָד
　...lōʼ nāpal mimmennû dābōr ʼeḥād
(And now I am about to go the way of
all the earth, and you know in your
hearts and souls, all of you, that not
one thing has failed of all the good
things which the Lord your God promised
concerning you: all have come to pass
for you,) not one *of them* has failed. (Josh. 23:14, RSV)

(3)　....וַיַּכּוּ מִמֶּנּוּ אַלְפַּיִם אִישׁ
　...wayyakû mimmennû alppayim ʼiš
(And they turned and fled toward the
wilderness unto the rock of Rimmon:
and they gleaned of them in the highways
five thousand men: and followed hard after
them unto Gidom,) and smote *of them*
two thousand men. (Judg. 20:45, JPS)

(4)　....וַיּוֹתֵר מִמֶּנּוּ מֵאָה רָכֶב
　...wayyôtēr mimmennû rākeb
(And David took from him a thousand
and seven hundred horsemen, and twenty
thousand footmen: and David houghed
all the chariot horses,) but reserved
of them for a hundred chariots. (II Sam. 8:4, JPS: also I Chron. 18:4)

That the singular 'mimmennû,' "of him," was used in these four instances to express the plural "of them" permits the question why 'mimmennû,' in Genesis 3:22 could not be another instance when the third person, masculine, singular was used by the narrator to mean "of them." If, indeed, such be the case, the new meaning yielded by 3:22 accords perfectly with the hypothesis concerning the sexuality of the degraded angels:

> And the Lord God said, "Behold the man is become as one of them, to know good and evil. . . ." (after JPS)

Why the narrator chose to use 'mimmennû' to say "of them" is not known. Perhaps for stylistic reasons he retained this word, having used it six times before in Genesis 2 and 3[76] in connection with the fruit of the forbidden tree, to highlight the relationship between the tree of sexual consciousness and these divine beings of lower rank. Or perhaps the narrator simply wanted to repeat his use of a singular form to express the plural, as in Genesis 2:19 with לוֹ, 'lô,' the collective for wild beasts and birds:

> .... לִרְאוֹת מַה־יִּקְרָא־לוֹ
> . . . lire'ōt mah-yiqrā'-lô
> (And the Lord God formed out of the
> earth all the wild beasts and all the
> birds of the sky, and brought them to
> the man) to see what he would call *them*. . . . (NJPS)

But whatever his reason, the narrator maintained God's separateness from the degraded angels through his use of 'mimmennû,' as meaning "of them."

This special classification of the demoted divinities permitted the narrator to pick up this theme of Genesis 3 and weave it into his story in chapter six.[77] He even indicated what he was doing by his use of a number of identical words from chapter 3 and, in one case, words closely alike.

Genesis 3:6			*Genesis 6:2*
וַתֵּרֶה. 'wattēre"	"saw"		וַיִּרְאוּ. 'wayyir°û'
כִּי. 'kî'	"that"		כִּי. 'kî'
טוֹב. 'ṭôb'	"good"		טֹבֹת. 'ṭōbōt'
וַתִּקַּח. 'wattiqqaḥ'	"took"		וַיִּקְחוּ. 'wayyiqḥû
מַאֲכָל, 'ma'ăkāl'	"food"		
	"of all (any)"		מִכֹּל. 'mikkōl'

Now, in Genesis 6:2 the degraded angels, instead of the woman, did the looking, and what they saw was also "good": the sexually alluring daughters of man, like the forbidden fruit, appeared enticing enough for plucking. These divine beings, endowed with the ability to procreate, presumably waited until there were enough women to satisfy their sexual desires. And the daughters of Eve, their eyes opened, were not found wanting.

The Depraved Nephilim

The disastrous results of such mixing were seen in the persons called Nephilim:

> The Nephilim were on the earth in those
> days, and also afterward,
> when the sons of God came in to the daughters
> of men,
> and they bore children to them.
> These were the mighty men that were of old,
> the men of renown. (Gen. 6:4, Cassuto)[78]

At first glance there is not the slightest suggestion of opprobrium. In fact, it seems that the narrator was saying just the opposite. The Nephilim were depicted as renowned mighty men, celebrated heroes. Yet, how strange it is that men of such renown were mentioned only one other time—when the Israelite spies, evaluating their chances of invading the land of Canaan, described the Nephilim as men of such gigantic stature that they seemed as grasshoppers in comparison.[79] And even this reference is regarded as being unrelated to the Nephilim in Genesis, because it was simply an example of "the historization of the mythical," where later individuals of great stature were compared with the antediluvian mythological Nephilim.[80] The etymology of the word also argues against anything suggesting adulation and honor. Nephilim, coming from נָפַל, 'nāpal,' "fall," hardly suggests warriors of stature, unless perhaps they were dead heroes, fallen on the field of valor. Since the narrator mentioned nothing about battles or slain warriors, it may be assumed that he was not talking about fallen heroes. Finally, it is improbable that the offspring from the licentious union of degraded angels and mortal women would turn out to be valorous, courageous, and honored. These objections to the usual interpretation of the Nephilim require that an effort be made to learn what the narrator might have meant when he used this term.

Nephilim, derived from the passive nominal formation of 'nāpal,' and translated as "fallen ones,"[81] is related by an interchange of middle consonants to נָבֵל, 'nābēl,' a word that was used on occasion in the sense of "to fall":

כִּנְבֹל עָלֶה מִגֶּפֶן
'kinbōl 'āleh miggepen'
As the leaf falleth off from the vine. . . . (Isa. 34:4, JPS)

כְּאֵלָה נֹבֶלֶת עָלֶהָ
'ke'ēlāh nōbelet 'ālehā'
like an oak falling as to its leaves[82]

From the root נָבַל, 'nābal,'[83] come נַבְלוּת, 'nablût,' "shamelessness, lewdness,"[84] and נְבָלָה, 'nebālāh,' "disgraceful folly, a wanton deed."[85] In the previous example of the Benjaminites of Gibeah, who were bent upon the homosexual rape of the Levite, the elderly host used 'neḇālāh' to describe their carnal intentions. In this episode 'neḇālāh' was used with a form of רַע, 'raʿ,' to do wickedly, to behave depraved." Coincidentally—or was it by design?—the word רָעַת, 'rāʿat,' "depravity," appeared in the sentence following the introduction of the word "Nephilim" in the Genesis story.[86] In view of the close relationship between נָפַל, 'nāpal,' and נָבַל, 'nābal,' this proximity strongly suggests that Nephilim projects the same idea as 'neḇālāh' in the book of Judges. Thus, Nephilim means the "depraved ones" or the "lewd ones." In this sense they would be the "fallen ones," not from having fallen to earth from their original abode in heaven,[87] but for having fallen into depravity.

The Sexual Voracity of the 'Gibbōrîm'

If Nephilim is interpreted as the "depraved ones," גִּבֹּרִים, 'gibbōrîm,' commonly translated as "heroes, mighty men," must be reexamined. It seems so discordant for the narrator to describe the offspring of the union between the divine beings and mortal women as depraved and then in the next line refer to them as "stalwart heroes."

Accordingly, the reexamination of 'gibbōrîm' begins with closely related words found in mishnaic Hebrew, a vital source of information for the essential meaning of many Hebrew roots and their precise usage.[88] "As a language with roots in the daily preoccupations of its speakers— agriculture, the handicrafts, animal husbandry, etc.—and their mode of living, it reflects in its richness and its earthy, pithy, and precise phrasing the basic meaning carried by the Hebrew root."[89]

Excellent examples of such pith and earthiness are found in the mishnaic derivations of 'gābar,'[90] the root of 'gibbōrîm':

גַּבְרָא , 'gaberā',' "male, man"[91]
כֹּחַ גַּבְרָא, 'kōaḥ gaberā',' "virile potency"[92]
גֶּבֶר , 'geber,' "phallus"[93]
גִּיבָּרָא , 'gîbbārā',' "hero, giant"[94]
גִּיבָּרָא , 'gîbbārā',' "phallus"[95]

Not only do these mishnaic derivations of גָּבַר, 'gābar,' embody the idea of masculinity and virility, but most important for an understanding of 'gibbōrîm' is the connection between the hero-giant and the sign of virility in the word גִּיבָּרָא, 'gîbbārā',' "hero, giant" and "phallus." This relationship, so obvious in mishnaic Hebrew, was also found in Psalm 19, though not so pronounced as in mishnaic Hebrew.

The Psalmist compared the sun to a bridegroom coming out of his bridal chamber:

> To the sun he gave a tent:
> Then like a bridegroom it goes forth from
> its bower, rejoicing like a warrior to
> run its course. (Ps. 19:5–6)[96]

The sun was as radiant as a bridegroom emerging from the bridal chamber after having proved to himself, and to his wife, that he was virile. Like a

גִּבּוֹר, 'gibbôr,' "a virile man" (not a "warrior") the sun rejoiced in the knowledge that he had the capacity, the virility, the staying power, to begin and to finish the course he would run in the heavens that day. To translate 'gibbôr' as "warrior" would not make sense, since there would not be any parallelism with "bridegroom"; but to regard 'gibbôr' as a virile man with pronounced masculine characteristics fits in perfectly with the picture the Psalmist probably had in mind when he used the figure of the bridegroom. That שֶׁמֶשׁ, 'šmš,' the root for "sun," is also the mishnaic Hebrew root for שַׁמָּשׁ, 'šammāš,' a euphemism for "phallus"[97] and שָׁמַשׁ, 'šāmaš,' a euphemism for "to perform the marital duty,"[98] strengthens the hypothesis that the Hebrew words for all three—"a virile man, sun, and bridegroom"—are related to some kind of sexual manifestation of masculinity.

In the context of this passage in Genesis, 'gibbôr,' the person of unquestioned virility, must be understood in the sense of a "rutter" or "sexual athlete." By associating these rutters with the Nephilim, the narrator underscored the lecherous character of the Nephilim. With 'gibbōrîm' as "rutters" the sentence makes excellent sense:

> It was then that the Nephilim appeared on earth—as well as later—after the divine beings had united with human daughters. Those were the men of old with the reputation[99] of unlimited sexual voracity and capacity.

Man's Animal Appétite

The denunciation of the Nephilim was matched by the narrator's scathing condemnation of man:

> בְּשַׁגַּם הוּא בָשָׂר
> 'bešaggām hú bāśār
> since he is but flesh (Gen. 6:3)[100]

The lexicon describes בְּשַׁגַּם, 'bešaggām,' as the infinitive construct of the root שָׁגַג, 'šāgag,' "to go astray, commit sin or error."[101] Closely parallel to 'šāgag' in meaning and structure is the root שָׁגָה, 'šāgāh,' "go astray, err,"[102] which as "ravish" in the books of Proverbs conveyed a sense of passionate, unending abandonment.[103]

> A lovely hind, a graceful doe—
> Let her breasts intoxicate you always,
> With her love be continually ravished. (Prov. 5:19, Chicago)

This use of the word presents an interesting possibility. If a form of 'šāgāh' meant sexual abandonment in the book of Proverbs, בְּשַׁגַּם, 'bešaggām,' another form of the same verb, might be rendered in Genesis 6:3 as "in their ravishing" or "in their being ravished"—a wording that depicted mankind as caught up in an endless succession of sexual encounters. Such behavior was judged by the narrator as animal—only animals, rutting without letup, would behave in this fashion—for he concluded:

הוּא בָשָׂר
'hû bāśār'
he is an animal.[104]

Rutting is associated with roaring, as is known from the English word "rut," which comes from the Latin 'rugire,' "to roar," so called from the noise made by deer in rutting season.[105] The Hebrews must have observed the same phenomenon and made the same association, for 'šāgāh' with its idea of rutting has a close structural parallel in שָׁאַג,'šā'ag,' "to roar."[106] This fact suggests that the narrator selected this particular word to present both a verbal picture and the sound track to accompany it: to the shrieks of women being ravished was heard the uproarious bellowing of the ravishing men.

The narrator's use of בְּשַׁגָּם, 'bᵉšaggām,' to convey both the ideas of ruting and roaring implies a close familiarity with the *Atrahasis Epic,* the second millenium prototype of the *Gilgamesh Epic.* He must have known that the story in this epic dealt with man's sins and his consequent punishment by plagues followed by the deluge.[107] In the Old Babylonian Version of the epic, it charged the people on earth with being so noisy in their animal-like roaring and bellowing that they disturbed the sleep of the gods.

> [. . .]
> The land became wide, the peop[le became
>   nu]merous,
> The land *bellowed* like wild oxen.
> The god was disturbed by their uproar.
> [Enlil] heard their clamor
> (And) said to the great gods:
> "Oppressive has become the clamor of mankind.
> By their uproar they prevent sleep."[108]

The biblical narrator, familiar with the behavior of animals in their rutting season, very likely understood the people in the *Atrahasis Epic* to be bellowing like wild oxen because they acted like animals in their wild, rutting orgy. Accordingly, he called man a בָּשָׂר, 'bāśār,' "animal," because only an animal could behave with such sexual abandonment. The indictment against man was complete.[109]

4

NOAH—THE SECOND ADAM

A Call to Repentance

To sentence mankind to annihilation without a divine warning of punishment and a call for repentance would have been totally out of keeping with
the biblical concept of justice. The prophets issued calls for repentance
along with threats of punishment. And when repentance was impossible
to achieve, as with the inhabitants of Sodom and Gomorrah, at least
Abraham and Lot were warned of the forthcoming destruction. In accordance with this spirit of justice, God would be expected to issue a
warning for repentance, particularly where all mankind—not just a city
or a nation—was concerned. And this was precisely what God did. His
warning to the earth's population was clear and unmistakable:

> My spirit shall not abide in man for ever. (Gen. 6:3, JPS)

What has been translated as "abide" is mere guesswork based upon
context[1] and is better translated as "expiate, answer for" or "shield, protect."[2] This part of the sentence then reads: "My spirit shall not shield
man forever...."[3] This announcement that God, His patience exhausted,
would continue no longer to shield the guilty from the punishment he
deserved forewarned man that henceforth he would have to shoulder the
consequences of his behavior. But man had a period of grace to repent
and reform:

> ...let the days allowed him be one hundred and twenty years. (Gen. 6:3, NJPS)[4]

Man had one hundred and twenty years to change his behavior. Significantly, this period of grace[5] was accorded to the individual, each man having
the same chance as Noah to save himself. Whether anyone bothered to
heed the warning is beside the point. What is important is the realization
that the narrator depicted divine justice as operative, allowing each man
sufficient time to heed the warning and repent his ways.

The Special Significance of One Hundred and Twenty Years

Why was the period of grace one hundred and twenty years, and not fifty
or one hundred and fifty years? The style and thought process of the nar-

rator caution against ascribing an arbitrariness to him. He worked with too much deliberation and direction to have selected any random number that popped into his mind. Therefore, the narrator must have had something quite definite in mind in using the figure of one hundred and twenty years. Since he gave no reason for this choice, this time span evidently would have been understood immediately by those to whom it was addressed. On his assumption, the search for clues begins by reviewing the facts presented by the text.

Noah was six hundred years old when the waters flooded the earth; at some time after his five hundredth year he fathered his first child; his other two sons were born in the span between his five hundredth and six hundredth year; the Flood coming in Noah's six hundredth year coincided with the death of Methusaleh, Noah's grandfather. Had it come one year earlier, Methusaleh's drowning in the Deluge would have marked him as one of the sexually depraved. Tradition hardly would have assigned such a designation to the son of Enoch, the man who "walked with God."[6] And so Methusaleh died a natural death in the year of the Deluge, preceded five years earlier by his son Lamech, Noah's father.[7]

Had the period of grace been one hundred years, it could have been said that one hundred is a round number and conveniently fits between Noah's five hundredth year and the year of the Deluge. Also, it represented a commonly acknowledged unit of magnitude, as in a Ugaritic diplomatic text[8] enumerating the tribute paid to the Great King, Shuppiluliuma: destined for the Queen and Crown Prince each was a gold cup studded with one hundred carbuncles and one hundred stones of lapis lazuli, and for each of the court dignitaries a silver cup studded with one hundred carbuncles and one hundred stones of lapis lazuli. With the number one hundred denoting an amount of respectable proportions, a divine warning of one hundred years would have signified a most adequate period of time for repentance. But the divine warning was one hundred and twenty years. Since the first unit, the one hundred years preceding the Flood, surely implies a sufficient period of grace, why was the remaining unit of twenty years added?

The Levitical legislation dealing with the release of people who had been pledged to the sanctuary provides the first clue. Though they had been set apart for the performance of auxiliary cultic services,[9] they could obtain their release from the fulfillment of such vows by a money payment calculated according to age and sex:

> When a man explicitly vows to the Lord the equivalent for a human being, the following scale shall apply: If it is a male from twenty to sixty years of age, the equivalent is fifty shekels of silver by the sanctuary weight; if it is a female, the equivalent is thirty shekels. If the age is from five years to twenty years, the equivalent is twenty shekels for a male and ten shekels for a female. If the age is from one month to five years, the equivalent for a male is five shekels of silver, and the equivalent for a female is three shekels of silver. If the age is

sixty years or over, the equivalent is fifteen shekels in the case of a male and ten shekels for a female. (Lev. 27:2-7, NJPS)

The money payment for release from the sanctuary vow clearly recognized age twenty as the beginning of adulthood, the decisive year separating the adult from the adolescent.

Far removed from the fulfillment of sanctuary vows, age twenty also was used as a line of demarcation determining who was to live and who was to die. As with the generation of the Flood, only this time with the Israelites in the desert, God's patience was exhausted. Addressing Moses and Aaron, God pronounced judgment upon the Israelites:

How much longer shall that wicked community keep muttering against Me? Very well, I have heeded the incessant muttering of the Israelites against Me. Say to them: "As I live," says the Lord, "I will do to you just as you have urged Me. In this very wilderness shall your carcasses drop. Of all of you who were recorded in your various lists from the age of twenty years up, you who mutter against Me, not one shall enter the land in which I swore to settle you—save Caleb son of Jephunneh and Joshua son of Nun." (Num. 14:27-30, NJPS)

The condemned were those Israelites "from the age of twenty years up." Those below this age evidently were regarded as not being responsible for their deeds. These age specifications in Numbers and Leviticus would seem to establish age twenty as the period of adulthood, when one assumed responsibility for himself.

With the twenty-year unit in the period of grace designating the age at which adulthood and responsibility began, the narrator seems to have been saying that God wanted to insure that everyone entering the one hundred-year grace period was an adult who legally could be held responsible for his actions. Hence, the infants of twenty years ago would have become adults like Noah; and like Noah they too would have had one hundred years in which to raise a family and be judged. That Noah was five hundred years old did not alter the fact that he entered this period like any other married, childless person. His advanced age of childlessness may indicate that the conception of children was not that frequent and that those born twenty years prior to the one hundred-year grace period probably started off married but childless like Noah. Presumably, during the one hundred years preceding the Flood, the earth's adult population had sufficient time to beget and raise children to maturity like Noah. However, it is no accident that Noah's sons did not father children until after the Flood. In accordance with the dictates of divine justice the narrator probably wanted to convey the idea that the sons and daughters of the generation of the Flood were childless like Ham, Shem, and Japheth at the time of the Deluge. Their childlessness would scotch the idea that God had abandoned His precepts of divine justice and destroyed the innocent, nonadult population along with those over twenty.

While this hypothesis may not answer all the questions pertaining to the grace period of one hundred and twenty years, it does suggest an explanation for what was meant by the words "in those days" and "also after that":

> The Nephilim were in the earth in those days, and also after that, when the sons of God came in unto the daughters of men, and they bore children to them. . . . (Gen. 6:4, JPS)

"In those days" was the period when divine beings *first* began consorting with the daughters of men, presumably long before mankind had sunk into depravity; "also after that" probably referred to the warning period of one hundred and twenty years. Sexual license practiced "in those days" continued unabated "also after that"—in the period of grace. God's warning failed to change their behavior. Consequently, God had no other alternative than to "blot out from the earth" the men, beasts, creeping things, and birds of the sky with the cleansing waters that ultimately would revivify the polluted, foul-smelling earth.

The Tranquilizing Sacrifice

After the earth was completely dry, God instructed Noah to lead forth, along with his family, all the living creatures from the ark so that they could "swarm on the earth and be fertile and increase on earth" (Gen. 8:17, NJPS). Having completed this assignment, Noah

> built an altar to the Lord and, taking of every clean animal and of every clean bird, he offered burnt offerings on the altar. The Lord smelled the pleasing odor, and the Lord said to Himself: "Never again will I doom the world because of man, since the devisings of man's mind are evil from his youth; nor will I ever again destroy every living being, as I have done." (Gen. 8:20–21, NJPS)

This is truly confusing. All along the narrator had indicated that God destroyed mankind because of man's depravity and his propensity for evil. But in these verses it seems God resolved to preserve man precisely because he was born with a mind that had this capacity for evil. Such a glaring contradiction of purpose is, in the opinion of one scholar, ultimately insolvable.[10] If, indeed, this analysis of God's words and acts is correct, it lays God open to the charge of implementing a deformed concept of justice—an accusation far more devastating than the charge of fickleness leveled against the Babylonian gods, who drowned mankind for disturbing the quiet of the heavenly abode.

Confusion and paradox aside, the picture of God presented here is shocking: God was so taken with the pleasing odor of burnt offerings that He vowed never again to visit mankind with devastation. A deity who could be influenced by sacrificial smells did not stand too many levels above those Babylonian gods who crowded around the offerings of Utnapishtim like hungry flies.[11] So utterly disparate is this postdiluvian picture of God from that of the deity whose sensitivity to moral depravity could not tolerate man's presence on earth that obviously what the narrator was saying has been misunderstood. To accuse the narrator, so brilliantly coherent and consistent up to this point, of inconsistency does not seem reasonable. Therefore, this picture of a fickle, paradoxical god must be rejected and an interpretation that does justice to the god he was portraying must be found.

The first clue toward a new understanding of this passage lies in the word נִיחֹחַ, 'nîḥōaḥ,' translated as "sweet,"[12] "pleasing,"[13] and "soothing."[14] Sounding so much like נֹחַ, 'nōaḥ,' "Noah," as to suggest a play on words, 'nîḥōaḥ' also has been defined as "soothing, tranquilizing,"[15] and "appeasing."[16] Since the idea that God could be soothed or appeased by Noah's sacrifice has been rejected, perhaps 'nîḥōaḥ' was meant to describe the intention of the sacrificer. Noah wanted to tranquilize God. Why? The answer to this question may be inferred from what God failed to tell Noah to do:

> Come out of the ark together with your wife, your sons, and your sons' wives. Bring out with you every living thing of flesh that is with you: birds, animals, and everything that creeps on earth; and let them swarm on the earth and be fertile and increase on earth. (Gen. 8:16–17, NJPS)

Noah was told to release all animal life so that they could begin the job of reproducing their species on earth. Note that these instructions pertained only to birds, animals, and everything that crept on earth. But what of man? What was Noah told to do regarding human repopulation of the earth? Not a word! God's silence would seem to leave mankind's fate in doubt. Were Noah and his family to perpetuate the race, or would God consign humanity to extinction upon the death of the survivors?

This glaring omission of any reference to man might well have frightened Noah into action. To convince God that man was worth saving, Noah constructed an altar and sacrificed to God. The odor of the burnt offerings conveyed his argument for man's right to survive and reproduce. By this means he seems to have been saying: "Before the Flood man's immorality and disobedience caused a stink. But now, O Lord, smell. The odor of my offering is not foul, because my actions and those of my family have been and always will be in accordance with the divine will. This soothing odor, in comparison to the odor of the antediluvian generation, is indeed of 'sweet savor.' Let my sacrifice be, therefore, a portent of the future, a promise that our actions will be as morally acceptable as the sweet, clean odor of our sacrifices." This argument, conveyed simply by the odor of burnt offerings, was both appeasing and "pleasing" to God, probably strengthening His conviction that man, as represented by Noah and family, could be trusted in the future to obey the divine dictates.

Noah's sweet-smelling sacrifice was by no means unique. The Babylonian flood survivor, Utnapishtim, also produced a "sweet savor" with a combination of cane, cedarwood, and myrtle.[17] However, the important difference is that the biblical narrator used the Utnapishtim precedent to develop a *rationale* for a certain form of sacrifice or for the entire institution of sacrifice: God's interest was not in burnt flesh per se but in the *odor* given off by such a sacrifice. The odor, as established by the precedent of Noah, affirmed the intent of the sacrificer to follow the example of Noah and fill the atmosphere with the sweet smell of obeisance and gratitude, not the foul odor resulting from disobedience and sexual depravity. The logic of this rationale, founded on the act of remembering, may be discerned when God reassured man that he need not worry about another devastating, universal flood. To this end God set His bow in the clouds to serve as a sign of the covenant that "never again shall all flesh be cut off by the waters of a flood, and never again shall there be a flood to destroy the earth" (Gen. 9:11, NJPS). Here the rainbow, like the burnt offering, stimulated the act of recall, causing God to remember man for blessing and perpetuity. Thus, when the clouds formed over the earth and the rainbow appeared in the clouds

> I will remember My covenant between Me and you and every living creature among all flesh, so that the waters shall never again become a flood to destroy all flesh. (Gen. 9:15, NJPS)

Divine Assurance of the Future

God's resolve never again to destroy "every living being" (Gen. 8:21), so explicit in its reference to all forms of life, went beyond the animate world to the inanimate in the first half of the verse:

> Never again will I doom the world because of man, since the devisings of man's mind are evil his youth. . . . (Gen. 8:21, NJPS)

Since God referred to living creatures in the concluding part of the sentence —"nor will I ever again destroy every living being, as I have done"—He must have been referring in the word הָאֲדָמָה, 'hāʾǎdāmāh,' "the earth," to the actual soil and not to the "world" as translated above. One biblical translation made this point quite explicit:

> When the Lord smelled the soothing odor, the Lord said to himself, "I will never again curse the soil because of man. . . ." (Gen. 8:21, Chicago)

God's resolve not to harm the actual soil presumably rested upon the acknowledgment that "the devisings of man's mind are evil from his youth." Yet, as was previously noted, this reason closely resembled God's justification for abandoning hope for the future rehabilitation of man: "every plan devised by his mind was nothing but evil all the time" (Gen. 6:5, NJPS). These grounds seemingly make God's motive utterly incomprehensible and totally confusing. First, God decided to destroy man because of the continual evil devisings of his mind; then He decided never to doom the soil because of these same evil devisings, which began in man's youth. Secondly, the concretization of the devisings of man's mind resulted in the pollution of the soil; yet, now these same evil devisings saved the soil from any spell of doom.[18]

The confusion is dissipated once it is realized that this verse, which speaks of the devisings of man's mind being evil from his youth, did not refer to events that precipitated the Flood but to the future: God at this moment was deciding the fate of man and regarded Noah as the *second Adam*.

The narrator had prepared the way for Noah's transition to the role of the second Adam by using the almost identical language and theme in the creation and flood stories—a stylistic parallelism indicative of a parallelism of content. A comparison of phraseology shows how closely the postdiluvian episodes continued the theme of the creation accounts.

Creation Story	*Flood Story*
Gen. 1:27, RSV[19] In the image of God he created him.	*Gen. 9:6, RSV* . . . God made man in his own image.
Gen. 1:28, RSV Be fruitful and multiply, and fill the earth and subdue it; and have dominion over the fish of the sea and over the birds of the air and over every living thing that moves upon the earth.	*Gen. 9:1–2, RSV* Be fruitful and multiply, and fill the earth. The fear of you and the dread of you shall be upon every beast of the earth, and upon every bird of the air, upon everything that creeps on the ground and all the fish of the sea; into your hand they are delivered.
Gen. 2:19, RSV every beast of the field and every bird of the air. . . .	*Gen. 9:2, RSV* every beast of the earth, and upon every bird of the air. . . .
Gen. 3:17, RSV cursed is the ground because of you. . . .[20]	*Gen. 8:21, RSV* I will never again curse the ground because of man. . . .

Even without these stylistic similarities the relationship between Noah and Adam is apparent from the fact that both men were the progenitors of mankind: Adam, father of the first race of man; Noah, father of the second. In this frame of reference with Noah as the second Adam, God reflected upon the future of man.

Removal of the Spell

God resolved not to burden this second race of man with the punishment imposed upon Adam and the first race of mankind as a consequence of Adam's eating the forbidden fruit. Noah and his children would not have to wrest food from the earth in anguish,[21] and harvest crops of thorns and thistles,[22] when "the devisings of man's mind are evil from his youth"— that is to say, when man's sexual consciousness, now an innate phase of his psycho-physiological development, becomes acute at the age of puberty. That the narrator used נַעַר, 'na'ar,' "youth," to indicate that sexual awareness occurred at puberty, roughly thirteen years old, can be inferred from a similar use of the word in Isaiah's Immanuel prophecy. Pointing to a young pregnant woman nearby, the prophet declared that Judah's foes would be exiled before the woman's unborn child, 'na'ar,' would know how "to refuse the evil and choose the good" (Isa. 7:16, JPS), that is, before the child became sexually conscious.[23] Isaiah's prediction could not have been more accurate, for the destruction of Samaria occurred exactly twelve years later. In short, divine justice would have compelled the removal of the supernatural spell from the earth: no more would man reap in anguish, no more would the earth be destined to yield thorns and thistles.

Having assured the fertility and productivity of the earth for man, God then proceeded to the matter of the earth's inhabitants themselves and vowed never again to destroy every living being as He previously had done. Nor did God stop with life: even time, characterized by the change of day to night and the variation of seasons, would not cease so long as the earth endured.[24] So ended God's declaration of purpose that formed the basis of the covenant He made with Noah. God's promise to Noah to lift the spell from the earth, thereby guaranteeing the continuation of life, bore out the prediction made by Lamech, Noah's father, when he named his son נֹחַ, 'nōaḥ,' a word corresponding in sound, if not origin, to יְנַחֲמֵנוּ, 'yᵉnaḥămēnû,' "will provide us relief." Lamech correctly foretold that "this one will provide us relief from our work and from the toil of our hands, out of the very soil which the Lord placed under a curse" (Gen. 5:29, NJPS).

These exegetical difficulties disappear in the light of this new interpretation. What some scholars believed to be the height of paradox turns out to be simply and easily explained, once these verses are read in the context of Noah as the second Adam.

Blood and the Souls of Animals

The fate of man thus decided, God turned to Noah and affirmatively answered the question implicit in the tranquilizing sacrifice: "Be fertile and increase, and fill the earth" (Gen. 9:1, NJPS). But God went even further. Man was to exercise absolute dominion over all terrestrial and marine life:

> Every creature that lives shall be yours to eat; as with the green grasses, I give you all these. (Gen. 9:3, NJPS)

God imposed, however, one significant restriction:

> Only flesh with its lifeblood still in it shall you not eat. (Gen. 9:4)[25]

Man was not to eat flesh with its blood because the blood contained the life of the animal. But such an interpretation, based upon the translation of נֶפֶשׁ, 'nepeš,' as "life," misses the point of God's prohibition.[26] Only when 'nepeš' is translated as "soul" does the reason for this prohibition become fully intelligible:

> Only flesh with its soul, that is, its blood, you shall not eat. (Gen. 9:4)

Any prohibition God imposed upon this new race of man can be assumed to refer in some way to the sins of the generation of the Flood. To believe otherwise would be to deny the existence of divine goodness, for surely God, to prevent a repetition of the causes that precipitated the Flood, expressly would forbid those practices that ultimately doomed antediluvian man. The most egregious sin was man's bestial sexuality, which polluted the earth and its atmosphere. So unrestrained, so wild, so voracious was man's sexual ravishing that he was called an animal[27] by the narrator. Surely, the ancients must have asked how man could have fallen so low as to have acquired the qualities and characteristics of a beast in the rutting season and to have cohabited with animals. Presumably, they found the answer to their question in the prohibition forbidding the eating of flesh with the blood still in it: man became animal-like by absorbing its blood along with ingesting its meat. The soul of the animal was believed to be in its blood;[28] consequently, anyone drinking the blood of an animal received its soul into his own body. Once inside the human being the animal soul transformed the human qualities into the instincts and characteristics of the animal.[29] To avoid a repetition of humans behaving like rutting animals, God had to prohibit animal blood from being consumed along with its flesh as a means of preventing human qualities from being subverted to those of an animal.

That animals possessed souls is a matter of debate, but the evidence apparently was present in the Hebrew text:

> And God said, The waters shall bring forth abundantly the prolific creature, a living soul, and fowl that may fly above the earth in the face of the expanse of heaven. (Gen. 1:20)[30]

> And God created the great huge creatures, and every living soul that creepeth, which the waters brought forth abundantly, after their kinds.... (Gen. 1:21)[31]

> And God said, The earth shall bring forth the living soul, after its kind, beast, and creeping thing, and animal of the earth after their kind: and it was so. (Gen. 1:24)[32]

concept of animals possessing souls can be inferred from the following item of Levitical legislation:

> If any man of the house of Israel slaughters an ox or sheep or goat in the camp, or does so outside the camp, and does not bring it to the entrance of the Tent

of Meeting to present it as an offering to the Lord, before the Lord's Tabernacle, bloodguilt shall be imputed to that man: he has shed blood; that man shall be cut off from among his people. (Lev. 17:3–4, NJPS)

What is remarkable about this piece of legislation is that "bloodguilt," used elsewhere in the Bible only with human beings, was associated here with animals.[33] Furthermore, the hypothesis is strengthened by the belief that "the killing of an animal not in accordance with sacrificial procedure is compared to the killing of a human being."[34]

The existence of the animal soul also may be inferred from this item of Levitical legislation cited previously:

If a man has carnal relations with a beast, he shall be put to death; and you shall kill the beast. If a woman approaches any beast to mate with it, you shall kill the woman and the beast: they shall be put to death—their bloodguilt is upon them. (Lev. 20:15–16, NJPS)

Here again the bloodguilt of an animal implied the existence of a soul, which could incur sin and guilt, even though it had not been endowed with a sense of moral discrimination. In the case of carnal relations between a man and an animal, the law sentenced the animal to death seemingly for two reasons: first, as the unfortunate victim of man's sexual hunger, it had become tainted by this act of human depravity and thus posed a threat to the cleanliness of the earth and atmosphere; second, it might have been feared that were the animal to conceive, it might have given birth to an issue half-animal and half-human, something like the mythological Centaurs, Satyri, and Sileni. In the case of the woman, a possible third factor might be inferred: the animal stood condemned by the very state of its sexual excitement as a willing, and thereby guilty, accomplice to the act.

Aside from textual references, perhaps the most telling evidence of the ancient Hebrew belief that the character-soul of the animal could be absorbed with the drinking of its blood is in the Hebraic and Aramaic derivatives of 'dām,' "blood":

Hebrew	Aramaic
דָּם , 'dām,' "blood"[35]	דַּם , 'dam,' "blood; life"[37]
דָּמָה , 'dāmāh,' "be like, resemble"[36]	דְּמָא , 'dᵉmā',' "blood; life"[38]
	דְּמָא , 'dᵉmā',' "to resemble"[39]
	דָּמִים , 'dāmîm,' "blood" (pl.)[40]
	דָּמִים , 'dāmîm,' "equivalent"[41]

How logical for the Hebrew word for "resemble" and the Aramaic word for "equivalent" to derive from the word דָּם , 'dām,' "blood," once it is assumed that by drinking a creature's blood, some or all of its qualities were absorbed, thereby manifesting the character of that creature.

Punishment for Homicide

From animal blood God proceeded to the subject of human blood: God required an accounting from anyone shedding human blood. Of whom would God require this accounting? First, from animals:

> ... of every beast will I require it. ... (Gen. 9:5, NJPS)

That the wild beast should be held accountable for acting in accordance with its nature, namely, killing a human being or animal for food, would be manifestly unjust unless, of course, the ancient Hebrews believed that animals, by virtue of their souls, were endowed with sufficient moral awareness to know that shedding human blood, or allowing itself to be used in an act of sodomy, or in the case of an ox, goring a man or woman to death was an evil for which they were held accountable. But such belief was ruled out when no explicit mention or inference that animals were created with a sense of moral discrimination could be located in the text.

Rather, the justification for holding the animal accountable for taking human life is found in the idea of requiring the return of the murdered man's soul from his murderer, expressed by the phrases דָּרַשׁ דָּמִים, 'dāraš dāmîm,' and דָּרַשׁ דָּם, 'dāraš dām,' "to require the blood." This biblical formula of retaliation could arise only if the murderer was believed to be in control of the victim's soul through the shedding of his blood. The family of the murdered man, moved not so much by vengeance as by the need to get back what had been lost, sought the life of the murderer in order to wrest away the soul of the slain, which had come under the control of the slayer.[42] Thus, retaliation became restitution; by killing the murderer, the family recovered the victim's soul.

In light of this explanation God's statement that He would require the blood of every man-killing beast is more easily understood. Far from a desire to exact vengeance or punishment, God required the death of the beast to effect the release of the soul of the slain from the control of the animal and, quite possibly, to prevent it from acquiring those human qualities that might cause it to initiate some act of sexual depravity with a human.

Next, God said that He would "require the blood" of any man who committed murder; no man would be allowed to gain control over another man's soul. With so inclusive a prohibition, why did the narrator have to add that God would require the blood of "man, his brother"[43]—here דָּרַשׁ דָּם, 'dāraš dām,' "require the blood of," and דָּרַשׁ נֶפֶשׁ, 'dāraš nepeš,' "require the soul of," are identical in meaning. The answer may lie in the Hebrew concept of retaliation. A family retaliated to regain possession of the soul. But what happened when the murderer was a brother or close kin of the victim, as in the case of Cain and Abel? Did retaliation have to be sought against the brother, since the soul of the slain remained in the family? The answer was yes, for though the family itself was not weakened by the loss of a soul, retaliation would preserve the family structure by preventing the stronger from destroying any weaker opposition within the family. Henceforth, under the general law of no mixing of souls, the crime of Cain was to be punished by death, not banishment.

This principle of retaliation, spoken perhaps at the time of the pronouncement of the death sentence or its execution,[44] concluded with the words:

> Whoever sheds the blood of man,
> By man shall his blood be shed;
> For in the image of God
> Was man created. (Gen. 9:6, NJPS)

This punishment was executed by a man commissioned by God to act as His agent or by one commissioned by God's agent. It appears that only one so designated could execute the death sentence without becoming guilty of shedding blood.

5

GOD'S AGENT

A Rationale for Retaliation

The idea of a divinely commissioned agent to execute God's judgment is contained in the special meaning צֶלֶם, 'ṣelem,' "image," acquired when used in the verse:

> For in the image of God
> Was man created.

Heretofore, these words have been given entirely different interpretations. One scholar understood this clause to mean that to slay a human being was to expunge God's image from the world;[1] another suggested that to touch man was to touch God himself, of whom every man was an image;[2] and a third interpreted the phrase as saying that to make man in God's image was to safeguard man from becoming submerged in nature or merged in the laws of the cosmos.[3] Clearly, each of these interpretations regarded this part of the verse as justification for the retaliatory shedding of human blood. But such a rationale for retaliatory punishment cannot account for the sentence bestowed upon Cain after murdering his brother. Cain was punished, but not at the cost of his own life. Rather, God banished him with the words:

> You shall become a ceaseless wanderer on earth. (Gen. 4:12, NJPS)

Cain would be expected to be grateful for escaping with his life, but he was not. He protested that his punishment was far too severe; at the same time he expressed the fear that he would be killed by anyone who met him. Now, in view of the supposed rationale for taking the life of a murderer—"for in the image of God was man created"—God acted in a completely incomprehensible fashion: He calmed Cain with the assurance that His mark would protect him from those seeking to kill him.[4] Protecting the murderer instead of seeking his death clashes with this apodictic pronouncement that the death penalty would be meted out to whoever shed human blood.

This conflict between God's declared punishment of murderers and

61

His protection of Cain supposedly is resolved by the theory of multiple authorship, with the "J" author having written the Cain and Abel story and the "P" author responsible for the blessing and covenant sections in chapter nine.[5] Even if this hypothesis is accepted, there is still an inconsistency over this matter of bloodshed in the writings attributed to "P." The first chapter of Genesis, which described man as having been created in the image of God,[6] prohibited the spilling of blood. Clearly to be inferred[7] from the following verses of chapter one is the prohibition against the shedding of blood within the animal kingdom and human blood within the community of man:[8]

> See, I give you every seed-bearing plant that is upon all the earth, and every tree that has seed-bearing fruit; they shall be yours for food. And to all the animals on land, to all the birds of the sky, and to everything that creeps on earth, in which there is the breath of life, [I give] all the green plants for food. (Gen. 1:29–30, NJPS)

In chapter nine, which is generally assigned to "P" authorship, God has changed His position toward the eating of flesh and the shedding of blood:

> Every creature that lives shall be yours to eat. . . . (Gen. 9:3, NJPS)

Further, "P" now justified retaliatory killing with the words "for in the image of God was man created" (Gen. 9:6, NJPS); whereas, on the basis of chapter one, it was inferred that God prohibited the shedding of human blood for the reason that man was created in God's image. Clearly, God felt differently on the matter of eating flesh or shedding blood, but the Priestly author, assuming there was one, failed to record the reason for such a change. No satisfactory answer by those upholding the theory of multiple authorship has yet been produced to explain this change of attitude. However, these inconsistencies very possibly can be resolved if these chapters are regarded as the unitary creation of one narrator, which permits drawing upon those sections heretofore attributed to "J" for the answers to these apparent contradictions.

"Likeness" and Lineage

In answer to the question of how the rationale for prohibiting the shedding of blood later could be used to condone retaliatory bloodletting, return to chapter one of Genesis, where צֶלֶם, 'ṣelem,' "image," was used in connection with God and man:

> I will make man in My image, after My likeness. (Gen. 1:26, NJPS)

Alongside 'ṣelem,' "image," the word דְּמוּת, 'dᵉmût,' "likeness," seems repetitious, for "image" in this instance appears to imply "likeness."[9] But would the narrator, generally so careful in his choice of words, have used any excess verbiage to describe man's close relationship with God?

On this basis alone, the hypothesis can be posited that "image" and "likeness" have separate meanings of their own.

The distinctiveness of 'dᵉmût,' "likeness," appears in connection with lineage:

> This is the record of Adam's line.—When God created man, He made him in the likeness of God; male and female He created them. And when they were created, He blessed them and called them Man. (Gen. 5:1–2, NJPS)

When it is considered how the narrator occasionally emphasized a particular quality of a word or phrase by its location in a sentence or paragraph, 'dᵉmût,' "likeness," used alone without "image," can be seen to relate "likeness" to evidence of lineage; by tracing Adam's origin directly to God, the narrator established between God and man the special relationship of a father to his child.[10] The creation of man by God in the divine likeness established the claim of kinship in much the same way paternity is implied today when a child's close resemblance to the parent is observed. The narrator had a definite reason for using this grossly anthropomorphic term to establish the paternity of God and the "sonship" of man: he wanted to show that God had made a covenant with man, much along the same lines as that which prevailed among treaty relationships of the ancient Near East.

Lineage and Covenant

Prior to Israel's appearance on the scene of world history, the Semites of Mesopotamia and Syria and the non-Semites of Asia Minor used the covenant as a legally binding contract.[11] The Akkadians, Babylonians, and Hittites frequently couched their suzerainty treaties in kinship terms. "Brotherhood" was declared by partners of equal or unequal status[12] to define and establish a bond between them, which then would be protected by oaths and other acts.[13] In addition to "brotherhood" there was also the concept of "fatherhood" that was found in the statement authorizing the repudiation of a personal bond: "You are not my father (mother, wife, master, etc.)."[14]

Once having established kinship, the suzerainty treaty placed great emphasis upon the benevolence performed by the monarchical "father" or "brother" for his vassal "son" or "brother"; in return for these gifts the recipient assumed the obligation to obey his king. In effect, the vassal was exchanging "*future* obedience to specific commands for *past* benefits which he received without any real *right*."[15]

This pattern of vassalage and kinship is found in the first chapter of Genesis. The relationship between God and man, couched in terms of man being created in the divine likeness, followed the ancient treaty pattern of establishing the kinship of a father and son.[16] God benevolently bestowed upon man the gift of dominion over all life on earth—a gift that the monarchical "father" would give to the vassal "son":

> Be fertile and increase, fill the earth and master it; and rule the fish of the sea, the birds of the sky, and all the living things that creep on earth. (Gen. 1:28, NJPS)

This same covenantal gift of fertility and dominion was given by God to Noah and his sons, only in the later parallel text in chapter nine fear and dread qualified the nature of dominion:

> Be fertile and increase, and fill the earth. The fear and the dread of you shall be upon the beasts of the earth and upon all the birds of the sky—everyting with which the earth is astir—and upon all the fish of the sea; they are given into your hand. (Gen. 9:1–2, NJPS)

Following this reaffirmation of privilege for postdiluvian man, together with the regulations and prohibitions governing the eating of flesh with its blood and the taking of human life, the covenant was made explicit in God's declaration to Noah:

> I now establish My covenant with you and your offspring to come, and with every living thing that is with you—birds, cattle, and every wild beast as well— all that have come out of the ark, every living thing on earth. I will maintain My covenant with you: never again shall all flesh be cut off by the waters of a flood, and never again shall there be a flood to destroy the earth. (Gen. 9:9–11, NJPS)

This theory of a covenant with Adam at the beginning of creation is strengthened by the description of Seth, Adam's third son, reported to have been born in the likeness and image of Adam.[17] This description is significant because it was omitted in the descriptions of Cain and Abel. It would seem that information relevant enough to be mentioned in connection with Seth also would have been cited for Cain and Abel; for, as sons of the same father they also would have been expected to bear a strong resemblance to their father. That Cain and Abel were not so described does not present a problem to those alleging multiple authorship of the Pentateuch: "J", to whom is ascribed the Cain and Abel story, need not be expected to use the descriptive terminology of Seth's birth in the "P" account. While this theory of multiple authorship offers the easy way out of reconciling textual difficulties, a plausible explanation for this descriptive omission can be made without recourse to the theory of different authorship by concentrating upon the covenant relationship between God and man.

The words establishing kinship between God and man were repeated with Adam's third son because the covenant was to be continued through Seth and his seed. The narrator would hardly have used בִּדְמוּתוֹ כְּצַלְמוֹ, 'bid‘mûtô k‘ṣalmô,' "in his likeness after his image" (Gen. 5:3, NJPS), to describe Cain, for these words establishing kinship would have meant that God had made a covenant with a murderer and his future progeny. Nor would the narrator have related these "kinship" words to Abel, the murder victim, for that would have meant that God had concluded a covenant with a "son" whose hope for succession died on that bloody field. Consequently, to indicate that the covenantal relationship passed from Adam to Seth, the narrator focused attention upon the implications of 'dᵉmût,' "likeness":

> This is the record of Adam's line.—When God created man, He made him in the likeness of God; male and female He created them. And when they were created, He blessed them and called them Man.—When Adam had lived 130 years, he begot a son in his likeness after his image, and he named him Seth. (Gen. 5:1-3, NJPS)

In this genealogical review of the line of Adam, the narrator restated the kinship (coterminous with covenant) established by God with the first man and then recorded that this same kinship and covenant were continued through Seth, who received through his parents the same characteristics they had acquired at creation: the 'dᵉmût,' the divine likeness. This information was more than an aside about the close resemblance Seth bore to his father. If the narrator really were interested in such petty details, why did he not mention something of the physical characteristics of Adam's other sons and daughters? That he did not do so seems to indicate that he used 'dᵉmût,' "likeness," not as a physically descriptive term but as the accepted term establishing a kinship-covenant relationship. The covenant established with Adam was to continue with Seth and his children.

The "Image" as Agent

Having established the strong probablility that "likeness" is a specific term conveying kinship, the evidence suggesting that 'ṣelem,' "image," has acquired in certain instances the special meaning of "agent" or "representative" of God requires investigation. A human being as an agent of divinity was a common feature in many of the treaty texts concluded in the ancient Near East. In these covenants, the king was thought of as "the choice and representative of the gods."[18] In fact, "the human king seems to have felt himself strengthened and confirmed when he could act as agent of the gods."[19] At times, such representation or agency was expressed in terms of "images," as in the vassal treaty of the Assyrian king Esarhaddon:

> (Ashur, king) of the gods, and the great gods, my lords, whether the image of Esarhaddon, king of Assyria, or the image of Ashurbanipal, the crown prince, ... You will raise no claim against the seal of Ashur, king of the gods, which is set in your presence.[20]

The idea of "image," as reflected in the Assyrian usage of the word in connection with the concept of the king as agent of the deity, must have been known to the author of Deuteronomy, for he displayed a thorough familiarity with the traditions underlying the thought and language of Assyrian vassal treaties. This inference derives from the close similarity of maledictions between Deuteronomy and the vassal treaty of Esarhaddon:

Deut. 28:23, RSV
And the heavens over your head
shall be brass, and the earth
under you shall be iron.

Vassal Treaty of Esarhaddon 528–531
May they (the gods) make your
ground like iron so that no one
can plough it; just as rain does
not fall from a brazen heaven, so
may rain and dew not come down
upon your fields and your pastures.[21]

Deut. 28:27, RSV
The Lord will smite you with boils
. . . and scurvy.

VTE 419–420
May Sin, the lantern of heaven
and earth, clothe you with leprosy.[22]

Deut. 28:28–29, RSV
The Lord will smite you with madness
and blindness and confusion of mind:
and you shall grope at noonday, as
the blind grope in the darkness, and
you shall not prosper in your ways;
and you shall be only oppressed and
robbed continually, and there shall be
none to help you.

VTE 422–424
May Shamash, the light of heaven
and earth, not render you a just
judgment/not give you a reliable
decision; may he deprive you of
the sight of your eyes (so that)
they will wander about in darkness.[23]

Deut. 28:30a, RSV
You shall betroth a wife, and another
man shall lie with her.

VTE 428–429
May Venus, the brightest of the stars,
make your wives lie in your enemy's
lap while your eyes look (at them).[24]

This striking resemblance between the words and associations of the Deuteronomic curses of leprosy and judicial blindness and the curses in the vassal treaty of Esarhaddon could be explained by assuming that "the pairing of these two concepts—which is comprehensible only in the light of Mesopotamian religion—was literally transcribed from a Mesopotamian treaty copy to the book of Deuteronomy."[25] If this assumption is correct, such direct borrowing from Assyrian treaty documents[26] would make it highly unlikely for the narrator of Deuteronomy *not* to have known that the king was considered to be the agent of the deity and that the word "image" was used in connection with this royal, but human, agent. However, it need not be assumed that this striking similarity between Deuteronomy and the vassal treaty of Esarhaddon depended on direct Hebrew borrowing at all. It is entirely possible that Deuteronomy and the vassal treaty reflect a common tradition going back into the second millenium and extending over much of the ancient Near East.[27]

To conclude, however, that the Deuteronomist knew of such Assyrian nomenclature or drew from the same source reflected in this Assyrian document is not to assume automatically that the narrator of Genesis knew of it—if the critical theory is accepted that Deuteronomy and Genesis were written at different times by different people. If no such theory of multiple authorship of the Pentateuch existed, it could have been concluded forthwith that the author of Genesis, being also the author of Deuteronomy, certainly was aware of the same covenantal tradition found in Assyrian thought when he worked through the Genesis material. However, even with such a theory, subscribed to by many biblical scholars, there is a strong possibility that a relationship does exist between these two books on the basis of a similarity of covenantal theme and expression.

For example, both the Noah narrative and Deuteronomy used the phrase "walking with God." Noah, the righteous man, blameless in his age, "walked with God" (Gen. 6:9). Because Noah's righteousness and blamelessness saved him and his family from the devastating waters of the Flood, "walked with God" has been interpreted as being synonymous with these virtues.[28] But this particular phrase, occurring as it does in Micah's threefold covenantal requirements[29] and in the Deuteronomist's requisites for divine aid in dispossessing more powerful nations,[30] suggests the idea of covenantal loyalty. It was because Noah was "righteous" and "blameless" that he may be said to have observed the terms of the covenant, as established with Seth, by acting as a proper and fit agent of God. Noah was saved, therefore, because he faithfully represented his Creator; true to the terms of the covenant, he did indeed "walk with God."

Dread—a Concomitant of Dominion

The covenant between God and Noah was reaffirmed after the flood water had subsided and Noah had disembarked. Noah and his sons were told to "be fertile and increase, and fill the earth" (Gen. 9:1). Then Noah was assured by God that "the fear and the dread" of him and his offspring would be upon all the living creatures of the world.[31] This capacity to cause fear and dread can be understood in light of the terror-inspiring aspect of kingship found in Assyrian texts describing royal conquests. Thus, Shalmaneser III (858–824 B.C.E.) wrote of his conquests:

I spread the terror-inspiring glare of my rule over Hatti.[32]

In the year of (the eponym) Daian-Ashur, in the month of Aiaru, the 14th day, I departed from Nineveh. I crossed the Tigris and approached the towns of Giammu on the river Balih. They became afraid of the terror emanating from my position as overlord, as well as of the splendor of my fierce weapon....[33]

In Shalmaneser's annalistic reports, he attributed his terror-inspiring capacity to the deity Ashur:

In the month Aiaru, the 13th day, I departed from Nineveh; I crossed the Tigris, by-passed the countries Hasamu and Dihnunu and approached the town of La'la'te which (belongs to) Ahuni, man of Adini. The terror and the glamor of Ashur, my lord, overwhelmed [them] . . . and they dispersed.[34]

In these excerpts it is shown that those favored by the deity possessed the common characteristic of producing terror in others. In fact, this capacity to invoke dread was synonymous with a reign of complete domination over captive peoples. The Deuteronomist, so strongly influenced by the tradition underlying the language of the Assyrian vassal treaty, also seemed to partake, along with the Assyrians, of a traditional way of depicting absolute sovereignty, for he promised Israel that it would acquire a similar capacity to instill fear as a reward for observing the terms of God's covenant:

> The Lord your God will put the dread and the fear of you upon all of the land in which you set foot. . . .(Deut. 11:25, NJPS)

Evidently, the Deuteronomist regarded the dread and fear that Israel would inspire in her neighbors as the mark of divine favor, which would culminate in complete sovereignty.

These examples from Assyrian annalistic literature and Deuteronomy suggest that the fear cast by Noah upon the surviving living creatures was nothing more than a commonly accepted way of expressing absolute power wielded by any true agent of God. God could hardly promise Noah dominion over mankind when the Deluge left hardly any mankind to speak of; so He expressed the degree of sovereignty He was conferring upon His human representative by granting him the power to inspire terror in the only living substitute for man: the creatures who had survived the Flood.

The Babylonian Agent

This discussion of the similarity between Assyrian covenantal and annalistic literature and certain passages in Deuteronomy and Genesis underscores the high probability that the underlying traditions influencing Assyrian thought and usage extended to the word 'ṣelem,' "image," in these first nine chapters of Genesis in connoting the Assyrian concept of agent or representative.

Another reason for interpreting צֶלֶם, 'ṣelem,' as "agent" is derived from its close structural similarity with סֶמֶל, 'semel.'[35] The rabbinic sages recognized this similarity when they equated the ladder Jacob saw in a dream with Nebuchadnezzar's image simply by transposing the ל, 'l,' and מ, 'm,' of סֻלָּם, 'sullām,' "ladder," to arrive at סֶמֶל, 'semel,' "image."

> "And behold a ladder." This is the image of Nebuchadnezzar. Semel is identical with sulam. The letters in this word are the letters in that.[36]

By equating סֶמֶל, 'semel,' a type of image erected by Manasseh in the Temple,[37] with סֻלָּם, 'sullām' (צֶלֶם, 'ṣelem'), the rabbis were saying in effect that 'ṣelem' could be translated as "image."[38]

The possibility of parallelism between 'ṣelem' and 'semel' leads to that passage in the book of Ezekiel where 'semel' denoted not an image but a man dealing with the commercial transactions of purchase and sale.[39]

Analysis of this word shows that it can be traced back to an Akkadian term meaning "*the commercial agent*" who buys and sells under orders of the wholesale merchant.[40]

In the Hammurabi Code a commercial agent, living abroad, was often responsible for ransoming prisoners. To these prisoners he undoubtedly was an "agent of deliverance."[41] Upon entering the Hebrew language as a loan word, this term for commercial agent thereupon acquired the additional meaning of an "agent of deliverance." Hence, the idea that "a good deed, a gift to God in fulfilment of a vow, the erection of a stele, or the like might be an 'agent of deliverance'" meant that Manasseh's gift to the deity, his 'semel,' "image," served as an "agent of deliverance."[42] Having traced 'semel' back to its original meaning of "agent," it is highly likely that its parallel word 'ṣelem' should be understood as "agent," in the first, fifth, and ninth chapters of Genesis.

Man's Functional Similarity to God

Once צֶלֶם, 'ṣelem,' is interpreted as "agent," a hitherto unsuspected logic and coherence in the first chapter of Genesis is discovered:

> And God said: "Let us make man in our image, after our likeness; and let them have dominion over the fish of the sea, and over the fowl of the air, and over the cattle, and over all the earth, and over every creeping thing that creepeth upon earth." (Gen. 1:26, JPS)

By inserting בְּצַלְמֵנוּ, 'bᵉṣalmēnû,' "in our image," alongside "after our likeness" the narrator established man as God's agent, whose action in exercising supremacy and domain over all life in the universe was answerable ultimately to God, with whom he had entered into a covenant. Mindful also as to why man should have been singled out of all the works of creation for honor and responsibility, the narrator inserted the word for "after our likeness" to show that man's lineage, traced directly to God, established him as different from all other forms of life, as someone "closer" to his Creator.

God made provision that His creation of man, once begun, would become self-perpetuating:

> And God created man in His own image, in the image of God created He him; male and female created He them. (Gen. 1:27, JPS)

Here the narrator amplified upon the concept of "man" by introducing the two sexes necessary for procreation: "male and female created He them." Evidently, the narrator, in reasserting that man was created in God's image, wanted to leave no doubt that woman also shared to some extent in the work of transmitting the divine gift of dominion, thereby insuring that her offspring, born "in the image of God," would inherit the gift of divine authority without any further intervention on God's part. With the continuation of the race thus secured by the process of birth, the narrator introduced Seth as the child of Adam and Eve, who was begotten in the "image" and "likeness" of his father and mother and through whom the covenant would be perpetuated.

The narrator might well have had another reason for asserting that God created both male and female in the divine likeness and image. Quite possibly he wanted to scotch any idea that the human being bore a physical resemblance to God by making it impossible for his statement to be taken literally. A literal interpretation would mean that God was bisexual, possessing both male and female characteristics. Surely, if the narrator intended to convey this idea, he would have portrayed evidence of divine bisexuality in other sections of the story. Such references are not to be found, of course, because this concept of divine bisexuality was utterly foreign to the narrator. Reference to the biblical God was always masculine, without the slightest hint of femininity.

The absence of any allusion to divine bisexuality strongly suggests that the narrator in this verse really was trying to express an abstraction regarding the relationship between God and man, despite the paucity of the Hebrew language in abstract terminology.[43] He was saying, in effect, that not physically but *operationally* does man resemble God. To understand the difference between physical and operational resemblance, it is helpful to look at the distinction between pictorial and operative imagery as drawn by Norbert Wiener in his discussion of the possibility of machines constructing their own progeny of machine:

> In order to discuss intelligently the problem of a machine constructing another after its own image, we must make the notion of image more precise. Here we must be aware that there are images and images. Pygmalion made the statue of Galatea in the image of his ideal beloved, but after the gods brought it to life, it became an image of his beloved in a much more real sense. It was no longer merely a *pictorial* image but an *operative* image.... These operative images, which perform the functions of their original, may or may not bear a pictorial likeness to it. Whether they do or not, they may replace the original in its action, and this is a much deeper similarity.[44]

According to Wiener, resemblance is confirmed if the image or likeness performs the *function* of the original, even though it may not bear a pictorial likeness. Injecting this concept into the biblical context shows how Adam and his descendants, acting on God's instructions, executed the will of their Creator and thereby functioned in the role of creator. In doing so, they became "operative images, which perform the function of their original," without implying any pictorial resemblance. The anthropomorphic terms "image" and "likeness," understood in this light, never were intended to be used for pictorial imagery. Rather, these terms were employed to convey special convenantal implications connected with lineage and agency. Man resembled God only by acting in the "operative" image of the Divine.

The cataclysmic destruction wrought by the Flood dispelled the belief that *all* men were born as "agents" of God, for God could hardly be expected to destroy His own designated representatives. Furthermore, only a select few could attain the position of God's agents, since the concept of agency implied differentiation and selectivity. An agent had to make representation *to* someone on behalf of someone else. God's "agent" had to represent the terms of the covenant established at the time of creation for all mankind. Thus, for the narrator to speak of God creating man in the divine image was to say that the man so selected has the *potential* of becoming the "agent" of the Creator. That this man was capable of becoming God's representative was manifested in the persons of Seth and Noah. But why were Seth and Noah so designated? And how was their potential actualized? To answer these questions necessitates a return to the events immediately preceding the birth of Seth, to the Cain and Abel conflict, when God first selected His "agent."

6

THE CRIME OF CAIN

The Rejected Offering

The Cain and Abel story, to make any sense at all, must be understood as the account of a struggle for the highest stakes imaginable—accreditation as God's צֶלֶם, 'ṣelem,' "agent." Cain's malevolence toward Abel, contrary to a widely proclaimed theory, did not reflect the age-old conflict between the pastoral and the agricultural ways of life,[1] for Scripture nowhere elevated one occupation above the other. It simply said that the brothers divided between them the labor necessary for the sustenance of the community.[2] Rather, Cain's hatred stemmed from the time when God rejected his bid for the office of צֶלֶם, 'ṣelem.'

The narrator set the stage for the murder of Abel first by introducing the first-born Cain as a farmer and his brother Abel as a shepherd. He then inserted the element of time: literally "at the end of days," but generally rendered "in the course of time" (Gen. 4:3). Such a phrase, while not enumerating the exact amount of time that had elapsed, conveys the impression that a lengthy span of time had passed. Thus the narrator was able to establish the fact that sufficient time had elapsed for the world's population to have increased from the first man and woman to such numbers that God needed an agent to remind the people of the terms of the covenant and to convey His wishes to them. This phrase, "at the end of days," also indicated that Cain and Abel had lived long enough to be compared, on the basis of their conduct, as to whom would qualify for the position of God's "agent."

Then, Cain brought an offering to God, closely followed by Abel with his sacrifice. Since God had not requested these offerings, were these offerings spontaneous and unsolicited? Or can it be assumed that the narrator omitted the reason for the offerings because it was so self-evident? If the occasion was the selection of God's "agent," no motive needed to be given, for the offerings would play the same significant role as those in the closely related ceremony of the installation of the Hebrew kings, during which the fat parts of the sacrificial animal also were offered.[3] But why did not Cain present such a fatted animal, if the proper and customary offering was the choice, fat parts of the animal? Was he not aware of what was

72

at stake? Did he not know that the circumstances of selection demanded the sacrifice of the fat parts of the firstlings of a flock?

From Cain's distress[4] at having been rejected by God, it seems that he was neither unaware nor indifferent to the importance of the occasion. Furthermore, he complied with protocol when he presented the fruit of the soil as an offering, for these also were accounted the "fat parts," as when the sacrifice of the fat parts of the firstlings of a flock?

> Say to your brothers, "Do as follows: load up your beasts and go at once to the land of Canaan. Take your father and your households and come to me; I will give you the best of the land of Egypt and you shall live off the fat of the land." (Gen. 45:17–18, NJPS)

The book of Daniel said that the aggressor would wreck havoc "upon the fattest places of the province."[5] And the infirm and blind Isaac, thinking that he was blessing Esau, mentioned the "fat of the earth" in bestowing his blessing upon Jacob:

> See, the smell of my son is as the smell of the field that the Lord has blessed. May God give you of the dew of heaven and the fat of the earth, abundance of new grain and wine. (Gen. 27:27–28, NJPS)

Clearly, these examples indicate that by offering the fruit of the soil—the "fat parts" of the earth—Cain was complying with the requirements of the selection and installation ceremony. Moreover, his offering refutes the charge that God rejected his presentation because of his begrudging attitude:[6] an offering of the "fat parts" of the earth reflected Cain's concern for the appropriate gesture.

The offerings having been presented, God then made His selection:

> The Lord paid heed to Abel and his offering, but to Cain and his offering He paid no heed. (Gen. 4:4–5, NJPS)

The word וַיִּשַׁע, 'wayyiša',' variously translated as "had regard for"[7] or "show regard for,"[8] prompts the question of how God paid heed or showed regard for Abel and his offering. Was there some outward manifestation to indicate to Cain then and there that he and his offering had been rejected? It has been suggested that God showed His pleasure with Abel by bestowing the blessing of fertility upon Abel's flock and withholding it from Cain.[9] While such a blessing might have been apparent over an extended period of time, it scarcely would have become manifest quickly enough for Cain to respond to the adverse decision with pique and dejection. It must be assumed, therefore, that in some way God's will manifested itself speedily. Since וַיִּשַׁע, 'wayyiša',' is the only word describing God's response to the offerings, it must have been selected by the narrator to express an immediately perceptible sign of divine pleasure.

The usual translation of the root שָׁעָה, 'šā'āh,' is "look upon, gaze."[10] Accordingly, the translators concluded that to gaze upon something was to "pay heed" or "show regard" for that object. However, an additional meaning of 'šā'āh' may be discerned in the fact that a number of Hebrew words, or their cognates, also embodying the concept of seeing or gazing, mean "shine" or "be bright":

נָבַט, 'nābaṭ' (Pi., Hiph.), "see, look"[11]
　　　　original meaning: "be bright, shine"[12]
　　　　'nabâtu' (Assyrian), "shine"[13]
צוּץ, ṣûṣ (Kal), "shine, sparkle"[14]
　　　　(Hiph.), "gaze, peep"[15]
חוּר, 'ḥûr'
　　　　(Syriac) 'ḥar'; (Babylonian) 'haru,' "see"[16]
　　　　(Mishnaic) חַוַר, 'ḥāwar,' "be bright, look with
　　　　　　gratification (of eyes)"[17]
חָרַר, 'ḥārar,' "be aglow"[18]

As is evident, these words display a relationship between "glowing" and "gazing." Turning now to 'šā'āh,' the same pattern of the aforementioned words is seen, in that the basic definition of the root forms[19] is "bright."[20] These words attest to the development in biblical thought of a belief that God, on occasion, could and did disclose the object of His pleasure and regard by enveloping it in an aura of light. The brightness revealed to the populace the one whom God had selected for the role of transmitting His will to the people.[21] Thus שָׁעָה, 'šā'āh,' in the Cain and Abel story had the additional meaning of "envelop in radiance." The narrator presented a picture of God enveloping Abel and his offering in a glowing light[22] as He gazed upon him. It was this brightness that enabled Cain quickly to conclude who was selected as "agent" or "representative."

The Glowing Face of Moses

The most compelling argument substantiating the cogency of this theory is found in the scene where Moses, descending from Mt. Sinai a second time with the terms of the covenant, radiated a glow imparted to him by God. Presumably, Moses was infused with this glow when God, though hidden in the cloud, gazed upon him when He addressed him.[23]

Upon beholding the radiance of Moses' face, the Israelites shrank away from him.[24] But their reticence was not due to a fear that the light from Moses' face would harm them if they gazed upon it:

> But Moses called to them, and Aaron and all the chieftains in the assembly returned to him, and Moses spoke to them. Afterwards all the Israelites came near, and he instructed them concerning all that the Lord imparted to him on Mount Sinai. And when Moses had finished speaking with them, he put a veil over his face. (Ex. 34:31–33, NJPS)

Had Moses believed that anyone gazing upon his glowing face would be harmed by the glare, he never would have removed his mask *before* addressing the gathering; after all, he was talking to those regarded as loyal, those who had survived the purge. Significantly, the Israelites did not shrink from Moses thereafter when he removed his mask in their presence. That Moses veiled his face only *after* he finished speaking to the Israelites indicates that public viewing of this radiance was an important factor in communicating the terms of the covenant to the assemblage.

In fact, removing his mask became standard operating procedure for Moses:

> Whenever Moses went in before the Lord to speak with Him, he would leave the veil off until he came out; and when he came out and told the Israelites what he had been commanded, the Israelites would see how radiant the skin of Moses' face was. Moses would then put the veil back over his face until he went in to speak with Him. (Ex. 34:34–35, NJPS)

This act of removing his veil before God and the people must be understood as Moses' response to the crisis of leadership suffered by the Israelites.

After waiting forty days and nights for Moses to descend from Mt. Sinai,[25] the Israelites despaired of ever seeing him again[26] and so turned to Aaron for leadership. They prevailed upon him to make an idol—"Make us a god to lead us" (Ex. 32:23). Moses, returning with the two tablets of the Pact, heard the boisterous sounds of idol worship. He reacted swiftly and decisively. Calling the Levites to his side, Moses rid the camp of the hard-core defectors in a bloody purge.[27]

In this entire sequence of events, no mention was made of light radiating from the face of Moses. Consequently, it must be assumed that his face did not radiate any light. Yet, he must have been in as close contact with God in his first stay on the mountain as he was in his second. That Moses did not reflect this divine light means that one's skin did not always glow as a result of being addressed by God. This effusion of light, in all likelihood, depended on divine will; in the case of Moses, it resulted from a challenge to his leadership.

The loss of prestige and confidence suffered by Moses culminated in the worship of the golden calf. To restore his prestige and to silence any further challenge to his leadership, Moses needed a sign, instantly recognizable by the populace, that would designate him the representative of the divine. Such a sign was the glow that radiated from his face; the light signified that God still regarded him as His 'ṣelem,' His "agent." When Moses, glowing radiantly, descended a second time with the covenant, he was acknowledged without challenge by the Israelites to be God's "representative." In a mark of obeisance, often displayed by subjects to their ruler, the Israelites "shrank" from coming near him; whereupon Moses, to demonstrate that he spoke with the full authority of God's representative, exposed his glowing face to the populace while reading the terms of the Pact.

Thereafter, Moses revealed his radiance to the Israelites to strengthen his claim that he spoke as the "agent" of God. Upon entering the Tent of

Meeting to confer with God, Moses would leave off his veil[28] so that the people, observing his glowing face when he emerged from the Tent, would know that he spoke with God and that he thereby conveyed God's dictates to them.

The relationship of light to divine representation seems to have been extended later to the institution of the priesthood, where the flashing light from the golden, bejewelled breastplate of the High Priest, attached to the ephod and hung in such a way that the Urim and Tummim[29] in the breastplate were upon the heart of the High Priest, testified to the divine presence and lent validity to the divinations reached by the Urim and Tummim. Perhaps this line of thought can even be carried one step further to those references linking the Torah with light:

> For the commandment is a lamp
> And the Torah is a light. (Prov. 6:23)[30]

Here the Torah, either ancillary to the priesthood with its ephod or succeeding the priestly institution, is compared to a light since it too is representative of God and testifies to His wishes.

Another Meaning for "Abel"

If the aforementioned arguments have established the glow of light as an indication of the presence or selection of God's 'ṣelem,' "agent," then the depth of meaning contained in the name הֶבֶל, 'hebel,' "Abel," can be appreciated. That Abel's name was not "explained" along with the names of his brothers, Cain and Seth, suggests that the narrator felt the meaning of Abel's name to be so clear that it needed no explanation.

Some ancient and modern commentators have derived 'hebel,' "Abel," from its lexical definition of "breath" or "vapor,"[31] in the Hebrew a word connoting the brevity of human life; the name thereby becomes an appropriate allusion to the fate that ultimately befell Eve's second son.[32] Thus, the rabbinic sages quoted Eve as saying that she named her son 'Hebel' because "he was born but to die."[33]

Another interpretation, however, is suggested by two words used parallel to 'hebel' in Psalm 39: נִצָּב, 'niṣṣāb,' "false image,"[34] in verse six and צֶלֶם, 'ṣelem,' "phantom,"[35] in verse seven. While expressing the same vaporous, fleeting existence ascribed to הֶבֶל, 'hebel,' the following also mean:

> צֶלֶם, 'ṣelem,' "agent"
> נִצָּב, 'niṣṣāb,' "prefect, deputy"[36]

The fact that these two words, each embodying the idea of high office, were used parallel to 'hebel' in this psalm suggests that 'hebel' also may have the additional meaning of "prefect" or "agent." Such a dual designation, harmonizing so neatly with the events of the Cain-Abel story, eliminates any need for amplification of Abel's name; as the selected "representative" whose life was a mere breath, 'hebel' would be recognized immediately for its double function.

Cain's Second Chance

God's preference for Abel and his offering, as noted earlier, caused Cain to respond with anger and disappointment; this reaction in turn prompted God to ask why he was angry and disappointed. That God would ask this question to elicit information taxes credulity, for it is unthinkable that God did not understand the cause of Cain's bitterness. Nor should His question be regarded as a means of chastisement "to call the culprit back to the consciousness and confession of his own guilt."[37] What if God was not seeking an answer to a question that was really not a question? It seems that God was saying in effect: "Why should you be angry? What right have you to be distressed?" In other words, God was telling him that he had gotten what he deserved, that he should have expected Him to react to his misconduct in this fashion.

The theme of misconduct was introduced by God's next remark:

Surely if you do right. . . . (Gen. 4:7, NJPS)

The narrator left no doubt that Cain's rejection by God need not be absolute or permanent; everything would depend upon his conduct. If he "does right," then שְׂאֵת, 'śᵉʾēt.' This word 'śᵉʾēt' has been translated as "there is uplift" (Gen. 4:7),[38] "you shall be upstanding,"[39] "it shall be lifted up,"[40] "you should be happy,"[41] "you will be accepted,"[42] "it should mean exaltation."[43] These translations, while acceptable in other contexts, miss the mark here, for seemingly this word was meant to convey something much more definite than a generalized concept of being acceptable to God and man.

To understand 'śᵉʾet' in the context of Cain's reward for changing his conduct, its use in the blessings (rewards in a real sense) that Jacob bestowed upon his sons must be examined.

Addressing Reuben, his first born, Jacob blessed him with the words:

יֶתֶר שְׂאֵת

Exceeding in rank (Gen. 49:3, NJPS)[44]

Here 'śᵉʾēt' means "rank," a translation that would fit easily into the context of the Cain episode. With 'śᵉʾēt' as "rank," God was saying that if Cain acted properly, he would be elevated in rank. Though what the rank would be was not stated, in all likelihood it would be below that of Abel. The Akkadian laws governing fratriarchate attest to the fact that such distinctions between brothers were known in the ancient Near East.

Akkadian literature reveals that one of the brothers sharing the fratriarchate was *primus inter pares,* while the other was a *talîmu* brother. In addition there was a "vice-fratriarch" called *terdennu.*[45] Such distinctions between brothers are believed to be present in the biblical term 'mišneh' when applied to the second son. This title occurred with sufficient frequency to prompt an identification with *terdennu* in the technical sense of "vice-fratriarch."[46]

This fratriarchal distinction might have meant that the highest Cain could aspire to was the rank of "vice-agent." Had he been able to equal or surpass Abel in rank, he probably would not have been moved to eliminate his "higher ranking" brother. That he did so suggests that the promised elevation in rank still would have left him subordinate to Abel—a situation that he evidently could not tolerate.

God's Threat to Cain

Having informed Cain of what to expect for a reward, God revealed what his punishment would be if he did not heed God's warning and persisted in his present course of behavior:

> ... sin is the demon at the door, whose urge is toward you; yet you can be his master. (Gen. 4:7, NJPS)[47]

The character of Cain's punishment is confusing. It appears to involve sin, either as a demon or as something lurking by a door, but beyond this point, it is difficult to comprehend exactly how sin fitted into the description of a punishment. No one would question the obvious, that sin possessed the person who was not doing "right." Indeed, so self-evident is this fact that it is curious that the narrator inserted this information at all. But to have God reassure Cain in His threat of punishment that Cain could oppose and ultimately triumph over sin, even while succumbing to it by not doing "right," makes no sense at all. By reassuring Cain of his ability to master or rule over sin, God rendered harmless the threatened punishment by which He hoped to force Cain into a different course of behavior. Only the Revised Standard Version retains the flavor of a condition in stipulating that Cain *must* master sin to evade punishment, but to achieve this effect it had to depart from the literal translation of the text. In light of these incompatible[48] factors it can be easily understood why one scholar has judged this particular passage to be "one of the most difficult and obscure Biblical sentences."[49]

The Nature of Cain's Sin

To bring some measure of lucidity to this enigmatic passage, the nature of Cain's wrongdoing needs to be investigated. In what specific way did he not do "right"? With the office of "agent" at stake, the narrator would be expected to mention at least one act of Cain's that disqualified him for that lofty position. Proceeding on this assumption, it appears that Cain's activity consisted solely of presenting an offering to God. Presumably, therefore, his improper conduct was somehow connected with his presentation of the offering. Since the fruit of the soil, however, was always acceptable in the Bible as an offering, Cain's sin could not have stemmed from the *type* of offering, but from his *manner* of presentation. With no clue given in this simple statement regarding his offering, God's threatened punishment must contain some reference to his sin.

The investigation starts with the word לַפֶּתַח, 'lappetaḥ,' generally translated as "at the door." The noun פֶּתַח, 'petaḥ,' also can mean "an opening"[50] as with a cave,[51] and the verb פָּתַח, 'pātaḥ,' "to open," has been used with the opening or uncovering of a pit.[52] Since no specific dwelling was mentioned in the story, 'petaḥ' as "door" evidently did not apply to a house, cave, tent, or city. This leaves only one possibility—the ground. Cain was a tiller of the soil and he brought an offering from the fruit of the soil. Also, the verb 'pātaḥ' has been used as either to "open" or "uncover" a pit. On this admittedly fragile evidence, it may be assumed that 'petaḥ' referred to an opening in the ground, dug very likely with the implements Cain used to cultivate the soil. Accordingly, to לַפֶּתַח, 'lappetaḥ,' can be ascribed the tentative meaning of "at the opening"—of some sort of pit.

The usual translation of the next word, חַטָּאת,'ḥaṭṭā't,' is "sin." But 'ḥaṭṭā't' does not always mean "sin." It can also be "stepping" or "walking."[53] Consequently, it cannot be said categorically that here 'ḥaṭṭā't' means "sin." To determine its proper meaning, רֹבֵץ, 'rōbēṣ,' has to be defined, for only after its function is fully understood can the meaning of 'ḥaṭṭā't' that best fits the sense of the phrase be selected.[54]

Assuming that 'rōbēṣ' is an early loanword from the Akkadian, meaning "demon," there are two possible translations:

> (1) ". . . sin is a demon at the opening"
> (of the pit)
> (2) ". . . at the opening is the stepping
> (or moving) of a demon. . . ."

To accept the first rendition, that sin is a demon, requires an explanation of what special emphasis the narrator hoped to achieve by personifying sin as a demon, since such personification is not found anywhere else in the Bible.

On the other hand, the picture of a demon moving about the opening sheds valuable light upon God's reason for rejecting Cain as His "agent," for it marked Cain as participating in a pagan cultic practice. By digging a pit and placing an offering beside or in it, Cain enticed this demon to ascend from the infernal region. More evidence supporting this theory will be presented shortly in the interpretation of another passage in this story; until then it can be assumed that this was a chthonic demon that had responded to Cain's cultic act.

Eve's Punishment

The introduction of Cain's punishment is contrary to all appearances if judged from the usual translation:

> . . . whose urge is toward you. . . . (Gen. 4:7, NJPS)[55]

The narrator, it seems, wanted to show that a relationship existed between this phrase and the punishment of Eve, because he used almost identical language in both passages. If the precise nature of Eve's punishment can be ascertained, the nature of God's threat to Cain should be clarified. Hence, the description of Eve's punishment needs to be examined.

As a consequence of eating the forbidden fruit of the Garden of Eden, Eve was told that she was to suffer the pains of childbirth and also lose her position of equal status with Adam. That she enjoyed equal status can be seen in Adam's vain attempt to place the responsibility for his transgression upon her. Adam hardly could have expected this attempt to succeed if he were the dominant figure, for he would be responsible for his actions, no matter what role a subordinate might play.

The narrator, evidently cognizant of the demarcations of responsibility, established Eve's equal status by describing her as עֵזֶר כְּנֶגְדּוֹ , "ēzer k⁵negddô':[56] not a helper in the sense of an assistant,[57] but as "a partner who suits him."[58] Such a translation derives its justification from the unsuitability of animals as companions of Adam. Since God created woman only when the animals did not fulfill their desired purpose, it may be concluded "that the woman was not thought of at first as a helper."[59] Though this raises the question of why Adam needed a helper when no tasks had been assigned to him in the Garden, Adam's need for a partner-companion cannot be questioned. Consequently, when God imposed the second part of the punishment upon Eve, He did so upon the copartner, not the subordinate, of Adam:

> Yet your urge shall be for your husband
> And he shall rule over you. (Gen. 3:16, NJPS)[60]

This translation obviously reflects some difficulty with the word תְּשׁוּקָה, 't⁵sûqāh.' And the reference in the Song of Songs does not help, because it is "radically different in spirit,"[61] expressing the joyous desire of the lovers for each other.[62] Fortunately, with assistance from the cognate Arabic,[63] it is learned that 't⁵sûqāh' can mean "urge,"[64] in the sense of the act of advocating earnestly or pressingly.

As an act of prodding or urging, 't⁵sûqāh' formed the basis of Adam's claim of innocence; behind his protestation seemingly lay the legal principle of liability, which would explain Adam's unchivalrous behavior of blaming Eve for his sinfulness on the ground that she was the one who gave him the forbidden fruit to eat. At first glance, Adam's defense seems ludicrous: even if given the fruit by Eve, he did not have to eat it. But this was precisely what Adam did claim: he *did* have to eat the fruit because he could not withstand the force of Eve's 't⁵sûqāh,' "prodding." Adam seems to have attributed to 't⁵sûqāh' an animating force similar perhaps to that attributed to the head of an axe that "flies from the wood and finds the other man."[65] Conceived as some kind of an object, 't⁵sûqāh' thus would come under the laws governing liability.

The chief basis of liability, as in the case of a man's animal falling into a pit dug by another man[66] or one man's ox killing another man's ox,[67] was ownership of the object causing the damage.[68] Since Eve "owned" her תְּשׁוּקָה, 't°šûqāh,' this pressing force responsible for breaking Adam's resistance to the point of eating the forbidden fruit, Eve thereby became liable for Adam's wrongdoing under the law of ownership of the damaging object.

Implicit in such a reconstruction are the assumptions that Adam had not readily acquiesced to Eve's proffering and that Eve's pressure upon him must have been considerable for him to transgress God's prohibition not to eat of the "tree of knowledge of good and bad."[69] Such assumptions are confirmed by God's explicit reference to Eve's persuasiveness in describing Adam's sin:

> To Adam He said, "Because you heeded your wife and ate of the tree about which I command you saying, 'You shall not eat of it. . . .'" (Gen. 3:17, NJPS)

The word "heeded" indicates that the narrator never intended to give the impression that Adam, without a word from Eve or an objection from himself, simply took the fruit when it was handed to him and bit into it.

Adam's maneuver to clear himself of blame was not accepted, and no reason was given. It is not known precisely on what legal ground God rejected his protestation of innocence. Evidently, the narrator must have taken it for granted that the reason would be so well-known as to render further elaboration unnecessary. Consequently, God must be assumed to have rejected Adam's argument on the ground that he, like the owner who had been warned of his goring ox, had been warned not to eat the forbidden fruit and, therefore, could not escape responsibility for his actions. Whatever the legal reason, God declared Adam culpable. He was guilty not only of eating the fruit of the forbidden tree, but, equally significant, he was punished for heeding his wife instead of God.

Turning now to Eve and her power to cause Adam to "heed" her words, God punished Eve by taking this power from her and giving it to her husband:

> Your urging will be your husband's. . . .[70]

The effect was twofold: not only was Eve deprived of her effectiveness and strength of persuasion, but Adam, upon receiving this gift of the 't°šûqāh' was made all the stronger because of its possession.

The equal-status relationship was radically altered as a consequence of God's decree. Eve was made subordinate to Adam because he had gained that which was taken from her. The narrator expressed this change of status with emphatic irony:

> And he shall rule over you. . . .

With the personal pronoun הוּא,'hû',' "he," inserted for emphasis, the narrator was saying that *he,* Adam, and not Eve, would be doing something that ordinarily Eve would be expected to do. That something was contained in the word יִמְשָׁל, 'yimšāl,' which probably meant here "to exercise authority over someone."[71] In essence, the narrator seems to have been saying something along these lines:

> Now with your תְּשׁוּקָה, 't⁴šûqāh,' belonging to your husband, *he*—and not you, Eve—will exercise authority through that which is yours,[72] namely your 't⁴šûqāh.'

The last part of the sentence can be translated thus:

> and *he* will exercise authority through yours.

This understanding of the usage of 't⁴šûqāh,' "urging," should help to clarify the passage dealing with Cain.[73] In this sentence, God said that the 't⁴šûqāh,' "urging," of the demon would be his, in the sense of working through him:

> And his "urging" will be yours. . . .

By possessing the demon's 't⁴šûqāh,' Cain would have the power to exercise authority. Here the narrator emphasized how unusual would be the situation where *Cain,* and not the demon, would exercise this authority:

> and *you* will exercise authority through his.

Where the demon ordinarily would be expected to exert his influence through his 't⁴šûqāh,' Cain would do so for he would possess the demon's 't⁴šûqāh,' "urging."[74]

Cain at last would have gained his objective of exercising authority, but not as God's צֶלֶם, 'ṣelem,' "representative." His relationship to the demon had disqualified him for that exalted office, leaving him only the authority and power granted him by the demon of the netherworld. In this way God warned Cain that he could not possibly hope to represent God in any capacity subordinate to the official "agent" if he persisted in maintaining his connection with the inhabitant of the infernal regions. God's threatened punishment portended no harm to Cain's person. Even when manifesting ritual allegiance to a demon, Cain was to suffer no physical injury nor any severe deprivations or penalties. His only punishment would come through himself as a logical consequence of his actions: he could not hope to represent God while having truck with a demon. Utterly absent was any spirit of vindictiveness on God's part. Cain's punishment would not be God's doing but his own.

Premeditated Murder

Possibly because he realized that he could never hope to gain the top office of "agent," Cain elected to seek power and position with the aid of the demon. Accordingly, he moved against his brother:

> And Cain said to his brother Abel. . . . (Gen. 4:8, NJPS)

This translation causes difficulties. The narrator did not indicate what Cain said to Abel to lure him to the fields, there to meet his death. The text recorded nothing of the conversation; yet Cain must have said something since the verb אָמַר, "'āmar,' "to say," is not used without an object.[75] Modern scholarship, following ancient exegetical traditions,[76] completes the verse with the words Cain is believed to have said to his brother: something on the order of "Let us go outside."[77]

To assume that this entire phrase was left out attributes a highly improbable degree of carelessness to those responsible for the transmission of the text. Certainly, it seems incredible that an omission, which appears so obvious, could have been overlooked. Yet, the guardians of the text must be so charged if—and here the "if" looms very large indeed—'āmar' is translated as "said." But there is another definition for "'āmar' that eliminates the need to postulate a scribal omission: that meaning is "to lie in wait for."

In the Akkadian, and probably the Ugaritic, the original meaning of the Hebrew "'āmar' was "to see," not "to say."[78] The Psalmist used "'āmar' in the sense of "to see" in the following instances where the act of seeing was linked with hostile intent:

> How many who eye my life! (Ps. 3:3)[79]
> How can you lie in wait for my life . . .? (Ps. 11:1)[80]

Since hostile intent was present in the Cain-Abel story, these examples from Psalms lend force to the suggestion that "'āmar' should be translated as "to lie in wait."

> And Cain lay in wait for Hebel, his brother. . . . (Gen. 4:8)

Such a rendition is strengthened by the legal implications contained in the term "to lie in wait" as illustrated in the law pertaining to accidental homicide:

> And if a man lie not in wait, but God cause it to come to hand; then I will appoint thee a place whither he may flee. (Ex. 21:13, JPS)

The inference is that anyone who lay in wait was guilty of premeditated murder. When the narrator stated that Cain lay in wait for his brother, he was implicating Cain on the legal grounds of malice aforethought, possibly to exonerate God of any responsibility for Abel's death.[81]

The narrator also might have used אָמַר, "'āmar,' "to lie in wait for," to direct attention to the similar sounding word אִמָּר, "'immār,' "lamb."[82] Choosing a word because of its similarity in sound to another word is an example of *talhin*,[83] a Semitic rhetorical figure whereby the author selects a particular word, not a synonym, to suggest both meanings simultaneously to the reader's consciousness. One is the primary meaning; the other, the secondary concept, adding another dimension to the idea expressed by the author. In this particular passage, the narrator probably wanted to invoke the picture of a lamb for one of two reasons. Either he wanted to portray Cain as some ravenous beast stalking his prey until that fateful moment when he leaped upon his unsuspecting, defenseless, lamb-like brother. Or, he wanted to heighten the idea that Abel was used as a lamb for sacrificial purposes.

Cain's Disavowal of Responsibility

The widespread impression, fostered principally by religious school texts, is that Cain killed Abel out of jealousy. Cain's jealousy had been raised to such a feverish pitch that it could not be assuaged until the object of this jealousy, Abel, lay dead at his brother's feet. A careful scrutiny of the text reveals, however, that the narrator was most careful to avoid any suggestion that Cain's anger and disappointment was directed in any way at Abel. That Cain became "very angry and downcast"[84] was stated clearly, but the narrator did not say at what or at whom he was angry. Neither does the text suggest, even indirectly, that the object of Cain's anger and disappointment was Abel. The narrator easily could have inserted this information if this were the case, but his failure to mention Abel as the object of Cain's anger leads to the conclusion that Abel was not that object.

If Cain did not murder Abel out of jealous rage, why then did he kill his brother? The answer to this question is found in the competition for the office of "agent": Cain murdered Abel in a desperate move to invest himself with the power of the "agent." Not in the jealousy of siblings but in a consuming quest for the authority emanating from the office of צֶלֶם , 'ṣelem,' lay the underlying motive for murder.

The first clue pointing to Cain's persistent interest in the issue of the 'ṣelem' appears in the repetition of the phrase הֶבֶל אָחִיו, 'hebel 'āḥiw,' translated until now as "his brother Abel." Naturally, this raises the question of why the narrator took such pains to add the word "brother" when there was no possibility of mistaking the fraternal relationship between the two brothers. One scholar understands the Bible as deliberately employing this unusual stylistic feature[85] to emphasize the fraternal relationship, for by doing so it established "the moral principle that man *is* indeed his brother's keeper and that all homicide is at the same time fratricide."[86] This interpretation, while certainly a possibility, prompts the question of why the stylistic device to emphasize the brother relationship was not used in verse four, where consistency of purpose would have dictated that the narrator insert אָחִיו,'āḥiw,' "his brother," immediately after הֶבֶל, 'hebel,' "Abel," the first word of the sentence.

The answer to this question lies not in a particular stylistic technique emphasizing fraternity but in a new translation of 'hebel.' In verses eight and nine 'hebel' should be translated "agent" or "deputy," a title synonymous with 'ṣelem,' and one which the narrator preferred using so as to suggest through the rhetorical figure of *talḥin* the secondary idea of 'hebel,' meaning "Abel." Accepting the translation of 'hebel' as "agent" explains why the phrase 'hebel 'āḥiw' was not used in verse four: Abel had not yet been designated "agent"; this was to come in the second half of the sentence. The first 'hebel' had to be the proper noun Abel; as such it had no need for any further clarification. But after being named God's representative, Abel henceforth was referred to by his title 'hebel' with ''āḥiw,' "his brother," in apposition to the title.

That Cain still regarded his relationship to his brother as governed by the office and responsibilities of the 'ṣelem' is evident in his answer to God's inquiry regarding the whereabouts of Abel. Pleading ignorance, Cain substantiated his denial with a counter question:

> Am I my brother's keeper? (Gen. 4:9)

Far from disavowing the responsibilities of brotherhood, Cain really was asking through the use of the emphatic pronoun אָנֹכִי, ''ānōkî,' "I," how *he* could be expected to know of his brother's whereabouts since, not being the "agent," he did not have the responsibility of being in charge of his brother.

Had Reuben's relationship with Joseph prevailed for Cain and Abel, Cain would not have been allowed by the laws governing brothers to deny this responsibility for his brother. Judging from Reuben's distress[87] upon discovering that his younger brother was missing from the pit, it may be surmised that "there existed a practice of holding an elder brother responsible for the younger."[88] Hence, God's query to Cain concerning Abel's whereabouts most likely was meant to be understood within the context of the older brother's responsibility for the younger. How then could Cain deny his responsibility? Evidently, he did so on the grounds that the new "agent" relationship invalidated the previous obligation of the older brother. That Cain would have wanted to invoke the rules governing this fraternal relationship may be inferred from his reaction at being rejected in favor of the younger brother. His failure to attain the position of "agent" signified to Cain that his rights as the older brother had been abrogated by God. Consequently, he now asked with a sense of justification how he could be held accountable for Abel, when—and here, presumably, must have been the thrust of his argument even though the narrator did not state it explicitly—his brother by virtue of being deputized as God's "agent" actually exercised juridical authority over *him*.

Cain's Cultic Sacrifice

God rejected the reasoning behind Cain's question by countering abruptly with the actual evidence of wrongdoing:

> What have you done? (Gen. 4:10, NJPS)

This translation has been interpreted as a rhetorical question with the force of interjection: "See now what you have done! How could you do so terrible a thing?"[89] While this interpretation plausibly fits the sense of the story, an alternative meaning is possible if עָשָׂה, ''āśāh,' is translated as "to cover."[90] God's question then is seen as a presentation of evidence by the divine prosecutor-judge. God accused Cain by asking: "What have you covered?"

This single question effectively limns in the details of the murder scene. Cain was standing by a hole that was covered, presumably with loose soil; beneath this covering was the blood of Abel. If Cain had meant to hide the evidence of this violent deed, he certainly was thwarted by Abel's blood crying from the ground. God continued:

> Hark, your brother's blood cries out to Me from the ground! (Gen. 4:10, NJPS)

Cain said nothing, for what else was there to say? He stood convicted by this incontrovertible and damning evidence. God then pronounced sentence upon him, and in so doing He revealed for the first time the enormity of Cain's transgression:

> Therefore, you shall be banned from the soil. . . . (Gen. 4:11, NJPS)

The word אָרוּר, ''ārûr,' invariably has been translated as "curse," a rendition that on occasion is either misleading or demonstrably wrong.[91] In the Akkadian the basic sense of the term is "to bind, hem in with obstacles, render powerless to resist,"[92] an effect that could be achieved by magical means. This idea of the magical or supernatural spell underlay ''ārûr' when it was used in connection with Balak's request to Balaam to put a curse upon Moses and the children of Israel (Num. 22:6). In time, and in view of Israel's progressive aversion to magic practices, this word lost its earlier occult connotation and came to be another word for "curse" in the conventional sense of the term.[93] In this narrative, however, ''ārûr' had not yet lost its occult connotation: this quality of rendering something powerless is best conveyed by translating ''ārûr' as "banned." This supernatural spell banning Cain from the אֲדָמָה, ''ădāmāh,' "earth," prevented him from obtaining what he initially desired from the "earth."

As is quite apparent by now, ''ădāmāh,' "earth," was not ordinary soil; it was personified to the extent of having a mouth and intentionally swallowing blood:

> . . . opened its mouth wide to receive
> your brother's blood from your hand. (Gen. 4:11, NJPS)

This particular episode in which the "earth" was personified by the act of swallowing is not to be equated with the time when "the earth opened its mouth and swallowed"[94] Dathan, Abiram, and their rebel followers, causing them to disappear from sight before the entire populace. These two episodes were entirely different, for nothing of the sort happened to the blood of Abel. Had the earth parted, causing the blood of the murder victim to flow into its crevice, Cain would have had to have been standing on the spot where he had shed the blood of his brother. Furthermore, in the Dathan and Abiram story the ''ădāmāh,' "earth," swallowed the dissidents at God's behest;[95] in the Cain narrative the "ădāmāh" acted independently of God, suggesting that the "earth" might have conspired with Cain to accept Abel's blood. Since the geological phenomenon that would have accounted for the swallowing of the rebels was absent in the Cain-Abel story, it must be inferred that the "mouth" of the earth was *man-made*.

In fact, one further step designates the "mouth" as the same or similar פֶּתַח, 'petaḥ,' "opening, entrance," mentioned by God in His warning to Cain. This suggestion need not seem extreme once it is realized that both פֶּה, 'peh,' and פֶּתַח, 'petaḥ,' mean the "mouth" or "opening" of an abyss, cave, or well.[96] Since a pit or hole in the ground fits into this broad category, the words—'peh' and 'petaḥ'—are synonymous.[97] If this hypothesis is correct, it means that Cain dug a pit into which he poured the blood of his brother. What these few words contain is a gruesome description of Cain's cultic sacrifice of his brother.

Cain previously must have covered the "mouth" or pit with loose soil, but then uncovered the aperture so that the "earth" could receive the sacrificial blood. Indeed, the narrator explicitly used the expression "from your hand" to convey the picture of a pouring action: either Cain poured the blood of Abel from a container in his hand into the hole he had dug, or he held the slain Abel over the pit so that his blood oozed into it.

The purpose of this cultic sacrifice is revealed in the first half of the following verse:

If you till the soil, it shall no longer yield its strength to you. (Gen. 4:12, NJPS)

This translation reveals no hint of a cultic sacrifice. However, by selecting alternative meanings for some of the Hebrew words, a translation that accords with the theory of cultic sacrifice can be obtained:

Though[98] you serve[99] the earth, it shall no longer bestow[100] its power[101] upon you.

Cain, having abandoned all hope of obtaining the office of "agent" from God, presented a blood sacrifice to the chthonic demon, אֲדָמָה, "ădāmāh," "earth," to secure its help in acquiring this much coveted position. How the assistance was to be given is not known; but the text is quite explicit that Cain had "served" the earth with a particular rite to obtain "power" from this infernal demon. Perhaps this power was to enable him to stand up to God, if need be, once God learned that he was the new "agent."

In this procedure Cain probably followed a practice common to the Canaanites, Hittites, Assyrians, and Greeks. A pit was dug with any appropriate instrument,[102] once the practitioner had determined a propitious spot for his act of sorcery.[103] Then such food offerings as loaves of bread, cheese, butter, white barley were lowered into the pit or arranged around its mouth, presumably to entice the spirit or spirits up out of the pit to eat and drink.[104] The liquids suitable for libations ranged from the *Odyssey*'s honeyed milk, sweet wine, and water to the Hittite oil and beer.[105] "But the beverage which these denizens of the underworld craved more than honey, beer, and wine was the blood of sacrificial animals."[106] The following excerpts from the Hittite texts illustrate the important role played by this sacrificial blood:

> He smears the nine *a-a-bi*'s [pits] with blood. Then for the nine *a-a-bi*'s (there are) nine birds and one lamb.[107]

> The queen comes forth, and the diviner opens up an *a-a-bi* before the storm-god of *marapši*. The diviner offers one sheep to the storm-god of *marapši*, and down inside the *a-a-bi* the diviner slaughters it. The blood he lets flow down into a goblet, which he places on the ground before the storm-god of *marapši*.[108]

In the Greek *Odyssey* similar importance was attached to the blood sacrifice:

> ... I took the sheep and cut their throats over the pit, and the dark blood ran forth. Then there gathered out of Erebus the spirits of those that are dead. ... These came thronging in crowds about the pit from every side, with a wondrous cry: and pale fear seized me.[109]

These excerpts closely resemble the biblical narrative in such features as the "mouth" or pit, the sacrificial blood flowing either directly into the pit or into a container from which it was then poured into the pit, the sounds of the dead, as in the case of the *Odyssey*. Here, the "wondrous cry" of the dead spirits out of Erebus strikingly resembles the cry of the slain Abel.

Within the context of this cultic slaying it now may be assumed that the narrator used אָמַר, "āmar," "to lie in wait," to evoke the image of אִמָּר, "immār," "lamb." In all likelihood the narrator wanted to emphasize that Cain lay in wait for his brother, who was to serve as the sacrificial lamb.

Only by regarding Abel as the sacrificial lamb can the heinousness of Cain's transgression be comprehended. Far from surrendering to an uncontrollable burst of jealous anger, Cain was moved to kill his brother by a coldly conceived and methodically executed plan to gain the coveted position of 'ṣelem,' "agent." At one stroke he eliminated his rival and at the same time offered Abel's blood as an oblation to the infernal demon in order to secure the services of an ally in his rebellion against God. If Cain merely wanted to rid himself of a rival, he need not have gone through the ritual just described. He could have killed Abel, and that would have been the end of it. However, Abel was more than a rival: he was the lamb to be sacrificed—the means to an end. In this murder Cain was not possessed by a rage bursting all bonds of self-control; this murder was nothing less than the dispassionate taking of life to advance a goal. Viewed in this light, Cain's murderous act stands as the first instance when human life was sacrificed for selfish goals or, as is more frequently the case, in a cause that later turned out to be nothing more than an exercise in self-aggrandizement. In the very beginning of its chronicle of the history of humanity, the Bible declared as heinous that callous, cold disregard for human life that knows neither the anguish of grief nor the torment of guilt.

7

THE AFFLICTION OF CAIN

The Divine Response

Cain's sin was no ordinary sin, for his was no ordinary murder. By killing the divinely appointed צֶלֶם, 'ṣelem,' he in effect openly challenged the sovereignty of God. In the Dathan and Abiram crisis, the only other insurrection against the divinely appointed "agent," the אֲדָמָה, 'ădāmāh,' "earth," was described as having "opened its mouth."[1] The seemingly deliberate use of identical phraseology draws attention to the profound change that had occurred with the 'ădāmāh' from the time of the first challenge to the divinely designated "agent" to the second. In the Dathan and Abiram episode the 'ădāmāh' dutifully obeyed God's command, thereby showing complete docility to God. In the Cain and Abel story, however, the 'ădāmāh,' far from exhibiting servility, actually entered the struggle against God by accepting the blood sacrifice from Cain.

This recognition of the different roles played by the 'ădāmāh,' "earth," introduces yet another ramification of Cain's sin: idolatry. The similarity between Cain's 'ădāmāh' and Môt, the Canaanite god of death and the King of Sheol, is close enough to suggest that the 'ădāmāh' must have been derived from Môt. To go down to Sheol, in the phraseology of Canaanite poetry, was to enter the mouth of Môt—the very Môt, who brings the dead to his mouth and "drinks their blood in a cup the size of a jug."[2] But the narrator, presumably unable to countenance the existence of any deity other than the God of Israel, reduced Môt from the status of a deity to that of a demon.[3] This demon turned out in the Cain and Abel story to be none other than the 'ădāmāh,' the Hebraic substitute for Môt and personification of the netherworld. It was to the 'ădāmāh,' this demonic rival of God, that Cain paid obeisance; it was to the 'ădāmāh' that he brought blood, the favorite beverage of the pagan deities; and it was with this former Canaanite deity, now reduced to a demon, that he sought an alliance against God. In the aftermath of this abortive revolt, God so completely subdued the 'ădāmāh' that, by the time of the Dathan-Abiram insurrection, the 'ădāmāh' had become God's willing instrument of destruction.

With the occult connection between Cain and the infernal demon severed, God pronounced sentence upon Cain:

You shall become a ceaseless wanderer on earth. (Gen. 4:12, NJPS)

Relegating Cain to the role of a "ceaseless wanderer" hardly seems commensurate with the gravity of his crime. Hence, the key words נָע וָנָד, 'nāʿ wānād' must be reexamined for a possible alternative translation.

The root נוּע, 'nûʿa,' from whence the word נָע, 'nāʿ,' is derived, means "to tremble, totter, stagger";[4] נָע, 'nāʿ,' therefore, would be a "totterer."[5] Its companion word נָד, 'nād,' comes from the root נוּד, 'nûd,' which means "to flutter, wave, shake,"[6] as well as the generally accepted "to wander." Thus 'nād' is translated as a "shaker." Together 'nāʿ,' "totterer," and 'nād,' "shaker," convey a sharply etched picture of Cain's physical transformation: Cain had become a spastic, a "shaking totterer."

Within the context of the thought patterns and behavior of the biblical world such divine response is understandable.[7] This trembling condition of Cain's insured that no part of the spirit of the murdered "agent" could be transmitted to the progeny of Cain. Previous chapters have shown how Jacob received the special qualities of leadership through a blessing, how Ham acquired potency by staring, and how Noah prevented the stolen potency from being bequeathed to the son of Ham by cursing Canaan.

In all likelihood, Cain knew that by killing Abel he not only eliminated his successful rival but also acquired his נֶפֶשׁ, 'nepeš,' that special quality of the former "agent" he needed to succeed to that office. Perhaps for reason of this theft did Abel's blood cry out in bitterness from the netherworld. Cain's possession of the 'nepeš' of his brother, the "agent," also explains why he was not struck dead on the spot by God: evidently, the special quality in the 'nepeš' of the "agent" protected its possessor from any harm, no matter who the person. Such a reason explains why Ham was never visited directly with a punishment. If to safeguard the 'nepeš' of Abel, God refrained from retaliating physically against Cain, He at least made sure that the progeny of Cain could never partake of Abel's 'nepeš' by incapacitating Cain's limbs and head, the transmitters of potency.

The Procreative Power of the Head and Limbs

To appreciate fully this precautionary measure, some of the ideas current in the Mediterranean world regarding the function of a man's head and limbs need to be reviewed to see if those ideas had their counterparts in the Hebrew mind. The Greeks believed that the head contained the stuff of life, the seed, and in it the procreative life-soul.[8] In the latter half of the fifth century Hyppocrates, while stating that the seed was drawn from the whole body, made it plain that the seed gathered to the spinal marrow and that most of it flowed from the head.[9] A later Pythagorean taught that "the seed is a drop of the brain containing in itself warm vapour. . . ."[10] Homer and his audience knew that during life the brain, a fluid mass, is-

sued forth to begin a new life.[11] Accordingly, Zeus could dispense with
the mother when he wished to have a child by giving birth to Athene
"from his head."[12] Like the Greeks, the Romans believed that the *caput*,
"head," contained the seed, the very stuff of life, and the life-soul associated
with it.[13] The Roman name for the contents of the head, the brain, *cerebrum*,
is related to the verb *cereo*, "I beget, engender."[14] And the masculine form
of *Ceres*, the name of the goddess of fertility identified particularly with
the seed in the "head" of the cornstalk, is *Cerus,* "engenderer."[15]

Closely associated in the Greek and Roman mind with the procreative
power of the head was hair. Growth of hair was popularly associated with
sexual vigor. "'Hairy' men were believed to have the strongest sexual
bent—and loss of hair, baldness, was believed to be dependent upon loss of
seed."[16] This belief would explain why in one version Athene was born
from the chin, "from the beard" of Zeus.[17] The Roman *genius*, the life-
spirit in the head active in procreation, clarifies why the hair, naturally
related to this generative life-soul, was for Apuleius *genialis*.[18]

The procreative spirit was by no means restricted to head or hair. As
presented in an earlier chapter, the Greeks believed that it could be transmitted by the knees and the thighs. In addition, a new part of the body
is found to be endowed with the power of procreation—the hand. Epaphus
was begotten by Zeus upon touching Io with his hand.[19]

Just as close parallels were found between the concepts of 'nepeš' and
'thymos,' so too parallels are found between the Greek ideas of generativity
and those in the Bible. The Nazirite offering his hair to God (Num. 6:2–21)
"may perhaps be explained as an offering of the life-substance from within
the head."[20] Then, in the episode of David's cursing Joab for treacherously
murdering Abner, the general of the forces of Ish-boshet, Saul's surviving
son, David proclaimed his innocence by declaring:

> I and my kingdom are guiltless before the Lord for ever from the blood of Abner
> the son of Ner; let it fall upon the head of Joab, and upon all his father's house;
> and let there not fail from the house of Joab one that hath an issue, or that is
> a leper, or that leaneth on a staff, or that falleth by the sword, or that lacketh
> bread. (II Sam. 3:28–29, JPS)

In this statement the connection between the head and one's generative
ability is quite evident. Once the blood-guilt fell upon the *head* of Joab
and all his descendants, their procreative capacity would be so damaged
that they would beget children who would be defiled by both leprosy and
a continuous genital discharge, who would be a disgrace to the memory
of the virile Joab—the more accurate translation for "leaneth on a staff"
is "holding the spindle,"[21] a euphemism for femininity—who would fare
poorly on the battlefield, or who would lack the capacity to provide food
for themselves. Most significantly, no harm was to be visited upon the
person of Joab. Ordinarily, the inclination would be to ask how Joab
could escape the physical effects of this punishment when his murder of

Abner precipitated the curse in the first place. In view of the preceding theory, however, it can now be understood why the entire force of David's malediction was directed against that part of Joab that physiologically could determine the quality of his procreativity. David wanted to prevent the progeny of Joab from being enriched by the valor, the masculinity, and the vigor of the slain Abner; and so he directed the force of his curse against the procreativity lodged in Joab's head.[22]

Biblical Hebrew suggested that the hands and arms also were endowed with this generative capacity, as is seen in the relationship between the two words derived from the root זרע, 'zr‘':

זְרוֹעַ, 'z^erô‘a,' "arm"[23]
זֶרַע, 'zera‘,' "seed, offspring"[24]

Likewise, the relationship is evident in three words that, in addition to their usual meanings, also can mean a *phallus*:

אַמָּה ,'ammāh,' "forearm" (in biblical and mishnaic Hebrew)[25]
אֶצְבַּע,'eṣbba‘,' "finger" (in biblical and mishnaic Hebrew)[26]
יָד,'yād,' "hand" (in Isa. 57:8)[27]

These examples appear to illustrate the extent to which biblical man accepted the physiological beliefs regarding the effect of the head and other human organs upon the process of procreation then current in the eastern Mediterranean world. The reason for Cain's affliction can now be appreciated. Far from punishing him with a particularly cruel form of suffering, God caused Cain's head and limbs to move wildly and uncontrollably solely to prevent the spirit of the "agent" from being transmitted through birth to the unauthorized and unworthy. That God did not afflict man ever again with this spasticity, despite all the countless transgressions recounted in the Bible, strengthens the conviction that this shaking condition was meant to be regarded as a divine safeguard—never as a punishment.

Cain's Confession of Guilt

What was Cain's reaction to God's preventative measure? Did he go to pieces?[28] Did he plead for some alleviation of his condition?[29] Or did he suddenly become overburdened by the enormity of his crime, realizing that his iniquity was too great to be forgiven?[30] Each of these interpretations has been offered as an explanation for Cain's initial reaction to this divine judgment:

My punishment is too great to bear! (Gen. 4:13, NJPS)[31]

According to this translation, Cain apparently regarded his condition as a punishment and therefore was pleading for a mitigation of his sentence on the ground that God was being too punitive. Yet, in the context of this new understanding of the text, this interpretation is unacceptable. Only by recognizing that Cain was to be afflicted with a shaking and a tottering condition could a correct interpretation be obtained.

Cain's condition has been described as closely resembling a spastic state. In modern Hebrew the adjective "spastic" is עֲוִיתִי, "ăwîtî,"[32] related to the mishnaic word עֲוִית, "ăwwît," "spasm" or "convulsion,"[33] which in turn comes from the biblical root עָוָה, "āwāh," "to twist, bend."[34] Most likely this is another case of *talḥin*, where the word, עֲוֹנִי, "ăwōnî," "my iniquity," also derived from עָוָה, "āwāh,"[35] was chosen by the narrator to suggest the *result* of the sin within the word "iniquity" itself; that is, the state of being twisted or bent over.

An appreciation of the usage of נְשׂא, 'neśô',' necessitates a return to the word שְׂאֵת, 'śe'ēt,' "elevation in rank,"[36] used by God to describe to Cain what he might expect if he acted righteously. Significantly, both שְׂאֵת, 'śe'ēt' of verse seven and נְשׂא, 'neśô" of verse thirteen are infinitive absolutes of נָשָׂא, 'nāśā'.'[37] That two such unusual forms of the same verb were used in such close proximity suggests that 'neśô',' the second infinitive absolute, was used deliberately to highlight its connection with the first infinitive absolute, meaning "elevation in rank."

These observations amend the translation as follows:

> My iniquity [i.e., my resultant spasticity] is greater than my elevation in rank.

In this rendition Cain neither cried for a merciful diminution of the divine decree nor languished in a mood of self-recrimination and remorse. Rather, he confessed his guilt and admitted defeat. Heretofore, Cain had denied any knowledge of Abel's disappearance. Now he admitted his involvement by his use of 'neśô',' "elevation in rank"—a position he hoped to gain by murdering his brother. Second, he seemingly acknowledged defeat in declaring that his spasticity so bent him over that obviously whatever power he received from his elevation in rank at the time of the murder had been negated; a person so bent over could hardly lay claim to being raised in office or stature. This feeling of utter defeat is suggested by Cain's description of what now must be regarded as God's punishment for his murder of Abel—banishment:

> Behold You have banished me this day
> from the face of the earth. (Gen. 4:14)

Expelled from the physical terrain where he sacrificed to the infernal demon, Cain presumably was left weak and helpless—cut off from his sole source of strength, the ''ădāmāh,' "earth." Cain's statement cannot be construed as meaning that he had been driven out from the cultivated ground into the desert[38] or that he had been cast out from the whole earth, without a place to rest.[39] If the latter, the narrator scarcely could have described Cain as dwelling in the land of Nod, east of Eden,[40] for this implies one locale at least where he was not an outcast from the whole earth.

Estrangement from God

There is, however, more than loss of strength that comes with expulsion:

> And from Your face I shall be hidden. . . . (Gen. 4:14)

All Cain's scheming had come to nought. He, who sought to enjoy the privileges of the office of "agent," reflecting the divine radiance of his exalted rank, apparently realized that his banishment squashed any hope of deriving the benefits of his new position. His primary goal, after all, was to officiate as "agent"—not to rebel against God. With his estrangement from God complete, his plot had to be regarded as a total failure. Never again was he to address God or invoke His name. Yet, even now, in his defeat Cain presumably refused to repent.

The Protective Mark

Cain's grim evaluation of his situation led him to predict:

> . . . and I shall be a shaking totterer and anyone who finds me will kill me. (Gen. 4:14)

His shaking and tottering would have alerted anyone meeting him that he possessed the coveted 'nepeš' of God's agent and that his affliction prevented the transmission of the 'nepeš' to his descendants. Accordingly, anyone coming across him supposedly would have sought to kill him to acquire the 'nepeš' for himself and his offspring. The probability that another homicide would occur was so great that God issued a proclamation forbidding any such attempt upon Cain's life:

> Therefore, if anyone kills Cain, sevenfold vengeance shall be taken on him. (Gen. 4:15, NJPS)

God did not say that sevenfold vengeance would be taken on anyone who killed a human being. In fact, nowhere did the biblical laws dealing with murder state that punishment would be sevenfold vengeance, whether devised by God or man. Rather, this terrible price was to be exacted only for Cain's death.

Such a warning raises several questions. Why should Cain, of all people, enjoy such divine protection? Further, was "sevenfold" simply a description of vengeance "of the most thorough-going kind,"[41] or was it to be taken literally? According to the line of interpretation developed here, this punishment was to be taken literally. Death could not be the projected punishment, since a person could be put to death only once, not seven times. Nor is it likely that it meant another case of shaking and tottering, only seven times worse. In the interest of strict justice God surely would never have afflicted one murderer more harshly that He had the first. No, this penalty of sevenfold vengeance evidently meant that God would visit Cain's spastic condition upon seven generations of the murderer's offspring. Now it is understandable why Cain enjoyed such divine protection: God had to protect him from any would-be murderer to insure that the 'nepeš' of the slain Abel was not transmitted to any unlawful possessor. A possible assailant would be deterred from taking Cain's life, knowing that God's punishment would prevent him from passing the 'nepeš' on to his children.

As proof that He had spared Cain from death, God supplemented His proclamation of vengeance with a protective sign or mark:

> And the Lord put a mark on Cain,
> lest anyone who met him should kill him. (Gen. 4:15, NJPS)

This measure can be understood best in the context of a Hittite law dealing with a husband who apprehended his adulterous wife with her lover. According to the law, the husband could kill them both without risking retaliation. However, if the husband wished to spare the guilty couple from the death penalty, he first had to bring them to the gate of the palace and declare: "My wife shall not be killed."[42] Secondly, he had to spare also the life of the adulterer and "mark his head."[43] Significantly, a simple declaration sparing the adulterer was not sufficient: it had to be followed by a mark upon the adulterer's head. The parallelism with the biblical situation is obvious. Cain was liable under biblical law for the death penalty, but he was spared by the same twofold act: first, God proclaimed that Cain was not to be killed: and then He put a mark upon him, attesting to his release from death. Only after these precautionary measures did expulsion follow:

> And Cain left the presence of the Lord
> and settled in the land of Nod, east of Eden. (Gen. 4:16, NJPS)

8

THE AEGEAN—SOURCE OF
OF THE FLOOD

Evidence of the Mesopotamian Flood

The Noah story, superbly coherent in its reconstruction of the major events preceding and following the Flood, reported with what now appears to be remarkable fidelity the elements that joined together to visit this catastrophe upon the world of the narrator. So detailed was his description that there seems to be little doubt that such an event occurred; only where the Flood originated and how it was caused have yet to be determined.

Up until now the search for evidence of the Flood has centered in Mesopotamia—and for good reason: both the Sumerian cuneiform inscription of the flood, dated at about the close of the third millenium B.C.E.,[1] and the later Akkadian version so closely parallel the biblical account of the Deluge that they are regarded by many scholars as its model.[2] The Flood, these scholars concluded, must have taken place in the region of the Tigris and Euphrates Rivers. Support for this theory came with the uncovering of a "flood-pit"[3] by Sir Leonard Woolley in his excavation of the city of Ur in southern Mesopotamia. Here, the eleven feet of silt at the maximum meant that a flood not less than twenty-five feet deep must have inundated that area. A flood of this depth would have destroyed everything in the delta except for a few of the greater towns, which had grown up into mounds high enough to be out of the flood's reach.[4] These excavations convinced Woolley that this evidence of a flood represented the same flood mentioned in the Sumerian legend and later, in the Genesis story.[5]

Not all scholars are persuaded that the silt in Woolley's "flood-pit" leads to such a deduction; some regard it as nothing more than evidence of a purely local inundation.[6] In addition, they contend that the world-wide diffusion of the flood stories requires that the Flood be dated back to the Stone Age: to place it in the third millenium—the date of the tale of the Sumerian deluge—would be too recent by thousands of years to account for such wide dissemination.[7]

Others, more favorably inclined to Woolley's claim, regard the sedimentary

97

strata as representing deposits left by more or less violent overflowings of either one or both Tigris and Euphrates Rivers. One of these inundations was so destructive that it became one of the themes of cuneiform literature:

> This was *the* Flood, of which legend has no doubt exaggerated the violence and the destruction, whereas archeology indicates that not all the cities suffered equally.[8]

Whether or not Woolley's "flood-pit" represents the sediment left by the Great Flood some six thousand or more years ago or another inundation is immaterial to yet another body of opinion:

> The fact remains that there *was* a great flood. And it happened in lower Mesopotamia, in the 'Land of Shinar.'[9]

A more recent review of the pertinent flood data presents the Mesopotamian flood in yet another perspective. The biblical account of the Flood is believed to be based on an event that occurred in about 2900 B.C.E., or perhaps a century or two after. Traces of this flood have been found at the site of the ancient city of Shuruppak—not Ur!—where, according to the ancient tablets, King Ziusudra, the Sumerian Noah, first received warning of its coming; and these traces perhaps may be identified also with the earliest series of flood deposits at Kish. But the great flood deposit uncovered by Woolley at Ur is too ancient for identification with Noah's flood; and the later flood deposits at Ur seem to be too late for such identification. As for the extent of flood damage, according to this review, it never was of sufficient magnitude to interrupt the continuity of Mesopotamian civilization.[10]

Despite these somewhat diverse scholarly opinions regarding the date, location, and effect of the Mesopotamian flood, there can be no questioning the fact that parts of Mesopotamia were inundated by a flood or floods, and the cuneiform texts described just how the land was deluged. The Sumerian tablet listed "rainstorm," "rain flood" or "cloudburst," and "mighty winds" as bringing on the deluge;[11] the later Akkadian *Gilgamesh Epic* spoke of "destructive rain," "wind," "tempest," "downpour," "rainstorm" or "rain flood," and "evil wind" or "storm,"[12] and also added that the dikes of the canals and reservoirs were broken by the violent rise of the rivers. Clearly, in both versions, raging winds and heavy rain, not the annual overflow of the Tigris and Euphrates Rivers, caused the great flood.

Divergencies in the Biblical Narrative

The biblical story, while resembling the Mesopotamian legends in many respects, introduced several features not found in these earlier accounts. First, there was the eruption of the subterranean waters:

> All the fountains of the great deep burst apart,
> And the flood-gates of the sky broke open. (Gen. 7:11, NJPS)

Second, there was the duration of the downpour: not the seven days of destructive rain in the Mesopotamian stories, but the forty days and forty nights of rain in Genesis. These divergencies raise the question of why the narrator departed from the Mesopotamian versions, if indeed it had served as a model, to introduce these additional items.

Ordinarily, dissimilarities in the biblical and Mesopotamian versions of the Deluge would be ascribed to conflicting religious concepts.[13] It would be perfectly understandable for the monotheistic narrator to excise all traces of polytheism before using this material in his story. For this reason it is hard to understand why the narrator included the variations of the subterranean waters and the forty days and nights, since they hardly reveal points of fundamental religious divergence. Surely it cannot be argued that by disclosing a new source of flood waters or by lengthening the period of rainfall the narrator had strengthened the monotheistic theme of his story. Nor is it convincing that the narrator found it hard "to conceive that seven days of rain would suffice to flood the whole earth."[14] After all, should the same measure of realism not be accorded to the Mesopotamian author? If he could conceive of this possibility, why could not the biblical narrator? Even supposing that Scripture wanted to teach that God used the underground waters and the rain—blessings for the righteous—to blight a depraved humanity,[15] why could it not convey the same idea by mentioning either the rain or the subterranean waters instead of both? Plainly these speculations by biblical commentators fail to be convincing; and so it must be assumed that the biblical narrator had other grounds for adding these details. These reasons become evident only when attention is shifted from the Mesopotamian delta of the Tigris and Euphrates Rivers to the Aegean Sea, and, at the same time, shifted chronologically from the third millenium to the period around 1500 B.C.E.

The Subterranean Waters and the Eruption of Thera

In what turns out to be a most prescient passage, Thomas Mann wrote of the Flood:

> Just as the Babylonian account, known to Joseph, was only a reproduction of earlier and earlier accounts, so the flood itself is to be referred back to older and older prototypes: one is convinced of being on solid ground at last, when one fixes, as the original original, upon the sinking of the land Atlantis beneath the waves of the ocean. . . .[16]

For Thomas Mann, a catastrophe the magnitude of the Deluge had to be linked to nature's other cataclysm of equal enormity—the sinking of Atlantis. Plato said in his *Timaeus* that this powerful empire of Atlantis, based on an island "larger than Libya and Asia together" and situated in the Atlantic Ocean, was battered by violent earthquakes and floods and then disappeared into the depths of the sea in a single day and night. Recently uncovered evidence discloses that Atlantis, far from being the lost continent that sank into the Atlantic, now may turn out to be linked with the Aegean island of Thera,[17] which collapsed in a volcanic eruption into the sea.

This startling theory is explored in a fascinating account of archeological and oceanographical probing of this Aegean island by James Mavor of the Woods Hole Oceanographic Institution. Aided by the most modern oceanographic equipment available, Mavor substantiated the positions of Spyridon Marinatos, present head of the Greek Archeological Services, and Angelos Galanopoulos, Director of the Seismological Institute of the Observatory of Athens, that the sunken portion of the island of Thera was indeed part of the empire of Atlantis. In doing so, he accepted the hypothesis that the magnitude of Atlantis was due to an error of tenfold, which might have originated when the Egyptian word or symbol representing 100 was transcribed by Solon from his notes to represent 1,000.[18] Once the size of Atlantis had been reduced by a factor of ten, its Ancient Metropolis[19] fitted the dimensions of Thera, which collapsed into the sea as a result of a tremendous volcanic explosion around 1450 B.C.E.

Whether the Ancient Metropolis of Atlantis is to be located at Thera must be left to the classicists, the archeologists, and the scientific coterie of seismologists, vulcanologists, and oceanographers finally to determine. What cannot be doubted, however, is that a volcano erupted at Thera with overwhelming force. This volcanic convulsion, in all likelihood the most devastating explosion, natural or man-made, ever witnessed by a human being, is believed to have destroyed the Minoan civilization on neighboring Crete, seventy miles to the south.[20] Its unparalleled violence can be appreciated from these few statistics. Based on the volume of the part of Thera that sank into the Aegean, the heat energy released during this eruption has been calculated to have been four and one-half times that of Krakatoa; this fact becomes intelligible when it is realized that the total energy unleashed by the eruption of Krakatoa has been estimated to have been four hundred and thirty times more powerful than the explosion of an Eniwetok H-bomb.[21]

The excavations at Thera have revealed that on that awesome day the inhabitants had no time to leave the island or take anything from their homes. Tremendous quantities of pumice, then pumice mixed with ash, sand, lapilli, and bombs of every size, buried every living thing in a white shroud, the thickness of which was over one hundred feet, and at some points over one hundred and fifty feet.[22] After the magmatic chamber was emptied of these vast quantities of materials, a cavity of huge dimensions was formed under the central part of the island. The magnitude of this cavity caused the roof to crumple into the ocean, creating the largest caldera on the face of the earth.[23] The stupendousness of this collapse strikes the observer when, from the center of the harbor, he beholds the inner sides of the caldera rising about eleven hundred and fifty feet above sea level and realizes that the sea bed is as deep as the cliffs are high above him.[24]

Rushing into this abyss, hugh quantities of sea water violently recoiled upon striking the bottom of the cavity, thereby producing sea waves of prodigious heights. Though most of the collapse occurred within a twenty-four hour period, it is possible that other portions collapsed intermittently, perhaps over a period of a month. To imagine its effect upon the surrounding area, consider the rockslide in Lituya Bay, Alaska during the earthquake of 1958, where a single massive wave, formed by rock sliding into the sea, first surged up the mountain on the opposite side of the bay to an elevation of at least twelve hundred feet above sea level, and then moved down the bay out to sea at a height of about two hundred feet.[25] The energy released by the Thera collapse, calculated to be two thousand times greater than that released by the Lituya Bay slide, must have formed—after the pattern of the Krakatoa eruption—three ocean waves, each seven hundred feet high at Thera and eighty miles long.[26] These three seismic waves (tsunamis) very likely surged across the sea at a height of two hundred feet, crashed onto the Cretan coast, and then rushed miles inland to climb hundreds of feet up the mountainsides. So tremendous must have been the power of these sea waves that they easily radiated as far as the coasts of Africa and the Levant.[27] Just before smashing into coastal Greece and Turkey at heights of three hundred feet,[28] these seismic waves might have warned of their approach with a low and rumbling sound, "a kind of 'vrooooo' from the depths of the earth,"[29] similar to that heard by a rancher shortly before a thirty-foot-high wall of water, set off by the Alaskan earthquake of 1964, thundered up the channel to demolish the city of Kodiak.

Indeed, the memory of such a rumbling was contained in a tradition concerning a tidal wave in the region of Troezen and the Saronic Gulf, which Euripides attributed to Poseidon in his attempt to overwhelm Hippolytus. In the messenger's speech in *Hippolytus,* Euripides described the wave in these graphic terms:

> And when we struck into a desolate place—
> There lies beyond the frontier of this land
> A shore that faces the Saronic Sea—
> There came a sound, as if within the earth
> Zeus' hollow thunder boomed, awful to hear.
> The horses lifted heads towards the sky
> And pricked their ears; while strange fear fell on us,
> Whence came the voice. To the sea-beaten shore
> We looked, and saw a monstrous wave that soared
> Into the sky, so lofty that my eyes
> Were robbed of seeing the Scironian cliffs.
> It hid the isthmus and Asclepius' rock.
> Then seething up and bubbling all about
> With foaming flood and breath from the deep sea,
> Shoreward it came to where the chariot stood.[30]

Such a sound preceding the appearance of these giant sea waves might have strengthened the conviction of eyewitnesses that only subterranean waters, bursting from the depths, could have sent up this stupendous volume of water to flood the earth. But even without the rumble, other observable phenomena might have contributed to the belief in an underground upheaval. Data released by the National Academy of Sciences on the Alaskan earthquake of 1964 stated that swimming pools as far away as Texas were partially emptied as their water sloshed back and forth, while the water in Australian, African, and Eurasian wells pumped up and down in response to these severe tremors. The sloshing of water—known as a seiche—also occurred closer to the epicenter: in Kenai Lake, Alaska, the sloshing water and ice peeled bark off trees along the shore to a height of twenty feet; on Francois Lake in British Columbia a seiche drove water up through fishing holes in rhythmic geysers; and in Alaska the earthquake waves alternately squeezed and stretched the sodden terrain to produce thousands of "mud spouts" or "sand fountains" squirting in unison.[31]

Surely the earthquake waves accompanying the Thera eruption also caused the water in the wells, streams, lakes in the lands bordering the Aegean and eastern Mediterranean to slosh about or shoot up like geysers; perhaps they even produced those "mud spouts" or "sand fountains" seen in Alaska. Such phenomena, associated as they were with the eruption, and the seismic sea-waves—with or without the underground rumble—must have signified to the survivors that the subterranean depths had joined with the rain to flood their lands.

The Extraordinary Rainfall

The rain that followed the volcanic eruption of Thera could not have been any ordinary rain, judging from the eyewitness accounts of the rain that followed the eruption of Krakatoa. This convulsion hurled a vast quantity of vapor and pumice into the atmosphere, which, forming a great cloud, then fell upon the ships in the immediate area in a rain of dust, pumice, and water. Some pieces of pumice were said to have been the size of pumpkins.[32] This mixture of falling ash and water completely blotted out all light from the sky:

> At Batavia, situated about 100 English miles from Krakatoa, the sky was clear at 7 a.m., but began to darken between that hour and 10 a.m.; at 10.15 the sky became lurid and yellowish, and lamps began to be required in the houses; about 10.30 the first falls from the overhanging clouds took place in the form of fine watery particles, and this was succeeded by a few grains of dust; at 11 a.m. this increased to a regular dust-rain, becoming heavier till 11.20, when complete darkness fell on the city. This heavy dust-rain continued till 1, and afterwards less heavily till 3 p.m.[33]

With the Krakatoa explosion producing a dust rain that turned day into night for almost two hours, surely the Thera eruption—five times greater than that of Krakatoa[34]—must have spewed forth so great a quantity of ash that the resulting torrential downpour also blacked out the light of day. This rain of water and pumice, judging from the cores of sea-bottom sediment dug up by Mavor's expedition in a wide swing through the deep eastern Mediterranean, covered this entire region. One core sample, revealing an ash layer of seven feet about one hundred miles southeast of Thera, led Mavor to conclude:

> Here was solid data showing that explosions at Thera were of a dimension sufficient to visit great calamity upon the entire eastern Mediterranean.[35]

This rain of mud and ashes, to have been responsible for such widespread devastation throughout this area, certainly must have lasted more than the four and a half hours of Krakatoan rainfall, but how much longer is not known. The Greek myth of Deucalion, perhaps relating the effect of the Thera cataclysm, failed to mention how long the rain fell.[36] The lack of any precise information leads to the conjecture that the Thera eruption was powerful enough to have caused a blackout of all the daylight hours for one full day—if not more.

Seismic Waves in the Flood Story

It must now be apparent why the search for the location of the biblical Deluge has been shifted from the Mesopotamian delta of the Tigris and Euphrates Rivers to the Aegean Sea. The preceding reconstruction of the phenomena following the Thera eruption coincides so closely with details in the biblical story that obviously the narrator must have accepted the explanations current at the time of composition that the subterranean waters, gushing up to form seismic waves of enormous magnitude, were largely responsible for flooding the coastal regions of the eastern Mediterranean.

This thesis is greatly strengthened by the likelihood that mention was made of seismic waves in those parts of the narrative dealing directly with the Deluge. The investigation begins with 6:17, for the differences in various translations of this sentence suggest that scholars may have had difficulty correctly understanding the words of the verse. In two earlier versions this reading is found:

> And I, behold, I do bring the flood of waters
> upon the earth. . . . (JPS)

> For behold, I will bring a flood of waters
> upon the earth. . . . (RSV)

Later versions, however, differ in their construction of the sentence:

> For My part, I am about to bring the Flood—
> waters upon the earth—to destroy. . . . (NJPS)

> For my part, I am about to bring on the Flood—
> waters upon the earth—to eliminate. . . . (Speiser, *Genesis*)

> And I—behold, I am about to bring a flood,
> water upon the earth, to destroy. . . . (Cassuto, 2:55)

In these later versions, "flood" has been separated from "waters," even though "flood of waters" is a perfectly acceptable literal translation of

מַבּוּל מַיִם, 'mabbûl mayim.' The reason for this change stems from the word-ing of another sentence (7:6), where הָיָה, 'hāyāh,' "was," has been in-serted between "flood" and "water":

> Noah was six hundred years old when the Flood came,
> waters upon the earth. (NJPS)

> Noah was in his six hundreth year when the Flood came—
> waters upon the earth. (Speiser, *Genesis*)

> Noah was six hundred years old when the flood came,
> water upon the earth. (Cassuto, 2:77)

This particular wording, as explained by Cassuto, was an attempt by the narrator to convey some understanding of the meaning and nature of 'mab-bûl,' "flood," to those who had never witnessed a flood before.[37] Cas-suto assumed that this was the narrator's intention in 6:17, even though 'hāyāh,' "was," had been omitted, for he translated the verse to mean "a flood, water upon the earth, . . ." instead of "a flood of waters."

But would these few words adequately have conveyed an appreciation of the nature of a flood to one who never before had lived through this ex-perience. Might not Noah have been misled by this definition of "waters upon the earth" and equated this unfamiliar term 'mabbûl' with גֶּשֶׁם, 'gešem,' "rain," which also becomes "water upon the earth" during a downpour? Presumably, the narrator referred to "*the* flood"—instead of "a flood"—because he did assume that Noah knew what he was talking about.

Finally, there is this puzzling passage:

> I will maintain My covenant with you: never again shall all flesh be cut off by the
> waters of a flood, and never again shall there be a flood to destroy the earth.
> (Gen. 9:11, NJPS)

Did the narrator deliberately want to differentiate between two agents of destruction, "waters" and "flood," or was he saying the same thing, only varying his terms?

The question raised cast sufficient doubt upon the meaning of 'mabbûl,' "flood," is to require a reexamination of this word. Unfortunately, other passages in the Bible cannot be turned to for verification of this translation because this word is found only in Psalm 29:10; here its translation is of no help, for obviously the scholars have been guided by the accepted mean-ing of the word in the Noah story. Without the aid of other biblical pas-sages, the etymology of 'mabbûl' and its usage in the Flood story are the only sources of information about this word.

An etymological investigation reveals scholarly disagreement over its origin. Cassuto argued convincingly that מַבּוּל, 'mabbûl,' is formed from the stem יָבַל, 'yābal,' "conduct, bear along,"[38] and cited יָבָל, 'yābāl,' in יִבְלֵי מַיִם, 'yiblê mayim,' "watercourses"[39]—another derivative of 'yābal'— to show that 'mabbûl' was well-suited to the theme.

Assuming that Cassuto was correct, that 'mabbûl' is formed from the stem יָבַל,'yābal,' יוֹבֵל,'yôbēl,' "ram, ram's horn,"another derivative of יָבַל,'yābal,'[40] contributes greatly to an understanding of this word. The thrust of יוֹבֵל, 'yôbēl,' as 'ram's horn" is to focus attention upon what a ram does with his horns: a ram *charges* with his horns. In fact, so crippling can be the blow of a charging ram that the ancients named the instrument for knocking down fortified gates or making holes in the city walls a *battering ram*. Now, does anything connected with water demonstrate the same tremendous battering force observed in a butting ram? The answer is yes—a *wave*. Not an ordinary wave, but a *seismic wave;* for only a seismic wave manifests this terrible, punishing power.

Support for 'mabbûl' as "seismic wave" comes from the special designations given to other types of waves, similar to those in English. גַּל, 'gal,' formed from the stem גָּלַל, 'gālal,' "roll, roll away,"[41] must have designated a "roller," that long, heavy wave that rolls in upon the coast, particularly after a storm. And מִשְׁבָּר, 'mišbbār,' derived from שָׁבַר, 'šābar,' "break in pieces,"[42] must have been the term for "breaker,"[43] that type of wave that breaks into foam against the shore. Accordingly, then, 'mabbûl' is the specific term for those monstrous, two hundred-foot waves that smashed into the Israelite coastal regions.[44]

To test the validity of this theory, "seismic wave" must be substituted for "flood" in the aforementioned verses in the narrative where differences of interpretation were noted. The passage where God informed Noah of His intention to inundate the earth now reads:

And I, behold, I do bring the seismic wave of waters upon the earth. . . . (6:17)

The phrase "of waters" is clearly redundant, for a wave would be nothing else but water. In view of this redundancy is it possible that the narrator never intended the consonants מים, 'mym,' to be vocalized מַיִם, 'mayim,' "waters"? The answer to this question would have to be yes and the Masoretes would have to be made responsible for this error. Working centuries later to preserve the integrity of the biblical text by fixing the spelling and pronunciation as well as dividing the words, sections, paragraphs, and books of Scripture, the Masoretes did not know the precise meaning of 'mabbûl.' They evidently assumed from its context in the story that it was something connected with water. Consequently, when they saw מים, 'mym,' following 'mabbûl,' they must have concluded that מים, 'mym,' had to be vocalized מַיִם, 'mayim,' "water," since this was the word used so frequently in the Flood story.

There is an alternative way of vocalizing מים, 'mym,' that makes considerably more sense. מִיָּם, 'miyyam,' is simply read "from Yam." Here יָם, 'yam,' does not mean "sea"[45] but rather the *name* in Ugaritic and Canaanite literature for the god of the sea and the subterranean waters, who contended with Baal, the lord of the air and genius of the rain, for the position of lord and master of Earth.[46] Judging from the number of Scriptural references to Yam,[47] he certainly was well-known to the Israelites, but the Bible, disregarding his exalted position in Ugàritic-Canaanite literature, depicted him as a demon, who was decisively defeated in his bid to overthrow God:[48]

> God alone stretched out the heavens,
> and trampled the back of Yam. (Job 9:8)
>
> Was it not you that dried up Yam...? (Isa. 51:10a)
>
> You made your horses trample Yam. (Hab. 3:15)

Even what previously had been translated "sea" in Exodus might have been intended to be understood as "Yam":[49]

> The deeps congealed in the heart of Yam. (15:8)

Far from legitimatizing the Yam of the Ugaritic-Canaanite saga, these biblical references show how this pagan god was transformed into a vanquished demon, whose control over the watery primeval chaos was subject to the Divine will.

The name "Yam" would explain why the narrator used the emphatic form of the personal pronoun "I" in God's speech to Noah outlining His plan of destruction (6:17). Evidently, the narrator wanted it clearly understood that what was about to burst forth from the depths of the sea was God's doing, not Yam's. This use of the emphatic personal pronoun underscores *God's* role: "Make no mistake about it—I, and *only* I, will bring on this seismic wave. Though the wave will come from Yam's domain in the depths of the sea, it will be released by Yam only upon My command." Consequently, the מַיִם, 'mayim,' of 7:6, vocalized according to the Masoretic understanding of 'mayim' in 6:17, would read:

> Noah was six hundred years old when the seismic wave came [was] from Yam upon the earth.

Not until 7:10 is water first associated with 'mabbûl':

> And it came to pass at the end of the seven days
> that the waters of the 'mabbûl' were upon the earth.

If 'mabbûl' is translated as "flood," it is impossible to explain how at the end of the seventh day all the water of the flood could have covered the earth—note that the sentence does not say that the waters *began* to cover the earth—when on that very day the rains, which were to continue for forty days and nights (7:4), had just begun to fall. But if 'mabbûl' is accepted as "seismic wave," then it makes sense that *all* the water of the wave inundated the land just as the rains began to fall.

The simultaneous occurrence of rain and seismic wave conforms to the reconstruction of the natural phenomena following the volcanic eruption at Thera: (1) the spew of ash from the volcanic eruption of Thera triggered torrential rains, and (2) thirty minutes after the explosion seismic waves, born of the eruption, smashed into the island of Crete.[50] This time sequence indicates that seismic waves easily could have reached the coastal regions of the east Mediterranean on the same day the rains of ash, pumice, and water fell upon the area.

Furthermore, the parallelism in 7:10–12 seems to confirm the thesis that 'mabbûl' means seismic wave:

> Effect—the seismic wave hits the earth. (7:10)
> Cause—fountains of the deep burst apart. (7:11a)
> Cause—flood-gates of sky are opened. (7:11b)
> Effect—rain falls forty days and nights. (7:12)

Here the narrator's train of thought is followed as it proceeded from the cause of the first to the cause of the second to the effect of the second.

The continuous rainfall of forty days and nights becomes comprehensible in light of what presumably must have happened following the Thera eruption. Its towering vapor cloud following the major phase of the explosion, coupled with the smaller clouds formed by the minor phases of eruption, probably triggered a rainfall that lasted for days on end—the use of the number forty would be in keeping with the Hebrew practice to denote a period of unusual length. Furthermore, this rain—pumice and mud at least in its initial phase—would explain why daylight must have ceased for a while after the Flood:

> Day and night
> Shall not cease. (Gen. 8:22, NJPS)

Daylight, as was observed earlier, must have been completely blotted out by the ash rain following Thera's eruption for perhaps two or three days;[51] this phenomenon evidently was so disturbing to the inhabitants of the world of the eastern Mediterranean that God had to promise never again to interrupt the orderly cycle of light and darkness.

The 'mabbûl' continued on the earth for forty days (7:17). Translating 'mabbûl' as "flood" introduces a contradiction, for it later is learned that the waters had swelled on earth one hundred and fifty days (7:24). But with 'mabbûl' as "seismic wave," the sentence simply states that over a period of forty days seismic waves smashed into the coast. Since Thera collapsed in stages, thereby creating a series of seismic waves,[52] the narrator probably drew upon this information in portraying an onslaught that extended over a sizable length of time.

The narrator would be expected to state how long the fountains of the deep remained open, since he dealt with the duration of rainfall. And this he does—if 'mabbûl' is accepted as "seismic wave": the fountains of the deep remained open for forty days. Note that in 7:24 the narrator spoke only of הַמַּיִם, 'hammayim,' "the waters," and not מֵי הַמַּבּוּל, 'mê hammabbûl,' "waters of the Flood" (7:10). If 'mabbûl' is accepted as "flood," this explains the omission of "...of the Flood" as a stylistic variation. However, with מַבּוּל, 'mabbûl,' as "seismic wave" the narrator had to use the simple word מַיִם, 'mayim,' "waters," to include both the waters above and the waters below.

The narrator also might have intended to indicate that both these agents of destruction, working together, were stopped at the same time:

> The fountains of the deep and the flood-gates of the sky were stopped up. . . .

This impression accords with the interpretation of 'mabbûl' as one of a series of seismic waves that lashed the coastal regions for forty days. This verse did not mean to imply, however, that the waters of the deep and sky were stopped up at the end of one hundred and fifty days. In a one-sentence recapitulation (8:2) the narrator stated that the seismic waves and torrential rains had stopped at the end of forty days; the waters then maintained their crest for an additional one hundred and ten days. Only after this period of one hundred and fifty days did the waters begin to recede.

Finally, now God's distinction between "the *waters* of the seismic wave" and "seismic wave" in His covenant with Noah (9:11) can be better understood. If 'mabbûl' is accepted as "seismic wave," then God was promising that never again would all flesh be cut off by the waters of the seismic wave nor would the earth ever again be destroyed by a seismic wave. Knowledge of the effects of seismic waves suggests that the narrator was making a distinction between the *waters* of the seismic wave as it affected *life* on earth and the destructive power of the wave as it affected the soil and rock of the earth itself. Considering that the damage done by seismic waves is most severe when the receding waters of the wave undermine the physical properties of the earth itself,[53] the reason why the narrator distinguished between the waters, which drowned all life, and the *power* of the waves, which sucked away huge chunks of earth, is obvious.

Frightening Clouds

Even the clouds preceding and following the volcanic eruption had to be dealt with by the narrator, for they played a most prominent role in the covenantal terms God established with Noah:

> I have set My bow in the cloud, and it shall be for a token of a covenant between Me and the earth. And it shall come to pass, when I bring clouds over the earth, and the bow is seen in the cloud, that I will remember My covenant, which is between Me and you and every living creature of all flesh; and the waters shall no more become a flood to destroy all flesh. (Gen. 9:13–15, JPS)[54]

This preoccupation with clouds becomes understandable once the emotional upheaval, sometimes bordering on terror, volcanic clouds can create in the beholder is appreciated. Such was the reaction of those who witnessed the volcanic eruption of Pelée on the West Indian island of Martinique on May 8, 1902. Four days before the cataclysm the captain of a French cable steamer, anchored in the harbor of St. Pierre, observed how the steady stream of black smut funneling out of the volcano formed an ever growing cloud that spread out over the sky like a giant black fan. This black evil mass was

> as the twilight of an eclipse settling over the land and sea. The spectacle of the advancing ash cloud, like a huge octopus overshadowing all, caused us all to direct our gaze upward, full of fear.[55]

Three miles away, on the slopes of Pelée, a food foraging party also saw a volume of cloud and ash—this time white, not black—"that fairly bewildered their senses":[56]

> Two miles and more, the column of white curling vapors was climbing—lifting, rolling and unrolling, until it lost itself in the general obscurity as the arching vapors thinned out and melted into the sky.[57]

On the day of the eruption, Pelée's upper flank opened at least three hundred feet wide and possibly as deep. From this gap a stupendous roar forced another black cloud to roll out in huge whorls:

> It mushroomed upward, forming an even blacker umbrella of darkness. This cloud roared down toward St. Pierre tumbling over and over. One moment it would clutch at the ground, the next it would rise perhaps a hundred feet before falling back to earth again. It seemed to be a living thing, glowing all the time, while from its center burst explosions that sent lightning-like scintillations high into the darkness. In less than a minute it had joined the first fireball which had demolished St. Pierre; they merged to blot out everything, and certainly to kill all they touched. The whole city was in flames.[58]

The types of volcanic clouds cited in these excerpts are representative of the clouds funneling out of a volcano preliminary to and in the process of exploding. It would seem reasonable to suppose, therefore, that these clouds, together with the monstrous vapor cloud, would have been regarded by the inhabitants of the Aegean and the eastern Mediterranean as harbingers of destruction. That this reaction to volcanic clouds probably was not restricted to a small area around Thera is inferred from the fact that the vapor cloud, ascending at least fifty thousand feet into the stratosphere, could have been seen by residents of the coastal regions of Asia Minor.[59] After witnessing such a phenomenon, these people naturally would have scrutinized thereafter any darkening clouds in the sky, fearful that they heralded another period of devastation.

Aware of these forebodings, the narrator assured man that he need never dread the reappearance of clouds that spread over the sky like a giant black fan; that curled, lifted, and rolled to the upper reaches of the heavens; that rose and fell, glowing and bursting within an umbrella of darkness; or that rose like a giant mushroom, seemingly to envelop the universe. Henceforth, God promised Noah, only rain clouds would be seen in the sky, distinguished from volcanic clouds by the rainbow in their midst. In sight of everyone, the rainbow would constantly reassure mankind that God would remember His promise never again to enlist volcanic clouds in the destruction of the earth.

In the passage where God said that He would remember His covenant when He saw the rainbow in the clouds, the narrator appeared to be dealing solely with the human factor. Since the Creator of the universe hardly would suffer from lapses of memory—thus He would not have to be reminded by rainbows of His obligations—the narrator evidently used this approach more to allay man's fear of ever seeing these horrifying clouds again. Whenever the rainbow is seen, man may rest assured that God also sees the rainbow and knows by the terms of the covenant not to flood the world again.

That the rainbow could not possibly have been intended to remind God not to flood the earth with *rain* is known from the fact that God used *two* means to inundate the earth: the subterranean waters and the torrential rains. Were the rainbow intended solely to remind God not to pour down a deluge of water upon the earth, what was to remind Him not to send the subterranean waters gushing up from the depths below? Secondly, the narrator avoided explicit mention of the word "rain"; instead, he used the word "the waters,"[60] further strengthening the deduction that were there a second flood, the underground waters would have to be used as well. For these reasons it appears that the rainbow in the clouds, far from signifying that there would be no second deluge from the rains above, was intended to still the fear that powerful volcanic clouds, gaseous and sooty, would reappear to participate in destroying the earth and its inhabitants.

Climatic Changes

Finally, God's promise not to permit nature's cycle of change to be reversed again implies that the Thera cataclysm drastically altered the orderly process of climatic change:

> So long as the earth endures,
> Seedtime and harvest,
> Cold and heat,
> Summer and winter,
> Day and night
> Shall not cease. (Gen. 8:22, NJPS)

This assurance of continuity apparently refers to different periods of time. It swings from the daily shift of light to darkness to the seasonal sowing of seed and harvesting of crops. The linking of these different time spans evidently indicates that the folk memory attributed both the disruption of the cycle of seedtime and harvest and the transformation of day into the blackness of night to the volcanic explosion of Thera. However, this is not to imply that these changes occurred simultaneously: no matter how long the mud rain blotted out the daylight, the blackout could not have lasted for months on end. More likely, the text was referring to changes that occurred years after the normal shift from night to day was resumed: the harvest had failed from lack of rainfall for so many concurrent years that people despaired of ever reaping crops again. Hence, God had to promise that no longer would continuous drought oppress man with starvation and force him to migrate.

That the Thera explosion could have produced perpetual drought even years later seems to be substantiated by the opinion of a number of geophysical authorities who regard volcanic eruptions as a primary cause of climatic change.[61] Not all volcanoes, of course, can exert this effect—only those that eject the fine pumiceous material to great heights in the atmosphere, there to persist for many years.[62] In fact, these submicron-sized particles are capable of remaining aloft for centuries. When they finally fall out from the turbulent atmosphere

> ... the atmosphere may have so few nuclei present that the cloud cover and precipitation activity are diminished. This would then give rise to the warm and dry climate characteristic of interglacial periods.[63]

It might have taken centuries for the Thera explosion to exert its effect upon the weather; then again its effect could have been more immediate. As with the explosion of one hundred megaton bombs,[64] it might have produced far-reaching climatic changes more rapidly by interfering with one of the small working parts of the weather system. But whether change came slowly or quickly, it is likely that the Thera explosion, equivalent to the detonation of four hundred and fifty hydrogen bombs, would surely have affected the weather pattern. The preceding interpretation of the text suggests that Thera produced the warm, dry climate characteristic of drought.

The Great Drought

Confirmation of this hypothesis comes from Rhys Carpenter, a distinguished classics scholar, who maintains that a drought lasting at least four hundred years was the prime cause for the disastrous cultural depression in Mediterranean civilization. From the close of the thirteenth to the ninth century B.C.E., a dropping of the food supply below the critical level of subsistence was responsible for the recession of civilization from one end of the Mediterranean to the other. Such a situation could have come about only through a climatic change of enormous proportions.[65]

Since there is no evidence of military defeat, Carpenter reasons that only famine satisfactorily explains why Mycenaeans abandoned the Aegean Islands and even the central Peloponnese, why the Ionians left Greece for the Asiatic mainland, and why the Hittites were forced to migrate from the interior plateau of Asia Minor southeast into northern Syria. This drought extending over centuries must have been caused by a change in the position of the trade wind belt. Today, the trade wind, by blocking the passage of the rain-bearing storms south of the Balkan mountain range,[66] is solely responsible for the long rainless summers of the Aegean. Postulating that a rise in planetary temperature produced a weakening of the high pressure polar front, thereby extending the trade wind's operation northward into the temperate zone, Carpenter argues that such a shift would mean that the trade wind had diverted the cyclonic rain storms away from their usual Mediterranean track. The result would be that the farmers of southern Greece, with eight months of continuous drought instead of the present four or five, could not harvest their crops.[67]

Archeological evidence suggests to Mavor a definite relationship between the great drought of 1200 B.C.E. and the Thera eruption of anywhere from 1450 B.C.E. to 1250 B.C.E. In seeking to reconcile these dates, Mavor suggests that inasmuch as he cannot confidently infer a date before which the Thera eruption occurred there is opened

> ... the exciting possibility that perhaps the Thera eruption and Cretan destruction both took place as much as 100 to 200 years later, tying in the great natural catastrophes of this era, the eruption and the drought.[68]

Even this time differential need not present a problem, for Thera could have erupted around 1450 B.C.E. and still be tied to the drought that followed two and a half centuries later, once granted that the fine, pumiceous material could have stayed aloft in the turbulent atmosphere for that long a period before affecting a climatic change with its fallout. Accordingly, Mavor's intriguing suggestion need not be discounted by the time factor: if the Thera eruption occurred around 1450 B.C.E. or even two hundred years later, it still could have exerted such an effect upon the weather pattern as to cause the most devastating drought ever to visit the eastern Mediterranean world.

Nature's Promise of Immortality

God's pledge to perpetuate seedtime and harvest, cold and heat, summer and winter, day and night, in addition to the assurance that henceforth the earth could always be depended upon to bring forth food, also faithfully preserved the *psychological* reaction of the survivors of the Thera eruption and resultant inundation. The phrases "cold and heat" and "summer and winter," while appending nothing to the basic idea that planting and harvesting would be continuous and steady, did emphasize the regularity of the natural processes, whether directly connected with raising food or not. This emphasis has been faithfully preserved by folk memory and reflects the yearning of the survivors for natural change, which works normally and with regularity. To appreciate the depth of feeling conveyed in this wish and to understand why it was so strong, insight is provided by the responses of some of the survivors of the atomic bomb attacks on Hiroshima and Nagasaki—those contemporaries who have come closest to experiencing a cataclysm that for many meant the end of the world.

In Dr. Robert Lifton's investigation of the psychological reactions of these survivors is seen as operative in a compelling need to maintain a sense of immortality in the face of certain biological death. This desire for immortality, present in the mind from the earliest periods of history and prehistory, represents

> a compelling universal urge to maintain an inner sense of continuous symbolic relationship, over time and space, to the various elements of life.[69]

The need for immortality may be expressed as living on through one's family or through one's creative works or human influences, as well as through a theology containing the belief of life after death. More pertinent to this study, a sense of immortality also may be achieved by being survived by nature itself, by perceiving that the natural elements remain. It is this concept of immortality that Dr. Lifton found among some of the Hiroshima survivors:

> I found this mode of immortality to be particularly vivid among the Japanese, steeped as their culture is in nature symbolism. . . . It is probably safe to say—and comparative mythology again supports this—that there is a universal psychic imagery in which nature represents an "ultimate" aspect of existence.[70]

So firmly imbedded is this belief in the persistence of nature that once it is shattered, once the "ultimate" aspect of existence has disappeared, a person may experience a sense of deep desolation, similar to that suffered by the Hiroshima survivor who heard a rumor that trees, grass, and flowers would never grow again in his city:

> I heard that no trees and flowers would grow. . . . I thought it would be forever. . . . I felt lonely . . . in a way I never had before. . . .[71]

To believe that life has been extinguished at its source is to experience that ultimate form of desolation that not only encompasses human death but goes beyond it.

The survivors of the Thera eruption and the resultant inundation, probably the two most stupendous natural catastrophes ever to have visited the ancient Aegean and eastern Mediterranean worlds, might well have experienced this ultimate form of desolation, believing as they did that not only the end of man but also the end of the earth and the natural processes had come. The proof that they had suffered psychic damage comes from the assurance that their nonhuman environment, the context of their existence, would never again be so fundamentally disturbed. Unerringly, the biblical narrator reinforced the idea that life was not being extinguished at its source by recording the promise that never would nature's rhythm be disrupted again. The natural elements would remain as always: the earth would produce crops to be harvested in the accorded time; the primary elements of cold and heat would be experienced either over long periods of time or within the brief span of twenty-four hours when the heat of the day was transformed so abruptly to the chill of the night; the months of aridity would be followed by the normal number of months of rain; and the light of day would be followed by the darkness of night. Only in the context of a universal need to maintain a sense of immortality—in this instance, by being reassured that nature, the ultimate aspect of existence, had not been destroyed—can the narrator's emphasis upon the survival of nature and its rhythmic regularity of change be fully appreciated.

Survivor Reactions of Lot's Daughters

That folk memory actually preserved the psychological reactions to disaster is substantiated by yet another portrayal of survivor reactions, that of the daughters of Lot. As previously discussed, after the destruction of Sodom and Gomorrah, Lot's daughters believed that they and their father were the sole survivors on earth; consequently, they resolved to perpetuate the human race by bearing the children of their father. Intellectually they must have known that only the cities of the Plain had been destroyed and that Zoar, their refuge before retreating to the mountains, had been spared. Yet psychologically they evidently believed that the destruction had been so great in the world that no male was left to father their children.

The despondency that drove the daughters of Lot to commit incest becomes comprehensible when viewed against the background of survivor reactions to the Hiroshima bombing. An uninjured Protestant minister, overwhelmed by the destruction all about him, expressed his hopelessness in this way:

> The feeling I had was that everyone was dead. The whole city was destroyed. . . . I thought all of my family must be dead—it doesn't matter if I die. . . . I thought this was the end of Hiroshima—of Japan—of mankind. . . . This was God's judgment on man. . . .[72]

And a Japanese woman writer despaired:

> I just could not understand why our surroundings had changed so greatly in one instant. . . . I thought it might have been something which had nothing to do with the war, the collapse of the earth which it was said would take place at the end of the world, and which I read about as a child. . . .[73]

The Protestant minister and the Japanese writer, two people of different sex and cultural backgrounds, also believed that the devastation they suffered was global, not restricted to any one locale. The response of the daughters of Lot to their crisis, corresponding so closely with that of these two Hiroshima survivors, strongly suggests that Hebrew folk memory had recorded accurately the emotional reactions of the survivors of the Deluge: God's promise that nature, henceforth, would manifest its persistence in its usual rhythmic changes is best understood as reassurance to a despairing people, dependent on nature for sustenance, that this ultimate source of life would continue as before the Flood.

The Blending of Two Flood Episodes

This investigation into the geographical origin and the distinctive features of the biblical Flood has led to a number of conclusions: (1) seismic sea waves following the Thera eruption were the subterranean waters mentioned by the narrator; (2) atmospheric changes created by the force of the eruption turned day into night, produced a prolonged rainfall, described as lasting forty days and nights, and caused a drought of unusual duration; (3) rain clouds with a rainbow, as distinguished from volcanic clouds, were acknowledged to be a portent of good. These hypotheses, even if only partially correct, still establish a causal relationship between the biblical Flood and the events preceding and following the volcanic eruption of the Aegean island of Thera.

But this is not to say that *the* Flood originated in the Aegean Sea rather than in the region of the Tigris and Euphrates Rivers. A chronological gap prevents the drawing of this conclusion. With 1500 B.C.E. established as the very earliest date Thera could have erupted and with the Sumerian flood story dated in the third millenium, this early Mesopotamian tale preserved a tradition of a devastating deluge occurring anywhere from five hundred to one thousand years before the Aegean inundations. So, there are traditions of two great floods, one—to accept Woolley's claim—extending over the delta of the Tigris and Euphrates Rivers, the other spreading out from the Aegean Sea to cover much of the Mediterranean coastal regions.

To account for the biblical Flood story incorporating such Mesopotamian themes as the hero-survivor, the ark, and the gathering of wildlife species, it must be understood first of all that the biblical narrator was engaged in writing the history of the universe in monotheistic terms. In the course of his work he had to come across the widely circulated story of a great flood. To have ignored it because its polytheism was theologically unacceptable probably would have rendered his history of the world incomplete, or even erroneous, in the eyes of his less intellectual contemporaries. Accordingly, he had to rewrite the early flood story to conform to his monotheistic faith.

Since the narrator wrote some time after the eruption of Thera, he could draw upon eyewitness reports or hearsay information to describe the physical phenomena of a mighty flood and the emotional damage it inflicted upon the stricken. He may have reasoned on the basis of the Thera cataclysm that a global flood would have manifested all the features of the Thera disaster—only to a much greater degree! During this world-wide flood the sun would have been blacked out for days; the seismic sea waves, soaring ever higher, would have come crashing down upon regions far inland; and the rains would have continued for at least forty days and nights.

By blending these details into the ancient flood story, the narrator certainly made his version more convincing, hence more acceptable. After all, in his chronicle of events, he was describing details of the Deluge that his contemporaries knew to be authentic. His description of the physical phenomena proven correct, they would be more inclined to accept his religious interpretation—so the narrator might have reasoned.

But there was another reason—as already indicated in this chapter—why the narrator integrated the details of the Thera cataclysm and inundation into his story: he was responding to the despondency of migrants fleeing the drought and to the fear created by the memory of darkness extinguishing daylight and black volcanic clouds whorling into the atmosphere. Because he could not divorce himself from the crises brought on by nature's upheaval, he so recounted the details of God's promise to Noah as to banish the lingering fear of a reoccurrence of the volcanic disaster and also assure the hopeless that the drought was never intended to be permanent. God's covenant with Noah thus declared an end to two extremes of natural visitation: no more would the earth be so submerged in water that a dove could not find a resting place; and no more would the earth so thirst for water that it could not sustain the scavenging raven.

In his account of the Flood the narrator not only presented a graphic picture of the physical and psychological effects following the Thera eruption, but in so doing revealed something of himself. Here was a man of deep compassion and sensibility, whose obvious concern was to mitigate fear and restore hope in the future.

APPENDIX

The Cainite Genealogy

God afflicted Cain not to exact vengeance but to prevent the נֶפֶשׁ, 'nepeš,' of the slain "agent" from becoming the permanent possession of Cain's descendants. In his shaking, tottering condition Cain somehow was rendered incapable of transmitting the 'nepeš' of Abel to the murderer's progeny. The Cainite genealogy attests to the effectiveness of this extreme measure: each descendant was distinguished by a quality, whether manifested in name or deed, that could never be ascribed to the children of God's agent; and, to describe the Cainite line "as the vehicle for mankind's technological progress"[1] would be warranted only if technology were regarded as a curse upon mankind. In fact, the biblical text designated the descendants of Cain as the source of evil and all that is culturally destructive.

The first of the line of Cain was Enoch:

> Cain knew his wife, and she conceived and bore Enoch. And he founded a city, and named the city after his son Enoch. (Gen. 4:17, NJPS)

It would seem from this translation that Cain founded a city and named it Enoch, after his son, but in the Hebrew text the city-builder was clearly Enoch, not Cain.[2] To add to the perplexity, the text appended the name "Enoch" after the word בְּנוֹ, 'bᵉnô,' "his son." Since Scripture recorded Cain as having only one son, the question is raised of why the narrator had to say that this son, who could not have been taken for anyone else, was Enoch. Further, how is naming a city after one's child to be explained? Nowhere in Scripture is a similar occurrence found. And for a city so distinguished as to have been named after one's child—why was it never heard of again? Totally discordant is the selection of Cain as the first of a line to serve as "the vehicle for mankind's technological progress." To so honor Cain counters the harsh treatment applied so consistently to Cain heretofore. These aspects require that the text be reexamined to see if more consistency can be restored to the narrative.

Beginning with the sentence dealing with the city,

> And he founded a city . . .

117

was it actually a "city" that was involved? Can עִיר , "'îr,' in this context mean something else? In the Hebrew lexicon the consonantal root for "city," עִיר, "'îr,' is the same as for "male ass," עַיִר, "'ayir,'[3] only the vowels differ. Yet even this difference is absent in עִירֹה, "'îrōh'[4] (to be read עִירוֹ , "'îrô'), "his ass": this possessive form of עִיר , "'îr,' has been shown to be a later development of the original עַיִר , "'ayir,' "ass.'[5]

If it is conceded that עִיר, "'îr,' is a later variation of עַיִר, "'ayir,' how can its use with בֹּנֶה, 'bōneh,' "build" be justified? The answer to this question is found in Genesis 2:22, where God "fashioned" into a woman the rib He had taken from Adam. The root form of the Hebrew word for "fashioned" is the same as the root of בֹּנֶה , 'bōneh'—בָּנָה, 'bānāh,' "build.'[6] In effect, God "built" Eve from Adam's rib. Here the narrator used the phraseology of Adam and Eve to describe a situation in which a male ass was being "fashioned."

Lest this theory be dismissed as too improbable, some facts relating to cultic representations of the ass need to be examined. From Egyptian sources it is learned that the god Seth, associated with various animals and later identified with the Canaanite Baal,[7] was depicted in the late Egyptian period as an ass or with the head of an ass.[8] Further, Scripture declared the ass to be an unclean animal.[9] On the basis of these two admittedly slender strands of evidence, it may be postulated that the narrator was saying that Enoch followed his father in pagan worship: Enoch fashioned a male ass either to invest his son with the power of the god symbolized by the male ass or to pledge his son and later progeny to the service of this god. If the suggestion to translate עִיר , "'îr,' as "male ass" is accepted, it is evident that Enoch was swearing allegiance to a deity by bestowing the name of this male ass upon his son:

וַיִּקְרָא שֵׁם הָעִיר כְּשֵׁם בְּנוֹ
wayyiqᵉrāʾ šēm hāʿîr kᵉšēm bᵉnô
And he gave the name of the male ass
as the name of his son

Furthermore, חֲנוֹךְ, 'ḥănôk,' "Enoch," cannot be in apposition to the next-to-last word, בְּנוֹ ,'bᵉnô,' "his son," because the next verse states that the name of Enoch's son was Irad—not Enoch. If Cain—not his son—was the one doing the naming, why did the narrator have to repeat the name "Enoch" after "his son," even though there was no possibility of mistaking the son for anyone else.

The reason lies in a special technique used by the narrator to express emphasis. The narrator placed the name "Enoch" at the end of verse seventeen to serve "as apposition with special emphasis'[10] to the entire preceding account. It was his way of using a dash, followed by an exclamation point:—Enoch! Working without marks of punctuation, the narrator expressed emphasis by the position of his words. By placing "Enoch"—"one who is trained'[11]—at the end of the sentence, the narrator was saying in effect: This is Enoch! *This* is the one who is trained to follow his father's example—an idol worshipper! In light of this interpretation the complete verse reads:

> And he gave the name of the male ass
> as the name of his son—Enoch!

Who was the person trained so well by his father that he gave his son the name of a male ass, fashioned by him for cultic purposes? Enoch!

Significantly, it has been suggested that עִירָד, "'îrād,' "Irad," is related to עָרוֹד, "'ārôd,' "wild ass" (Job 39:5).[12] This theme of the ass may be developed even further. עִירָד, "'îrād,' is probably a combination of two words: עִיר, "'îr,' רָד, 'rād.' This second word, רָד, 'rād,' could be a form of רוד, 'rûd,' "roam, wander restlessly." Used together, the two words read: "a male ass roams" or "a roaming male ass." In this order the last letter of the first word—ר, 'r'—and the first letter of the second word—ר, 'r'—coalesce (haplography) into a single ר, 'r.' Thus, the two words, רָד עִיר, "'îr rād,' become the single word עִירָד, "'îrād.' Whether its derivation is accepted as עָרוֹד, "'ārôd,' "wild ass," or עִיר רָד, "'îr rād,' "a roaming wild ass," "Irad" is identified with a male ass.

Ordinarily, to be named after an animal would not be especially significant since the Israelites and their Canaanite neighbors on occasion named children after animals, as with Hamor,[13] חֲמוֹר, 'ḥămôr,' "donkey," the father of Shechem; Caleb,[14] כָּלֵב, 'kālēb,' "dog," the son of Jephunneh; Nahash,[15] נָחָשׁ, 'nāḥāš,' "snake," the father of Hanun; and עתן, "'atn,' "she-ass," a personal name among the Canaanites.[16] But when "Irad" is viewed as the son of one who fashioned a cultic male ass, its relationship to words meaning "ass" becomes an important factor in substantiating the proposed theory.

Obviously, neither Enoch, a son trained in the ways of idolatry, nor Irad, the son dedicated to the ass cult, can be judged as praiseworthy in terms of Hebrew monotheism. The narrator consistently applied this standard to the entire Cainite line. Hence, the name of Irad's son, מְחוּיָאֵל, 'mᵉḥûyā'ēl,' "Mehujael," variously interpreted as meaning "whom God blots out, fattens, smites, quickens,"[17] or "the priest of God, the seer of God,"[18] must derive from another source, for the narrator hardly would have permitted אֵל, "'ēl,' the name of God, to constitute a part of the names incurring the punishment of Cain. More likely, the name is derived from a combination of מָחָה, 'māḥāh,' "exterminate,[19] smite,"[20] and יָאַל, 'yā'al,' "determine, show willingness."[21] Mehujael would thereby bear the characteristics of one who was "determined to smite" or "showed a willingness to exterminate."

Likewise, מְתוּשָׁאֵל, 'mᵉtûšā'ēl,' "Methusael," the son of Mehujael, far from being derived from the Akkadian "the man of God,"[22] probably comes from two Hebrew words: מַת, 'mat,' "man,"[23] and שְׁאוֹל, 'šᵉ'ōl,' "Sheol,[24] underworld." Sheol, perhaps derived from the root שׁאה, 'š'h,' expressing a sense of desolation or devastation,[25] has come to mean "the world (below our world) where are found shadowiness, decay, remoteness from God (Isa. 38:18; Ps. 6:6): Nothingness."[26] Far from being "a man of God," Methusael thus appears as "a man of desolation, Nothingness," or "a man remote from God."

This man remote from God was the appropriate parent to beget the murderous Lamech, who boasted to his wives of how he killed a young foe for bruising him—a rather unequal exchange, when "wound for wound, bruise for bruise,"[27] so listed at the end of the law of talion, indicated that these were the least important physical injuries that could be committed. Lamech exacted the harshest punishment for the slightest of injuries and then vauntingly declared:

> If Cain is avenged sevenfold,
> Then Lamech seventy-sevenfold. (Gen. 4:24, NJPS)

In this extreme of hyperbole,[28] Lamech declared his standard of vengeance to be far more exacting than God's. Whereas God would have exacted vengeance only if Cain was slain, Lamech would punish with death anyone who so much as bruised him. Not for him was the law that a bruise was to be repaid with a bruise.

Lamech's cruel nature precludes his name from being interpreted as "a strong youth"[29] or as designating one of a certain class of Mesopotamian priests.[30] Far from being a strong young man, Lamech was the slayer of a young man. Nor did he reflect credit on the Mesopotamian priesthood; for, no priest would boast of exacting greater vengeance than his god. Possibly, the name "Lamech" stems from the Hebrew root מָכַךְ, 'mākak,' "be low, humiliated,"[31] or a form of מוּךְ, 'mûk,' "be low, depressed, grow poor."[32] If the ל, 'l,' at the beginning of לָמֶךְ, 'lāmek,' "Lamech," is regarded as a *lamedh emphaticum*, an asseverative particle attached to the beginning of the word to lend emphasis to that word,[33] then מֶךְ —ל, 'lā-mek' conveys the idea of "truly low" or, simply, "the lowest!"—a remarkably apt description for that descendant of Cain who had no regard for human life.

Even the names of Lamech's wives contribute to this portrayal of their husband. Far from alluding to beauty,[34] עָדָה, 'ādāh,' "Adah," more likely is the female form of עַד, 'ad,' "booty."[35] Lamech must have claimed her as a prize in one of his raiding expeditions. The name of his second wife, צִלָּה, 'ṣillāh,' "Zillah," probably comes from the root צָלַל, 'ṣālal,' "tingle, quiver with fear."[36] Understandably, as the wife of Lamech, Zillah would quiver with fear lest she arouse his displeasure.

The narrative recorded that Lamech fathered three sons and a daughter. Adah bore Jabal, "the ancestor of those who dwell in tents and amidst herds" (Gen. 4:20, NJPS), and Jubal, "the ancestor of all who play the lyre and the pipe" (Gen. 4:21, NJPS). Zillah bore Tubal-cain, "who forged all implements of copper and iron" (Gen. 4:22, NJPS), and his sister Naamah. Such a distinguished list of accomplishments certainly would seem to dis-

credit the theory of the "bad seed" of the Cainite line. And there is no con-
testing the translation, for the text is clear and unmistakable. However,
before these activities can be judged as truly "the beginnings of human art,"[37]
it must be determined if these activities could have been evaluated differently
by the cultural standards of that ancient period. An indication of such a
possibility is found in the names of Lamech's sons.

All three names—יָבָל, 'yābāl,' "Jabal"; יוּבָל, 'yûbāl,' "Jubal"; and תּוּבַל,
'tûbal,' "Tubal"—come from the root יָבַל,'yābal,' "conduct, bear along
in procession."[38] That they stem from a common root seems to indicate
a composite group, made up of three elements that did not differ from one
another too greatly. This family group, to judge from the occupations of
the brothers, possessed herds of some kind, tents, musical instruments, and
bellows for working with copper and iron. Since all bear in their names the
idea of "bearing along in procession," the brothers and their children must
have composed a wandering group, something like gypsies or "camp-
followers," that streamed along from one camp site to another.[39]

The gypsy character of this seemingly new type of tent settlement[40] is
complete with the characteristics discerned in the name of Tubal-cain's
sister נַעֲמָה, 'na'ămāh,' "Naamah," a term used in connection with
singing and playing in both Canaanite and Hebrew.[41] The female element
added to the gypsy-character of this group with singing and the playing of
musical instruments. These ancient camp-followers must have resembled
their modern gypsy counterparts who gain their livelihood in Arab Asia:

> The travelling smiths or tinkers of modern Arab Asia, whether Ṣleib or Nawar
> (Gipsies), follow more or less regular trade-routes. With their asses and their
> tools these groups depend for their livelihood on their craftsmanship, supplement-
> ed by music and divination, in which the women excel. It is probable that the
> Kenites of the Bible, with a name derived from *qain,* "smith," resembled these
> groups somewhat in their mode of living. It can scarcely be accidental that
> Cain's descendant Lamech had three sons, each of whom is credited with
> originating one of the three occupational specialties of this form of society: tents
> and herds, musical instruments, copper and iron working. The famous party of
> Asiatics depicted on a tomb at Benai Ḥasan, belonging to the early nineteenth
> century B.C., probably represents just such a group: the number of individuals
> (thirty-seven) which constituted it, is about right. In keeping with the character
> of the group is the fact that it is represented as possessing asses, weapons,
> musical instruments and portable bellows for use in working copper.[42]

This description shows that the women represented by Naamah supplemented
such male activities as working with metals and tending herds of asses by
singing and practicing divination.

The gypsy children of Lamech, performing those jobs that were beneath
the dignity of the host population,[43] reflected the low estate of their
father and themselves. With them all mention of the Cainite line comes to
an end. The narrator had proved his point: all the children of Cain, culminating in the seventh generation, testified to the effectiveness of God's
measures to prevent the 'nepeš' of the slain Abel from being taken over

by the Cainites: no one ever enjoyed any status even remotely resembling that attached to the office of the "agent" of God. Further, God levied upon Cain the very punishment He threatened to impose upon Cain's would-be slayer: sevenfold vengeance, translated in terms of generations, showed the seven generations of the Cainite line depicted in the worst possible light.

The Sethite Genealogy

Having proved that the superior qualities of the צֶלֶם, 'ṣelem' never could have been transmitted to the seed of Cain, the narrator then introduced the new "agent":

> Adam knew his wife again, and she bore a son and named him Seth, meaning, "God has provided me with another offspring in place of Abel," for Cain had killed him. (Gen. 4:25, NJPS)

The text described Seth as resembling his father "in his likeness after his image"—a designation that, in an earlier chapter, identified the 'ṣelem' by the covenantal relationship between God and Seth. That Seth was morally qualified is shown in Eve's explanation of his name: God provided her with this boy as a replacement for Abel. With *God* providing the child, there could be no question as to his moral excellence. Hence, no qualifying moral test had to be given. With Cain, an entirely different situation prevailed. Yet, why was a moral examination given to Cain if, as the translations would have us believe, Eve explained Cain's name by referring to the assistance she received from God:

> I have gained a male child with the help of the Lord. (Gen. 4:1, NJPS)

Had Cain been born with the help of the Lord, surely he would have had the same moral certification of excellence Seth had. Why then was one son subjected to a test and rejected, while the other was accepted unqualifiedly as an "agent"? The answer again lies in the translation. To have God involved with the birth of a child and then have him turn out as morally reprehensible as Cain was so contrary to the narrator's theology as to be inconceivable. Hence Eve's words must have been mistranslated. This assumption is confirmed by another translation, which omitted any suggestion of God's help in the birth of Cain. Eve said:

> I have created a man equally with the Lord.[44]

With support from the Canaanite language, קָנִיתִי, 'qānîtî,' is rendered as "I have formed (created), gave birth to." Eve actually was boasting of her own generative and creative powers, which she equated with God's.[45] Far from acknowledging any debt to God, Eve declared that she had created Cain without any divine help. Her boast resolves the theological incongruity: God was not responsible for Cain's birth.

Seth's inauguration as "agent" occurred when he reached manhood, a period marked by his marrying and fathering a child. At this time was the name of the Lord invoked:

אָז הוּחַל לִקְרֹא בְּשֵׁם יְהֹוָה

’az hûḥal liqᵉrō’ bᵉšēm ădônay (Gen. 4:26)

Since classical Hebrew draws no distinction between the initial performance of an action and its reiteration, הוּחַל, 'hûḥal,' can signify both to commence and recommence. And so, in this verse 'hûḥal' is translated as "recommence":

Then it was begun once more to call upon the name of the Lord.

That the name of the Lord was invoked once more means that prior to his death Abel must have invoked the name of the Lord in the pursuance of his duties as "agent." Only after a period of seven generations of the Cainite line had elapsed[46] was a new "agent" designated, who presumably acted in God's name. Likewise, the populace, responding to the examples of the "agent," must have called upon the divine name.

The genealogical record of the descendants of Seth, far from being a simple matter of enumerating births, was used by the narrator to contrast the children of Seth, the "agent," with the Cainite line.

The first of the Sethites was אֱנוֹשׁ, 'ĕnôš,' "Enosh," the son of Seth. In the lexicon אֱנוֹשׁ , 'ĕnôš,' means "man, mankind."[47] Used as a name, it personifies those qualities that distinguish the humane person from the beast. The cognate Ugaritic root, אנש, 'anš,' "was gentle, kindly,"[48] seems to substantiate 'ĕnôš' as expressing the gentle, kindly character of the humane man.

The son of Enosh, קֵינָן, 'qênān,' "Kenan," is not to be confused with קַיִן, 'qayin,' "Cain," though these names are differentiated only by the addition of another ן (נ), 'n,' to קֵינָן, 'qênān,' "Kenan." Most likely the final ן, 'n,' is not an integral part of the root, but rather a nominal formative suffix[49] added to differentiate between the Hebrew names of Kenan and Cain. This suffix is found in:

עֵבֶר, "ēber' (Gen. 10:21) as against עֶבְרוֹן, "ebrōn" (Jos. 19:28)

חֶבֶר, 'ḥeber' (Gen. 46:17) as against חֶבְרוֹן, 'ḥebrôn (Num. 3:19)

Accordingly, "Kenan" seems to be derived from קין, 'qyn,' which has been traced to קָנָה, 'qānāh,' "create."[50] In the Ugaritic, קנה, 'qnh,' appears to be parallel with כּוּן, 'kûn,'[51] from which is derived the adjective כֵּן, 'kēn,' "right, veritable, honest."[52] The plural form of this word, כֵּנִים, 'kēnîm,' was used by the narrator five times[53] in chapter forty-two of Genesis to mean "honest men." Such derivation makes "Kenan" closely approximate the meaning of "the honest man."

Mahalalel, the son of Kenan, obviously comes from the two words, מְהַלַלְ־אֵל, 'mahălal-’ēl,' "praise of God."[54]

The son of Mahalalel is יֶרֶד, 'yered,' "Jared," which, when traced through

רָדָה, 'rādāh,' "have dominion, rule,"[55] has the force of "let him have dominion" or "he will have dominion"—a blessing in either case.

As head of the seventh generation from Adam, Enoch, the son of Jared, was accorded particular attention. Sharply contrasting with his Cainite counterparts, Jabal, Jubal, and Tubal-cain, the social pariahs, Enoch was described as having been elevated to the position of "agent" by the word וַיִּתְהַלֵּךְ, 'wayyithallēk,' "and he walked": Enoch "walked with God." In situations of exercising authority or responsibility of office, the word הִתְהַלֵּךְ, 'hithallēk,' "walked," could mean "carrying out a responsibility" or "fulfilling one's office." This connotation was present in Samuel's defense of his record as the premonarchical Israelite leader:

> And Samuel said unto all Israel: "Behold I have hearkened unto your voice in all that ye said unto me, and have made a king over you. And now, behold, the king walketh before you; and I am old and gray-headed; and, behold, my sons are with you; and I have walked before you from my youth unto this day. Here I am; witness against me before the Lord, and before His anointed. . . ."
> (I Sam. 12:1–3, JPS)

Samuel was not concerned that the newly anointed king happened to be walking about at the time; he used מִתְהַלֵּךְ, 'mithallēk,' "walketh," to describe the regal assumption of authority. And before Samuel challenged the people to find any wrongdoing when he was the official spokesman of God, he referred to his own record as leader with the same words: "I have walked before you from my youth. . . ."

Also, in King Hezekiah's prayer to God for the strength to recover from an illness, הִתְהַלֵּךְ, 'hithallēk' was used in the same context:

> Remember now, O Lord, I beseech Thee, how I have walked before Thee in truth and with a whole heart, and have done that which is good in Thy sight.
> (II Kings 20:3, JPS)

If "walking with God" were only synonymous with righteous conduct, Hezekiah need not have added that he walked before God "in truth and with a whole heart," for that would have been understood. The necessity of adding this description of his moral behavior indicates that this reflexive form of הָלַךְ, 'hālak,' did not convey the meaning of ethical wholeness. Hence, King Hezekiah's "walking" must be understood as an expression of tenure in the most responsible office of the land.

The term "walk," even when used in connection with God, carried the same special connotation found with Samuel and Hezekiah. God used the same reflexive form of הָלַךְ, 'hālak,' in explaining to David why He did not grant him permission to build the Temple:

> Shalt thou build Me a house for Me to dwell in? for I have not dwelt in a house since the day that I brought up the children of Israel out of Egypt, even to this day, but have walked in a tent and a tabernacle. In all places wherein I have walked among all the children of Israel, spoke I a word with any of the tribes of Israel, whom I commanded to feed My people Israel, saying: Why have ye not built Me a house of cedar? (II Sam. 7:5–7, JPS)

In seeking to smooth over an apparent difficulty in the literal translation of the text, the RSV translated the pertinent section of these verses in this fashion:

> ... but I have been moving about in a tent for my dwelling. In all places where I have moved with the people of Israel. . . . (II Sam. 7:6–7, RSV)

In this rendition the RSV reveals how it missed the point of the special meaning "walk." The Hebrew text was quite explicit: God had "walked" in a tent and in a tabernacle, not just in a tent. Nor did the text say that the tent and tabernacle moved about with God in it; rather it stated that God, not the tent or tabernacle, did the moving or "walking." The RSV, apparently unable to make any sense out of God saying that He "walked" for a long time in His tent and tabernacle, eliminated the difficulty by having the tent of God move about. What the RSV did not realize was that the word "walk" was being used in the same special sense encountered in the cases of Samuel and Hezekiah: "to discharge one's duty" or "to act as leader." God was saying that up until now He had led the Israelites and transmitted His wishes in the tent and tabernacle; since He had no need of a house of cedar then, He did not need it now.

Lastly, there is the example of "walk" in the narrator's description of Noah:

> Noah was a righteous man; he was blameless in his age; Noah walked with God. (Gen. 6:9, NJPS)

With the phrase "blameless in his age" parallel to Noah's righteousness, "walking with God" should be understood as meaning the execution of the responsibilities of one's office. Clearly, the narrator was referring to Noah's role as "agent": as God's representative he would be the one person to be informed of the impending annihilation of all life on earth.

Now that "walking with God" is understood as expressing the exercise of authority of an office, the theory can be pursued that Enoch played the special role of God's agent when he was described as "walking with God." That Enoch walked with God three hundred years means that Enoch acted as God's agent for that length of time.

The name "Enoch" is used both for Cain's and Jared's sons; however, the import of the name differed according to whether one was a descendant of Cain or Seth. For the son of Cain, Enoch signified "one who is trained" in the idolatrous ways of his father. In contrast, the name of Enoch, the son of Jared, also from חָנַךְ, 'ḥānak,' "dedicate, trained," designated Enoch as a man dedicated to God.

Enoch is best remembered for what happened to him at the end of his life:

> All the days of Enoch came to 365 years. Enoch walked with God; then he was no more, for God took him. (Gen. 5:23–24, NJPS)

This cryptic description of his end stimulated the creation of folk myths in the Book of Enoch, which told of angels who revealed God's appearance

in judgment to Enoch, of Enoch's intercession for the fallen angels, of
Enoch's journey from the prison of the fallen angels to the underworld, the
tree of life, the holy mountain in the middle of the earth.[56] These
wondrous tales arose because the usual formula of "and he died" was missing. In its stead there was the ambiguous phrase, "then he was no more, for
God took him." A number of biblical commentators read into these words
the type of end that later occurred with Elijah—ascension alive to the heavenly realm.[57]

Unquestionably the text is open to such an interpretation, but its acceptance would oblige the offer of at least some reason why this living translation to the divine sphere occurred with Enoch and with no one else in the
Pentateuch. Did Enoch possess greater merit than Abraham or Moses? The
silence of the text on this point is instructive: failure to mention any special
merit most likely means there was nothing worth noting. Must it then be
concluded that God acted capriciously, picking Enoch for no reason other
than mere whim? Such a conclusion seems unwarranted, for nowhere in the
passages investigated did God ever act on a whim; rather, the opposite was
true. Indeed, a capricious God would have been inconceivable to the narrator. The answers to these questions seem to open this sentence to a
different interpretation.

Examining the text, it is noted that Enoch, like Seth, began to act as
"agent" only after proving manhood with the birth of his first child. Then
followed the usual description: the number of years lived after the birth of
the first-born, the fact that other sons and daughters were born, and the
final total of his years. Ordinarily, this last item would conclude with וַיָּמֹת,
'wayyāmōt,' "and he died," but this word, strangely enough, was omitted.
That Enoch died seems evident from the preceding statement that "all the
days of Enoch were three hundred sixty and five years" (Gen. 5:23, JPS).
Why then did the narrator deliberately substitute this equivalent expression
for וַיָּמֹת, 'wayyāmōt,' "and he died"? The answer is to be sought in the
special importance of the seventh generation.

As previously noted with Cain and his descendants, the full weight of
God's punishment became manifest in the seventh generation. Would this
not also be true for the infernal demon, if he wanted to retaliate against
God's agent for the punishment of his servant Cain? Presumably, he would
have waited until this seventh generation of Adam and Seth to wreak
vengeance. To guard against the possibility that such an inference might be
drawn from the fact that Enoch "died," the narrator omitted the word וַיָּמֹת,
'wayyāmōt,' "and he died," because it might be construed as signifying
the presence of the demon Death, 'Mōt' (in the Canaanite), or מָוֶת,
'māwet' (in the Hebrew), a word directly related to וַיָּמֹת, 'wayyāmōt,'
"and he died." If this was the narrator's motive for omitting the usual "and
he died," it would also affirm that God was the sole determiner of life and
death, as enunciated in Deuteronomy:

I deal death and give life.... (Deut. 32:39, NJPS)

To express the idea of death without using the word itself, the narrator substituted the idea of cessation of function: וְאֵינֶנּוּ, 'wᵉʾênennû,' "and he was not" or "then he was not." When Enoch stopped "walking with God," he stopped functioning as God's agent: in other words, he stopped living. Viewed in this light, the text does not permit the interpretation that Enoch was translated to the heavenly abode.

The concluding words of the verse confirm Enoch's death:

> . . . surely God took him. (Gen. 5:24)

In Psalm 49, לָקַח, 'lāqaḥ,' had the specialized meaning of "to snatch." The psalmist pictured the demon Death as reaching out of Sheol to snatch his victims and drag them down into his miry lair, there to be consumed.[58] Such a picture of Death was totally unacceptable to the narrator of this Genesis passage. It was not the infernal demon, from his miry lair in Sheol, who selected God's agent as his victim and determined when he was to be snatched, but God. Hence, לָקַח, 'lāqaḥ,' used with God, means "take," thereby stressing that God, not Death, decided when His agent was to be taken—not snatched—from life. Underscoring this basic differentiation, the narrator introduced the clause by כִּי, 'kî,' an emphasizing particle translated in this particular instance, not as "for" or "because" but as surely":[59] ". . . surely *God* took him."

Where God took Enoch to is not known. The silence of the text suggests that the narrator was reluctant to specify exactly where God had taken His agent. Such omission seems to have stemmed from a resolve not to lend credence to any belief purporting to know the abode of the righteous dead—one such belief was that they dwelt in the Hebrew equivalent of the Elysian Fields[60]—on the grounds that it might be theologically suspect. As in the case of Moses, when the text said only that he died and that no man knew of his burial place, likewise with Enoch, it said only that God, and God alone, took Enoch from the realm of the living; where, it did not say.

Methuselah, the son of Enoch, was renowned for living a record nine hundred and sixty-nine years. His name appropriately reflected this longevity; for, Methuselah, מְתוּשֶׁלַח, 'mᵉtûšelaḥ,' seems to be a composite of three words: מְתוּ שֶׁל לַח, 'mᵉtû šel lēaḥ,' meaning "a man of vigor" or "a man of life-force."[61] The two words, שֶׁל לַח, 'šel lēaḥ,' "of vigor, life-force," illustrate haplography where one ל, 'l,' coalesces into מְתוּשֶׁלַח, 'mᵉtûšelaḥ.' With the doctrine reaffirmed that God was the sole determiner of the time of death, the narrator reintroduced with Methuselah the usual וַיָּמֹת, 'wayyāmōt,' "and he died."

Lamech, son of Methuselah and father of Noah, presents a problem, because his name was identical with that descendant of Cain whose name was interpreted as meaning "the lowest!" Naturally, this meaning cannot be applied to one of the Sethite line, particularly the father of the patriarch who survived the Flood. And so it is probable that לֶמֶךְ, 'lemek,' contains the idea of "strong youth," from the Arabic 'yalmakun,' "strong youth."[62]

The birth of Noah, the last of the prediluvian patriarchs, is a most suitable point in the narrative to look back upon the Cainite and Sethite lines for those characteristics that clearly distinguished one from another. A comparison of these two family trees shows that the narrator carefully recorded the age of the Sethite line while omitting it for the Cainite line; that the narrator stopped recording the births of the Cainite line after the seventh generation while continuing to do so with the Sethite line; and, that the genealogy of both lines, except for one instance, proceeded through the first-born son. An explanation of these differences adds significantly to an understanding of how one became God's agent.

As explained earlier, the narrator no longer needed to record the descendants of Cain beyond the seventh generation, once having demonstrated that the 'nepes' of God's agent Abel was not transmitted through the line of Cain. However, he had to continue recording the line of Seth to show that Noah, God's agent, survived the Flood. For God's agent to have perished in the Flood would have been inconceivable to the narrator.

Further proof that the antediluvian Sethite descendants occupied the exalted position of "agent" lies in their longevity. Paralleling a Babylonian tradition that told of an antediluvian period composed of ten generations of kings who, according to the Greek Berossus, lived a total of 432,000 years,[63] the biblical story ascribed remarkably lengthy life spans to the antediluvian patriarchs, though never approaching the mythological records of the Babylonian kings. Evidently the narrator accepted the tradition that longevity, as seen with the Babylonian kings, indicated high rank and status; and so the descendants of Seth, described as having lived long years, reflected their status as agents of God. The exact number of years lived by each patriarch is not important here; it is sufficient that the recording of longevity as a device for expressing the exalted position of certain people be acknowledged. Conversely, the descendants of Cain, whose names testify to their low status and degradation, never even had their ages recorded; to have done so would have indicated status and merit.

The first-born son seems to have transmitted the blessing or punishment, as the case may be. The blessing of the office of "agent" was handed down from father to eldest son, since with the one exception the first-born of the children was the only one mentioned in the narrative. That exception, of course, was Seth, the third-born of the sons of Adam, who with Abel dead and Cain banished, assumed in a very real sense the role of the first-born. Transmittal of punishment through the first-born occurred with the descendants of Cain, for only the name of the first-born son, again with one exception, was mentioned. Evidently, the narrator mentioned the first-born of the Cainite line to show that the "agent" was not to be found among those who ordinarily might have qualified to receive this blessing. That Lamech's children, Jabal, Jubal, Tubal-cain, and Naamah, were mentioned is the exception that proves the rule, for the characteristics of these four children combined to form a single unit of a pariah, gypsy-like tribe.

The function of the first-born reveals why Cain expressed anger when Abel was elevated by God to the office of "agent"; as the first-born, he assumed that he would gain this coveted position. That he did not establishes, with regard to the order of birth, a fundamental position of the Bible in this beginning of human history: the order of birth, while obviously important, was not the sole criterion for the acquisition of honor or wealth; one also had to possess moral rectitude. Where the necessary moral qualifications were lacking, the honor or position was granted to another, as when Jacob repudiated Reuben, the first-born.[64] Where the office passed without interruption through the eldest son, each first-born presumably possessed the requisite moral qualifications.

Naturally, this function of the first-born reflected not upon the acceptability of the second-born, but upon the demands of a particular type of society. This "preferential status of the first-born son had its origin and *raison d'être* in semi-nomadic and predominantly agricultural societies. The religious, social and economic obligations of the eldest son in such communities placed him second in rank to the *pater familias* and hence he was considered entitled to special prerogatives by virtue of that position."[65] Israelite Palestine, being mainly agricultural in the era of the First Babylonian Dynasty, accorded this privileged status to the first-born son. The reason why the narrator seemingly made a special effort to designate Enoch and Noah as God's agents—they "walked with God"—when, as the first-born of the Sethite line, they should have been recognized as God's agents, is explained by their particular role in the narrative. The narrator had to prove in the case of Enoch that the power of the infernal demon was ineffectual against God's agent: by describing Enoch, the head of the seventh generation from Adam, as "walking with God," he demonstrated that Enoch retained his position despite the anticipated attempt by the demon Death to wreak vengeance upon God's representative. With Noah the situation was different. The last of the antediluvian patriarchs, Noah was also the first of the postdiluvian patriarchs. As such he was the main personage in the unfolding of the first chapter of postdiluvian history. Consequently, the narrator, in his customary stylistic recapitulation,[66] reintroduced Noah, first as moral man, as a man set apart from his generation, "a man wholesome and unimpaired" (Gen. 6:9), and then in terms of the role he was to play as God's "agent": "he walked with God." The narrator thus set the stage for the cataclysm, the survivors, and the subsequent rebirth of humanity.

NOTES

NOTES TO CHAPTER I

1. R. Graves and R. Patai, *Hebrew Myths* (Garden City, New York: Doubleday and Co., 1964), p. 120.

2. *The Zohar* (London: The Soncino Press, 1956), 1:73a.

3. D. C. Allen, *The Legend of Noah* (Urbana, Illinois: Illini Books, 1963), p. 73.

4. G. von Rad, *Genesis* (Philadelphia: The Westminster Press, 1961), p. 133.

5. C. De Tolnay, *Michelangelo, The Sistine Ceiling* (Princeton: Princeton University Press, 1945), 2:25.

6. Sanhedrin 108a, *The Babylonian Talmud* (London: The Soncino Press, 1935).

7. *Pentateuch and Rashi's Commentary* (New York: Hebrew Publishing Co., n.d.), p. 39.

8. D. Garnett, *Two By Two—A Story Of Survival* (New York: Atheneum, 1964), p. 65.

9. *Ibid.*, p. 84.

10. *Letters From The Earth* (Crest Book; Greenwich, Connecticut: Fawcett Publications, Inc., 1963), p. 101.

11. J. Skinner, *A Critical and Exegetical Commentary on Genesis* (New York: Charles Scribner's Sons, 1910), p. 182.

12. C. A. Simpson, "Exegesis of Genesis," *The Interpreter's Bible* (New York: Abingdon-Cokesbury Press, 1952), 1:555.

13. E. R. Goodenough, *Jewish Symbols in the Greco-Roman Period* (New York: Pantheon Books, 1956), 6:25.

14. *Ibid.*

15. *Ibid.*

16. *Ibid.*, p. 47.

17. *Ibid.*, 5:167.

18. *Ibid.*, p. 166.

19. *Ibid.*, p. 169.

20. *Ibid.*, p. 196–197.

21. Translation and commentary by R. Gordis, *The Song of Songs* (New York: Bloch Publishing Co., 1954, 1961, 1973), p. 70.

22. *Ibid.*, p. 72.

23. *Ibid.,* pp. 26, 96.

24. *Ibid.,* p. 74.

25. *BDB,* p. 274.

26. Translation by H. W. F. Saggs, "The Branch to the Nose," *J.T.S.,* N. S. 11 (1960), 324.

27. Jastrow, p. 402.

28. Saggs, p. 326.

29. *Ibid.*

30. G. Bachelard, *The Psychoanalysis of Fire* (London: Routledge and Kegan Paul, 1964), p. 23.

31. *Ibid.,* p. 23–24.

32. *Ibid.,* p. 28.

33. *Ibid.,* p. 28–36.

34. *Ibid.,* p. 36.

35. *Ibid.,* p. 37.

36. *Ibid.,* p. 47.

37. *Ibid.,* p. 48.

38. *Ibid.,* p. 83.

39. *Ibid.*

40. Gen. 18:11–12.

41. Genesis Rabbah 36[7], *Midrash Rabbah* (London: The Soncino Press, English translation, 1939), pp. 290–291.

42. Gen. 19:15–26.

43. Genesis Rabbah 51, p. 447.

44. Genesis Rabbah 51[11-12], p. 448.

45. Genesis Rabbah 51[9], p. 448.

46. *Ibid.*

47. *Pentateuch with Rashi's Commentary,* p. 83.

48. *Ibid.*

49. E. A. Speiser, *Genesis* (Garden City, New York: Doubleday and Co., Inc., 1964), p. 145. Anchor Bible series.

50. In light of these biblical examples, it seems reasonable to conclude that the Hittites also believed in the power of wine to endow one with procreative potency, as may be seen in the advice given to Appuš by Ištanuš: "Go, get drunk, sleep well with your wife, and she will bear." H. A. Hoffner, Jr., "Birth and Name-Giving in Hittite Texts," *JNES* 27 (1968), 202.

Notes to Chapter 2

1. Graves and Patai, p. 121.

2. *Ibid.*

3. L. Ginzberg, *The Legends Of The Jews* (Philadelphia: The Jewish Publication Society of America, 1909), 1:165.

4. Graves and Patai, p. 122.

5. R. Graves, *The Greek Myths* (Baltimore: Penguin Books, 1955), 1:37.

6. Graves and Patai, p. 122.

7. Speiser, p. 61.

8. *Ibid.,* p. 62.

9. *Ibid.,* p. 61.

10. *Ibid.*, p. 62.

11. *Ibid.*

12. *Ibid.*

13. *Ibid.*

14. I Kings 19:13.

15. Gen. 19:26.

16. O. Fenichel, "The Scoptophilic Instinct and Identification," *The Collected Papers of Otto Fenichel* (New York: W. W. Norton and Co., Inc., 1953), first series, p. 391.

17. J. L. Palache, *Semantic Notes On The Hebrew Lexicon* (Leiden: E. J. Brill, 1959), p. 28.

18. *BDB*, p. 1003.

19. *Ibid.*, p. 1004.

20. Palache, p. 28.

21. *BDB*, p. 962.

22. Palache, pp. 29, 43.

23. *BDB*, p. 542.

24. D. Daube, *Studies in Biblical Law* (Cambridge: Cambridge University Press, 1947), p. 35.

25. *Ibid.*, p. 39. (Deut. 34:7)

26. Gen. 9:20.

27. U. Cassuto, *A Commentary On The Book Of Genesis* (Jerusalem: The Magnes Press, 1964), 2:159.

28. *Ibid.*

29. *Ibid.*

30. The theme of depriving a person of his sexual powers was known in ancient Near Eastern society. In locales where belief in the effectiveness of magic was current, sorcerers were employed in a limited number of cases to "neutralize" or eliminate an individual's present sexual powers. H. A. Hoffner, Jr., "Symbols For Masculinity and Femininity," *JBL* 85 (1966), 327f.

31. P. Seligman, "Some Notes on the Collective Significance of Circumcision and Allied Practices," *Journal of Analytical Psychology* 10 (1965), 9.

32. Daube, p. 5.

33. Gen. 39:11–19.

34. Translation from Cassuto, 2:158.

35. T. Gaster, *Thespis* (Garden City, New York: Doubleday Anchor Books, 1961), pp. 257–261.

36. *Ibid.*, pp. 257–258.

37. *Ibid.*, p. 258.

38. II Sam. 11:11.

39. Gaster, p. 259.

40. *Ibid.*

41. The NJPS version of Gen. 9:24 reads:

> When Noah woke up from his wine and learned
> what his youngest son had done to him. . . .

Obviously the earlier and later versions differ over the translation of וַיֵּדַע, 'way-yēdaʿ.' In the first rendition, "and he knew" seems to indicate that knowledge was gained by one's own efforts, whereas "and he learned" implies that one's knowledge came from others. This difference in the two translations reveals the dilemma faced by the translators of the later version. Perhaps asking themselves how could Noah have known what Ham had done when all the while he was asleep, they must have concluded that Noah could not have known anything of what happened while he lay in a drunken stupor; and consequently they had to translate 'wayyēda'' as "and he learned" to convey the idea that Noah's knowledge of the affair must have come from an outside source, presumably his sons.

42. R. B. Onians, *The Origins Of European Thought* (Cambridge: Cambridge University Press, 1954), p. 23.

43. *Ibid.*, p. 28.

44. *Ibid.*, p. 44.

45. *Ibid.*, p. 46.

46. *Ibid.*

47. *Ibid.*, p. 47.

48. *Ibid.*, pp. 47–48.

49. *Ibid.*, p. 50.

50. *Ibid.*

51. *Ibid.*, p. 55.

52. *Ibid.*, p. 56.

53. *Ibid.*

54. *Ibid.*, p. 67.

55. *Ibid.*, p. 68.

56. *Ibid.*, p. 69.

57. *Ibid.*

58. *Ibid.*, p. 73.

59. *Ibid.*

60. *Ibid.*

61. *Ibid.*, p. 74.

62. *Ibid.*, p. 75.

63. *Ibid.*, p. 79.

64. *Ibid.*, p. 80.

65. *Ibid.*, p. 31.

66. *Ibid.*, p. 32.

67. *Ibid.*

68. *Ibid.*

69. *Ibid.*, p. 33.

70. *Ibid.*, p. 66.

71. *Ibid.*, p. 77.

72. Aeschylus, *Eumenides,* in The Loeb Classical Library (New York: G. P. Putnam's Sons, 1930), 2:281.

73. Onians, p. 78f.

74. The word נֶפֶשׁ, 'nepeš,' "soul," is used no less than four times, and as Speiser correctly notes, the use of this term does not mean "that I may bless you myself." Its repeated use in the narrative suggests to him that the term carries some technical nuance, "but what that connotation may be is difficult to decide." (Speiser, p. 208.) This difficulty is evident in Speiser's translation:

> Then prepare it as a festive dish, the way I like, and bring it to me to eat, so that I may give you my very own blessing before I die. (Gen. 27:4)

Here, 'nepeš' becomes "my very own blessing." In the NJPS translation, 'nepeš' is rendered "my innermost blessing":

> Then make me a tasty dish such as I like, and bring it to me to eat, so that I may give you my innermost blessing before I die.

This technical nuance associated with 'nepeš,' suspected but unexplained by Speiser, becomes clear once the qualities of the 'thymos' are attributed to the 'nepeš.'

75. E. M. Good, *Irony In The Old Testament* (Philadelphia: The Westminster Press, 1965), p. 99.

76. Onians, p. 48.

77. *Ibid.*

78. *Ibid.*, p. 172.

79. Two other versions of Gen. 27:24:

> Still, as he was about to bless him, he asked again, "You are my son Esau?" (Speiser, *Genesis*)

> . . . so he blessed him. And he said: "Art thou my very son, Esau? (JPS)

80. It is quite possible that נֶפֶשׁ, 'nepeš,' as used in the Isaac-Jacob episodes, reflects a fusion with the concept of רוּחַ, 'rûaḥ,' that thereby made it possible to leave the body during life. Onians (p. 482) theorizes that 'rûaḥ,' "spirit," so closely identified with 'psyche,' "the procreative life-soul" (Onians, p. 483), fused with 'nepeš,' just as the separate entities of 'thymos' and 'psyche' later became united (Onians, p. 116).

81. Gen. 48:8. When the text uses "saw" or "beheld" with the blind Jacob, it means that he noted the presence of his sons or directed his attention to them.

82. Onians, pp. 175 and 491.

83. *Ibid.*, p. 491.

84. In the anointing of a king, the "spirit" or 'nepeš' was transmitted "by pouring actual liquid representing seed into one who thus becomes a 'son'" (Onians, p. 493). Such adoption explains why Jacob adopted Ephraim and Manasseh as his own sons, only in this case they received the seed from contact with Jacob's knees instead of anointment.

85. *BDB*, p. 302.

86. *Ibid.*, p. 303.

87. The same concept in rabbinic thought is illustrated by רָאָה, 'rā'āh,' "see" (Jastrow, p. 1435) and רֵאָה, 'rē'āh, or רֵיאָה, 'rē'āh,' "lungs" (*Ibid.*, p. 1472), where both words share the same root-consonants.

88. C. H. Gordon, *The Common Background Of Greek and Hebrew Civilizations* (New York: W. W. Norton and Co., paperback, 1965), p. 9. W. F. Albright traces the origins of the new ways of thinking which appeared among the Greeks in the early sixth century B.C.E. to a general intellectual movement, probably appearing first in Phoenicia. From there it spread both to Israel and to the Aegean shores, where it took different forms in these two different cultures. *Yahweh and the Gods of Canaan* (Garden City, New York: Doubleday and Co., Anchor Books, 1969), p. 259.

89. Interpreting the statement that Ham saw the nakedness of his father as meaning originally that he had sexual intercourse with his father's wife, F. W. Bassett concludes that Noah cursed Canaan because he was the fruit of this incestuous act. "Noah's Nakedness And The Curse Of Canaan—A Case Of Incest?"

VT 21 (1971), 235. For D. Neiman, however, the cursing of Canaan together with the blessing of Shem and Japheth constitute a passionate battle cry, uttered by Israel in the heat of the struggle against Canaan. Attributing this curse to Noah justified the rage of Israel; Canaan was not only evil in this period of battle (around 1230 B.C.E. or 1180 B.C.E.) but was inherently bad. Furthermore, the sons of Noah, as ancestors of the Hebrews and Hellenes, demonstrated how ancient was their alliance against Canaan, their common enemy. "The Date and Circumstances of the Cursing of Canaan," in *Biblical Motifs* (Cambridge, Mass.: Harvard University Press, 1966), pp. 121 and 132.

90. S. H. Blank, "The Curse, Blasphemy, the Spell, and the Oath," *HUCA* 23 (Cincinnati: Hebrew Union College-Jewish Institute of Religion, 1950–1951), 94.

91. H. C. Brichto, "The Problem Of 'Curse' In The Hebrew Bible," *JBL Monograph Series* 13 (1963), 100.

NOTES TO CHAPTER 3

1. Allen, p. 169.

2. *Ibid.*, p. 170.

3. C. Odets, "The Flowering Peach," in *The Best Plays of 1954–1955* (New York: Dodd, Mead and Co., 1955), p. 190.

4. *Ibid.*, p. 194.

5. A. Heidel, *The Gilgamesh Epic And Old Testament Parallels* (Chicago: The University of Chicago Press, 1946), p. 86.

6. *Ibid.*, p. 268.

7. Ginzberg, p. 158.

8. Genesis Rabbah, p. 213.

9. *Ibid.*, pp. 213–214.

10. *Ibid.* According to Raphael Patai, post-biblical Jewish literature regarded fornication as the arch-sin, the greatest crime, most hateful to God. *Man and Temple* (London: Thomas Nelson and Sons Ltd., 1947), p. 146.

11. Cassuto, 2:53.

12. Speiser, p. 47.

13. von Rad, p. 123.

14. N. M. Sarna, *Understanding Genesis* (New York: McGraw-Hill Book Co., 1966), p. 53.

15. *BDB*, p. 947.

16. Gen. 4:8–15.

17. R. Gordis, "The Knowledge Of Good And Evil In The Old Testament And The Qumran Scrolls," *JBL* 76 (1957), 131.

18. *Ibid.*

19. *Ibid.*, p. 132.

20. Gen. 19:7 and Judg. 19:23.

21. Gordis, *JBL* 76:133.

22. H. S. Stern, "The Knowledge of Good and Evil," *VT* 8 (1958), 414. A presentation of the major arguments for and against interpreting the knowledge of good and evil as primarily sexual in character is to be found in J. Bailey, "Initiation And The Primal Woman in Gilgamesh And Genesis 2–3," *JBL* 89 (1970), 144–147.

23. *Ibid.*, 406.

24. H. L. Ginsberg, translator of "Ugaritic Myths, Epics, and Legends," in *Ancient Near Eastern Texts* (Princeton: Princeton University Press, 1955), p. 132, (iii) lines 10–23. Hereafter, this volume will be referred to as *ANET*.

25. J. M. Powis Smith and E. J. Goodspeed, translators, *The Complete Bible. An American Translation* (Chicago: The University of Chicago Press, 1949). Hereafter this book will be referred to as Chicago.

26. M. Buber, *Good And Evil* (New York: Charles Scribner's Sons, 1953, paperback), p. 91; and *BDB*, pp. 427–428.

27. Speiser, p. 51.

28. *BDB*, p. 1007.

29. M. H. Pope, "The Word שַׁחַת in Job 9:31," *JBL* 83 (1964), 270 and 274.

30. A. Ehrman, "A Note On   in Mic. 6:14," *JNES* 18 (1959), 156.

31. Pope, p. 274.

32. *BDB*, p. 329.

33. Speiser, p. 47.

34. Gen. 6:11, NJPS.

35. Jastrow, p. 478.

36. *Ibid.*, p. 479.

37. E. Kautzsch, *Gesenius' Hebrew Grammar* (Oxford: Oxford University Press, 1949), p. 68. Through the change of final consonants in commutation fro the harsher, rougher sound of צ, 'ṣ,' to the softer שׁ, 'ś.'

38. *BDB*, p. 47.

39. *Ibid.*, p. 92.

40. L. Koehler and W. Baumgartner, *Lexicon In Veteris Testamenti Libros* (Leiden: E. J. Brill, 1958), p. 1056.

41. Jastrow, p. 167.

42. P. R. Ackroyd, "The Hebrew Root באשׁ," *JTS*, N.S. 1–2 (1950–51), 35–36.

43. In an Old Babylonian incantation for potency, which reflects the well-known excitability of goats in the presence of women, an imagined act of bestiality between a ram and a woman is witnessed by an impotent man to excite his lust. R. D. Biggs, *ŠÀ.ZI.GA—Ancient Mesopotamian Potency Incantations* (Locust Valley, New York: J. J. Augustin Publisher, 1967), pp. 33, 34.

44. *ANET*, p. 196, paragraph 187.

45. *Ibid.*, paragraph 188.

46. *Ibid.*, paragraph 199.

47. *Ibid.*, p. 197, paragraph 200 (A).

48. A. Büchler, *Studies In Sin And Atonement* (New York: Ktav Publishing House, Inc., 1967, reprint), pp. 219, 221.

49. *BDB*, p. 823.

50. Koehler and Baumgartner, p. 773.

51. Palache, p. 53.

52. The possessive form עֲוֹנָהּ, 'ăwônāh,' "its iniquity," should not be understood as the iniquity incurred by the earth as a result of its own wrongdoing; rather it conveys the idea that the earth now "possesses" (suffers from) this damage or "crookedness" perpetrated by its inhabitants.

53. Palache, p. 53.

54. E. R. Dalglish, *Psalm Fifty-One In The Light Of Ancient Near Eastern Patternism* (Leiden: E. J. Brill, 1962), p. 92.

55. The English translation of Targum Onkelos reads:

... and I will visit the guilt that is upon it....

Allowing for the change of tense, the insertion of the phrase "that was" eliminates the possibility of עָלֶיהָ, "ālèhā,' "upon it," being linked with the verb "will visit." It is not that God will visit *upon it* punishment, but that this "crookedness" or "iniquity" is to be found *upon it,* the land. J. W. Etheridge, translator, *The Targums of Onkelos and Jonathan Ben Uzziel On The Pentateuch* (New York: Ktav Publishing House, Inc., 1968, first printed in 1862), Vaiyikra, section 29, chapter 18, p. 121.

56. J. Barr, *Comparative Philology And The Text Of The Old Testament* (Oxford: Oxford University Press, 1968), pp. 96–98.

57. J. Greenfield, "Lexicographical Notes I," *HUCA* 29 (1958), p. 222.

58. This hypothesis of a correspondence of meaning is strengthened by the fact that פָּקַד, 'pāqad,' and בָּדַק, 'bādaq,' both mean "to search, examine" (Jastrow, pp. 141, 1206); פָּקַד, 'pāqad,' "pay attention to, observe with care" (*BDB*, p. 823).

59. S. Rin, "Ugaritic—Old Testament Affinities," *BZ* 7 (1963), p. 32. Also, cf. *BDB*, p. 754.

60. עַל, "al,' "from" in Job 24:9. M. Dahood, "The Phoenician Contribution To Biblical Wisdom Literature," in *The Role Of The Phoenicians In The Interaction Of Mediterranean Civilizations,* W. A. Ward, ed. (Beirut: The American University of Beirut, 1968), p. 138.

61. Had God desired vengeance, He need not have punished this evil generation with a flood. He might have rained down sulphurous fire upon them, as He did to the pederasts of Sodom and Gomorrah. But God did not blast the earth with this type of fiery holocaust because His purpose presumably was not motivated by the desire to punish.

62. Speiser, p. 45.

63. Cassuto, 1:293.

64. *Ibid.*

65. *Ibid.*

66. *Ibid.,* p. 294.

67. *BDB,* p. 103.

68. *Ibid.,* p. 104. This duality of meaning is found in the Aramaic as well. Jastrow, p. 155.

69. Palache, p. 14.

70. C. G. Jung, *Symbols of Transformation, The Collected Works* 5 (London: Routledge and Kegan Paul, 1956), 150–151. Shakespeare understood this symbolism when he wrote in *Anthony And Cleopatra:*

> She made great Caesar lay his sword to bed:
> He ploughed her, and she cropped. (II, ii, 625–628).

71. Esth. 2:12–14.

72. Lev. 19:19.

73. Deut. 22:10.

74. Lev. 19:19 and Deut. 22:9.

75. Lev. 19:19 and Deut. 22:11.

76. Gen. 2:17, 3:3, 3:5, 3:11, 3:17.

77. Starting with the premise that Hebrew linguistic and literary tradition is a continuation of the linguistic and literary tradition of the Canaanites, Cassuto

looks to these sources for information regarding the meaning of בְּנֵי הָאֱלֹהִים, 'bᵉnê hā'ĕlōhîm.' In both Ugaritic and Phoenician writings he finds the phrase, "the sons of god," connoting the congregation and assembly of the gods. But since the theology of the Israelites recognized only one God, it ascribed to angels those forces and tasks formerly attributed by pagans to their deities. Hence he would interpret בְּנֵי הָאֱלֹהִים, 'bᵉnê hā'ĕlōhîm,' as those divinities comprising the heavenly household. This term is common to all God's angels, both the higher and lower ranks, the good and the evil divinities (1:292–294). According to this new interpretation, however, the בְּנֵי הָאֱלֹהִים, 'bᵉnê hā'ĕlōhîm,' of Gen. 6:2 are the degraded angels of the lower ranks.

78. Cassuto, 1:291. Less literal but more emphatic as to the lineage of the Nephilim is Speiser's rendition:

> It was then that the Nephilim appeared on earth—as well as later—after the divine beings had united with human daughters to whom they bore children. Those were the heroes of old, men of renown. (Speiser, p. 44.)

79. Num. 13:33.

80. E. G. Kraeling, "The Significance And Origin Of Gen. 6:1–4," *JNES* 6 (1947), 195.

81. J. Morgenstern, "The Mythological Background of Psalm 82," *HUCA* 14 (1939), 83. The middle letter of נָפַל, 'nāpal,' is פ, 'p,' a labial consonant (Gesenius-Kautzsch, p. 34.), which on occasion has been interchanged (*Ibid.*, p. 68.) with the other labial consonant ב, 'b' (*Ibid.*, p. 34), as with the words קָפַץ, 'qāpaṣ' and קָבַץ, 'qābaṣ,' both meaning "to seize."

82. *BDB*'s translation of Isa. 1:30, p. 615.

83. *BDB*, p. 614.

84. *Ibid.*, p. 615.

85. *Ibid.*

86. Gen. 6:5.

87. Morgenstern, pp. 106–107.

88. R. Gordis, "Studies In The Relationship Of Biblical And Rabbinic Hebrew," in *Louis Ginzberg Jubilee Volume* (New York: The American Academy for Jewish Research, 1945), pp. 174–175.

89. Greenfield, p. 204.

90. *BDB*, p. 149.

91. Jastrow, p. 208.

92. R. Grossman, H. Sachs, and H. H. Segal, *Compendius Hebrew-English Dictionary* (Tel Aviv: Dvir Publishing Co., 1947), p. 154.

93. Jastrow, p. 208. In addition to the Mishnah, גֶּבֶר, 'geber,' in the Bible also denotes virility and procreative power, as well as physical strength, courage, and valor. Kosmala attributes the later use of this word for phallus in rabbinical language to its concomitant sexual meaning dating back apparently to most ancient times. H. Kosmala, "The Term *Geber* in the Old Testament and in the Scrolls," in *Supplements To Vetus Testamentum* (Leiden: E. J. Brill, 1969) 17:161–162.

94. Jastrow, p. 234.

95. *Ibid.*

96. Ps. 19:6 in M. Dahood, *Psalms 1–50*, Anchor Bible, vol. 16 (Garden City: Doubleday and Co., Inc., 1966), p. 120.

97. Jastrow, p. 1602.

98. *Ibid.*, p. 1601.

99. As Morgenstern has pointed out, "men of renown" can apply to people of disrepute to emphasize the magnitude of their deeds. *HUCA* 14 (1939), 94.

100. Speiser, p. 44. In his commentary on this verse Speiser admits that the obscurity of בְּשַׁגַּם, 'bᵉšaggām,' opens it to another rendition. "A different analysis of the components yields 'by reason of their going astray' (:he is flesh). But the first interpretation is superior, though still highly uncertain" (p. 44). Unfortunately, Speiser gives no reason why the first reading is to be preferred. If the sense of these verses is understood, Speiser's second reading, with some changes, must be preferred.

101. *BDB*, pp. 992–993.

102. *Ibid.*, p. 993.

103. J. Greenstone, *Proverbs* (Philadelphia: The Jewish Publication Society of America, 1950), p. 52.

104. Here בָּשָׂר, 'bāsār,' is translated "animal," exactly as rendered in Genesis 6:19 and 7:15, 16. The singular person, "*he* is an animal," is used though בְּשַׁגַּם, 'bᵉšaggām,' is plural—"in their ravishing" or "in their being ravished" to convey the idea that individual man, multiplied many times over, was responsible for this deplorably immoral situation.

105. *Webster's New International Dictionary of the English Language* (Springfield: G. and C. Merriam Co., 1913) p. 1862.

106. Jeremiah (5:7b–8) makes a similar comparison, though without using שָׁגָה, 'šāgāh': "When I fed them to satiety, they committed adultery and יִתְגֹּדָדוּ, 'yitggôdādû' [fornicated], in the houses of harlots. They were like well-fed, ruttish stallions, neighing to each other's wives." H. L. Ginsberg, "Lexicographical Notes," in *Supplements To Vetus Testamentum* (Leiden: E. J. Brill, 1967), 16:75.

107. *ANET*, p. 104.

108. *Ibid.*

109. Why the narrator used the rare form of בְּשַׁגַּם, 'bᵉšaggām,' can only be guessed. The literary master that he was, he perhaps wanted to draw attention to גֶּשֶׁם, 'gešem,' "rain," a word whose consonants closely resemble those of בְּשַׁגַּם, 'bᵉšaggām.' In fact, the words would be identical were it not for the interchanging of the שׁ, 'š,' and the ג, 'g':

בְּשַׁגַּם, 'bᵉšaggām'
הַגֶּשֶׁם, 'haggešem (Gen. 7:12)

In like fashion, the form שָׂתוֹת, 'śātôt,' in Isa. 22:13 appears to have been chosen for its similarity in sound to שָׁחֹט, 'šāḥōṭ,' which also appears in the same verse (Gesenius-Kautzsch, p. 210). By using words closely resembling each other, the narrator perhaps sought to underscore both the cause and the means of destruction. This hypothesis is strengthened by the narrator's sensitivity for sounds and word play, as seen in the series of words concluding with בְּשַׁגַּם, 'bᵉšaggām'; all end in 'ām.'

בְּאָדָם לְעֹלָם בְּשַׁגַּם
'bā'ādām lᵉōlām bᵉšaggām'

Even though לְעֹלָם, 'lᵉōlām,' and בְּשַׁגַּם, 'bᵉšaggām,' are disconnected in thought, the alliteration proves the narrator's feeling for style.

NOTES TO CHAPTER 4

1. E. A. Speiser, "YDWN, Gen. 6," *JBL* 75 (1956), 126.

2. *Ibid.,* p. 128.

3. Speiser, *Genesis,* p. 44.

4. One exegete understood these words as meaning that "God sets a maximum age beyond which man, who has increased his vital power in such an antigodly manner, cannot go" (von Rad, p. 111). But he did not tell us why God set a maximum age of one hundred-twenty years. Furthermore, since the text does not specify that the age limitation applies only to wicked men, it presents us with a seeming inconsistency: man is not to live beyond one hundred-twenty years, yet Noah lived four hundred-seventy years after God made this statement (Gen. 9:28). This apparent inconsistency disappears once these words are understood as the second half of the warning God issued to mankind.

5. Heidel, p. 230.

6. Gen. 5:22, 24.

7. Gen. 5:31

8. C. H. Gordon, *Ugaritic Literature* (Rome: Pontifico Instituto Biblico, 1949), pp. 120, 121.

9. M. Noth, *Leviticus* (London: SCM Press, Ltd., 1965), p. 204.

10. von Rad, p. 119.

11. *ANET*, p. 95.

12. JPS.

13. NJPS; RSV; Cassuto, 2:116.

14. Chicago; Speiser, *Genesis,* p. 50.

15. *BDB*, p. 629.

16. Koehler and Baumgartner, p. 614.

17. *ANET*, p. 95.

18. E. A. Speiser, "An Angelic 'Curse': Exodus 14:20," *JAOS* 80 (1960), 198.

19. The similarity of meaning shows up more quickly in the RSV, free of the archaic language of the King James or the early JPS versions.

20. This comparison between Gen. 3:17 and 8:21 shows a similarity of expression, except for the key words, translated herein as "curse": קָלַל, 'qallēl,' and אָרַר, ''ārar.' Though these two words are different in structure, they display the same parallelism of meaning that they do in Ex. 22:27, where the words are synonymous (Speiser, *JAOS* 80:199). It is likely, given the narrator's penchant for alliteration, that he used 'qallēl' instead of ''ārar' to approximate the consonantal sounds of הַקְלּוּ, 'hăqallû' (8:8), and קַלּוּ, 'qallû' (8:11). Such a reason would establish the same parallelism of style and meaning between 3:17 and 8:21 as prevails between the other selections from the creation and flood stories.

21. Gen. 3:17, NJPS.

22. Gen. 3:18, NJPS.

23. Gordis, *JBL* 76 (1957), 136.

24. Gen. 8:22.

25. Speiser, *Genesis,* p. 57.

26. Jacob Milgrom understood נֶפֶשׁ, 'nepeš,' "life," to be the life-essence that is distinct from the body, does not disintegrate in the dust, and departs from the body. "A Prolegomenon To Leviticus 17:11," *JBL* 90 (1971), 150.

27. Gen. 6:3.

28. J. Pedersen, *Israel* (London: Oxford University Press, photoprint, 1964), 3–4:315.

29. *Ibid.*, 1–2:483.

30. *Pentateuch with Rashi's Commentary*, p. 5.

31. *Ibid.*

32. Gen. 1:24. *Ibid.* Other references cited by Pedersen (1–2:511) are: Gen. 2:19:9:10, 12, 15, 16: Lev. 11:10, 46: 24:18: Ezek. 47:9.

33. Noth, p. 130.

34. *Ibid.*, p. 131.

35. *BDB*, p. 196.

36. *Ibid.*, p. 197.

37. Jastrow, p. 312.

38. *Ibid.*

39. *Ibid.*

40. *Ibid.*

41. *Ibid.*, p. 313.

42. Daube, p. 123.

43. Gen. 9:5.

44. O. Eissfeldt, *The Old Testament* (New York: Harper and Row, 1965), p. 68.

NOTES TO CHAPTER 5

1. Cassuto, 2:127.

2. E. Jacob, *Theology Of The Old Testament* (New York: Harper and Row, 1958), p. 169.

3. W. Eichrodt, *Man in the Old Testament* (Chicago: Henry Regnery Co., 1951), p. 30.

4. Gen. 4:15.

5. Speiser, *Genesis*, pp. 29 and 57.

6. Gen. 1:27.

7. Cassuto, 1:58.

8. von Rad, p. 59.

9. J. M. Miller hypothesizes that the Priestly writer used צֶלֶם, 'ṣelem,' "image," as a secondary term to clarify the implications of דְּמוּת, 'dᵉmût,' "likeness." "In the 'Image' and 'Likeness' of God," *JBL* 91 (1972), 301–304.

10. No special kinship of father to child pertained to animals since they were not created in His likeness.

11. D. J. McCarthy, *Treaty And Covenant* (Rome: Pontifical Biblical Institute, 1963), p. 4.

12. E. Gerstenberger, "Covenant And Commandment," *JBL* 84 (1965), 40.

13. *Ibid.*, 41.

14. *Ibid.*, 42.

15. G. E. Mendenhall, *Law And Covenant In Israel And The Ancient Near East* (Pittsburgh, 1955), p. 32.

16. That the treaty and covenantal terms of fatherhood and sonship were used in the ancient Near East for over a thousand years and were employed as such by the Hebrews is well documented by F. C. Fensham in his paper, "Father and Son as Terminology for Treaty and Covenant," in *Near Eastern Studies in Honor of William Foxwell Albright,* ed. H. Goedicke (Baltimore: The Johns Hopkins Press, 1971), p. 129.

17. Gen. 5:3.

18. McCarthy, p. 85.

19. *Ibid.*, p. 94.

20. *Ibid.*, p. 201.

21. M. Weinfeld, "Traces of Assyrian Treaty Formulae in Deuteronomy," *Biblica* 46 (1965), 417.

22. *Ibid.*, 418.

23. *Ibid.*, 418–419.

24. *Ibid.*, 419.

25. *Ibid.*, 422–423.

26. *Ibid.*, 423.

27. K. A. Kitchen, *Ancient Orient And Old Testament* (Chicago: Inter-Varsity Press, 1968), p. 100.

28. Cassuto, 2:50.

29. Micah 6:8.

30. Deut. 11:22.

31. Gen. 9:2. This fear and dread of man has been interpreted by one scholar to arise from the realization of the creatures who were saved that, having been granted life on account of Noah's righteous behavior, they "would realize more clearly the superiority of the human species" (Cassuto, 2:125.). Animals will fear man, according to another commentator, because he will now become flesh-eating (von Rad, p. 127.). Unfortunately, this explanation does not account for the fear that the creeping things, the insects, and fish would have for man. Nor need the ethical capacity to acknowledge the superiority of man because of his righteous behavior be attributed to animals.

32. *ANET*, p. 277, i6–ii5.

33. *Ibid.*, p. 278, ii78–102.

34. *Ibid.*, p. 277, i29–ii13. The Assyrian Adad-Nirari III (810–783 B.C.E.) likewise attributed his military success in Palestine to the god he represented:

> I marched against the country Ša-imēriši: I shut up Mari', king of Damascus (Imērišu) in Damascus (Di-ma-áš-qi), his royal residence. The terror-inspiring glamor of Ashur, my (text: his) lord, overwhelmed him and he seized my feet, assuming the position of a slave (of mine). *ANET*, p. 281, V (1–21).

Sargon II (721–705), the conqueror of Samaria, also gives credit to his god Ashur:

> Iamani from Ashdod, afraid of my armed force (lit.: weapons), left his wife and children and fled to the frontier of M[usru] which belongs to Meluhha (i.e., Ethiopia) and hid (lit.: stayed) there like a thief. I installed an officer of mine as governor over his entire large country and its prosperous inhabitants, (thus) aggrandizing (again) the territory belonging to Ashur, the king of the gods. The terror (-inspiring) glamor of Ashur, my lord, overpowered (however) the King of Meluhha and he threw him (i.e., Iamani) in fetters on hands and feet, and sent him to me, to Assyria. *ANET*, p. 285 (11–15).

35. With צ, 'ṣ,' and ס, 's,' as sibilants of equal phonetic value (Gesenius-Kautzsch, p. 34), the consonants ל, 'l,' and מ, 'm,' only need to be transposed (metathesis) to have almost identical words (*Ibid.*, p. 70.).

36. Genesis Rabbah 68[13], pp. 627–628.

37. II Chron. 33:7–15.

38. What the rabbis posited in their ancient homily is confirmed in the cognate Arabic, where the Arabic parallel for סֶמֶל, 'semel,' is the same for צֶלֶם · 'ṣelem.' A. Guillaume, *Hebrew and Arabic Lexicography* (Leiden: E. J. Brill, 1965), p. 12.

39. Ezek. 8:3–5.

40. H. Torczyner (Tur-Sinai), "Semel Ha-qin'ah Ha-maqneh," *JBL* 65 (1946), 294–295.

41. *Ibid.*, 300.

42. *Ibid.*, 301.

43. A. M. Honeyman, "Merismus In Biblical Hebrew," *JBL* 71 (1952), 18. And J. L. McKenzie, *Myths and Realities* (Milwaukee: The Bruce Publishing Co., 1963), p. 142.

44. N. Wiener, *God and Golem, Inc.* (Cambridge, Massachusetts: M. I. T. Press, paperback, 1966), pp. 30–31.

NOTES TO CHAPTER 6

1. Speiser, *Genesis*, p. 31.

2. Cassuto, 1:203.

3. R. Patai, "Hebrew Installation Rites," *HUCA* 20:163.

4. Gen. 4:6.

5. Dan. 11:24. Even though the word חֵלֶב, 'ḥēleb,' is not used specifically, the idea of fatness is associated with the soil.

6. Speiser, *Genesis*, p. 30. "Abel's act of worship was an inward experience, an ungrudging, open hearted, concentration devotion. Cain's noble purpose was sullied by the intrusion of self, a defect that blocked the spiritual channels with God." Sarna, *Understanding Genesis*, p. 29.

7. Cassuto, 1:204. Also, RSV.

8. Speiser, *Genesis*, p. 29.

9. Cassuto, 1:207.

10. *BDB*, p. 1043.

11. *Ibid.*, p. 613. Also, Palache, p. 45.

12. Palache, p. 45.

13. *BDB*, p. 613.

14. *Ibid.*, p. 847. Also, Palache, p. 45.

15. *BDB*, p. 847.

16. Palache, p. 27.

17. Jastrow, p. 439.

18. Koehler and Baumgartner, p. 336.

19. שָׁעַע, 'šāʿaʿ, שָׁעָה, 'šāʿāh,' and שְׁעִי, 'šeʿê.'

20. Palache, p. 72.

21. This theory is substantiated by a number of words which convey both the concept of the "select" of society, expanded from those picked by God as His "agents" to include the ruling class and the concept of radiance and glow:

חֹר, 'ḥōr,' "nobleman," *BDB*, p. 359.

חָרַר, 'ḥārar,' "be aglow," Palache, p. 26.

שַׂר, 'śar,' "ruler, chieftain," *BDB*, p. 978.

שָׂרָה, 'śārāh,' "princess, noble lady, Sarah," *Ibid.*, p. 979.

שְׂרַי, 'śāray,' "brilliance, Sarai," H. L. Ginsberg, "Ugaritic Studies And The Bible," in *The Biblical Archeologist Reader* (Garden City, New York: Anchor-Doubleday and Co., paperback, 1964), 2:49.

שָׂרַר, 'śārar,' 'rule,' *BDB*, p. 979.

שָׂרַר, 'śārar' (Assyrian), "rise in splendor" (of sun), *Ibid.*, p. 977.

בָּרַר, 'barar,' "select, purify; make shining, polish," *Ibid.*, p. 141.

Finally, שׁוֹעַ, 'śô'a' (Palache, p. 72), a derivative of שָׁעָה, 'śā'āh' (שָׁעַע, 'śā'a'— שֵׁעִי, 'ś°'ê') is defined as "nobleman." S. Rin, "Ugaritic-Old Testament Affinities," *BZ* 11 (1967), 177.

22. The narrator described Cain's chagrin at having been rejected with the word חָרָה, 'ḥārāh.' The translations correctly interpret the sense of the word to mean "distressed" (Gen. 4:5, NJPS) or "angry" (Gen. 4:5, JPS and Chicago), but literally the word means "to glow" or "to burn" (Palache, p. 26). This word must have been chosen deliberately to highlight the element of light in the narrative: Abel "glowed" in the light of divine favor; and Cain "glowered" because of divine disfavor.

23. Ex. 34:29. The older JPS correctly interprets this verse as meaning that God talked to Moses, and not the other way around as in NJPS: "Since he had spoken with Him."

24. Ex. 34:30.

25. Ex. 24:18.

26. Ex. 32:1.

27. Ex. 32:28–29.

28. Ex. 34:34.

29. E. Robertson, "The Urim and Tummim: What Were They?" *VT* 14 (1964), 73.

30. G. Vermes, "The Torah Is A Light," *VT* 8 (1958), 437.

31. *BDB*, p. 210.

32. L. Ginzberg, 1:107.

33. *Ibid.* A similar premonition, reflecting a possibly concealed etymology of his name, appears in a closely related Arabic phrase: "She was bereft of her son." A. Guillaume, "Paranomasia in the O.T.," *JSS* 9 (1964), 282.

34. M. Dahood, *Psalms 1–50*, p. 238.

35. *Ibid.*

36. *BDB*, p. 662.

37. G. R. Castellino, "Genesis IV 7," *VT* 10 (1960), 443.

38. Gen. 4:7, NJPS.

39. Cassuto, 1:205.

40. JPS.

41. Chicago.

42. RSV.

43. Speiser, *Genesis*, p. 29. The word הֲלוֹא, 'hălô,' sometimes used as a negative in the English translation of שְׂאֵת, 'ś°'ēt,' has been left out intentionally.

44. This translation accords with the elucidation by Stanley Gevirtz, who renders יֶתֶר שְׂאֵת, 'yeter ś°'ēt,' as "pre-eminent in authority." "The Reprimand Of Reuben," *JNES* 30 (1971), 98.

45. C. Gordon, "Fratriarchy," *JBL* 54 (1935), 228.

46. *Ibid.*, 230.

47. Also, Speiser, *Genesis*, p. 29. ". . . sin shall be a 'rōbhēṣ' at your door; its

desire shall be for you, but you will be able to master it" (Cassuto, 1:205).
". . . sin is couching at the door, its desire is for you, but you must master it" (RSV).
". . . sin coucheth at the door, and unto thee is its desire, but thou mayest rule over it" (JPS). ". . . sin will be lurking at the door. And yet he is devoted to you, while you rule over him" (Chicago).

48. G. R. Driver, "Theological And Philological Problems In The Old Testament," *JTS* 47 (1946), 158–159.

49. Cassuto, 1:208.

50. *BDB*, p. 835.

51. I Kings 19:13.

52. Ex. 21:33.

53. Prov. 13:6, Job 14:16. I. Eitan, *A Contribution To Biblical Lexicography* (New York: Columbia University Press, 1924), pp. 38–41.

54. Both Speiser and Cassuto interpret רֹבֵץ, 'rōbēṣ,' as the noun "demon," while the other versions translate it as the verb "to couch, lurk." If חַטָּאת, 'ḥaṭṭā't,' is accepted as meaning "sin" and 'rōbēṣ' as the verb "to couch," there is grammatical discord between the feminine 'ḥaṭṭā't' and the masculine verb form of 'rōbēṣ' (Cassuto, 1:210.). But if the stem רבץ, 'rbṣ,' is seen as matching phonologically the Akkadian 'rābiṣum,' "demon" (Speiser, *Genesis*, p. 33), it may be concluded with Speiser and Cassuto that 'rōbēṣ' is an early loanword from the Akkadian with the meaning of "demon." The grammatical irregularity coupled with the similarity of 'rōbēṣ' to the Akkadian 'rābiṣum' would seem to indicate that the figure of a demon rather than the verb "couching" or "lurking" is the more accurate translation.

55. Gen. 4:7, NJPS. In the translations cited previously, three versions translate תְּשׁוּקָה, 'tᵉšûqāh,' as "desire," and another as "urge": the meaning, however, is probably the same: the demon will try to get Cain into his power (Cassuto, 1:212). The fifth version differs considerably by picturing the demon as devoted to Cain. Though Speiser translates 'tᵉšûqāh,' as "urge" (*Genesis*, p. 22), he does not advance an understanding of the phrase that much further because it is not known how "urge" fits into the framework of biblical psychology. With 'tᵉšûqāh' found in only two other instances in the Bible, efforts to learn what it means in these other passages are severely limited.

56. Gen. 2:18.

57. von Rad, p. 80.

58. L. Koehler, *O. T. Theology* (London: Lutterworth Press, 1957), p. 246.

59. *Ibid.*

60. Other translations of this passage are:

> And yet you shall be devoted to your husband,
> While he shall rule over you. (Chicago)
>
> Yet your desire shall be for your husband,
> And he shall rule over you. (RSV)

61. Gordis, *The Song of Songs,* p. 95.

62. *Ibid.*

63. The Arabic verb 'sâqa,' "drove, urged on," is the phonetic equivalent of שׁוּק, 'sûq,' the root of 'tᵉšûqāh.' G. R. Driver, *JTS* 47:158.

64. *Ibid.*

65. Deut. 19:5 in D. Daube, "Direct And Indirect Causation In Biblical Law," *VT* 11 (1961), 253.

66. Ex. 21:33–34.

67. Ex. 21:35.

68. Daube, *VT* 11:258.

69. Gen. 2:17, NJPS.

70. *BDB* (p. 40) construction is similar to Hos. 3:3, where JPS used the possessive.

71. As in Ex. 21:8, NJPS. If the narrator wanted to say that henceforth Adam would exercise authority over Eve, he would not have to use the emphatic הוא, 'hû',' "he": he simply would have omitted the word, leaving יִמְשָׁל, 'yimšāl,' to convey the sense of the third person, masculine, singular. But the narrator, by inserting 'hû',' wanted to convey the idea that *he,* Adam—and not Eve—would be doing something that Eve ordinarily would be expected to do. To render יִמְשָׁל־בָּךְ, 'yimšāl bāk,' as "and he shall rule over you" does not make much sense, for this situation would be the natural, anticipated consequence of God's punishment and not something that Eve would have been expected to do. Certainly this does deal with the exercise of authority, but it was not over Eve, even though such subordination was the ultimate result.

72. Here בָּךְ, 'bāk,' is not translated as "over you" or "through you" but as "through yours" or "through that which is yours."

73. The relationship between these two passages is disclosed by their identical sentence structure:

וְאֶל־אִישֵׁךְ תְּשׁוּקָתֵךְ וְהוּא יִמְשָׁל־בָּךְ
wᵉ'el 'îšēk tᵉšûqātēk wᵉhû' yimšāl bāk (Gen. 3:16)
וְאֵלֶיךָ תְּשׁוּקָתוֹ וְאַתָּה תִּמְשָׁל־בּוֹ
wᵉ'ēlèkā tᵉšûqātô wᵉ'atāh timšāl-bô (Gen. 4:7)

In the first part of both sentences the narrator specified to whom the 'tᵉšûqāh' would belong, and in the second half he emphasized who would exercise authority and how this would be done.

74. בּוֹ, 'bô,' "through his" ['tᵉšûqāh,' "urging," (understood)]

75. Cassuto, 1:213.

76. *Ibid.,* p. 214.

77. Speiser, *Genesis,* p. 29.

78. The shift in meaning developed from the sense of "to show" to the idea of "to speak." W. F. Albright, "Northwest Semitic Names in a List of Egyptian Slaves from the 18th Century, B.C.," *JAOS* 74 (1954), 229, n. 47.

79. Ps. 3:3. Dahood, *Psalms 1–50,* p. 15.

80. Ps. 11:1. *Ibid.,* p. 68.

81. The selection of אָמַר, ''āmar,' to express the idea of "to lie in wait" and not צָדָה, 'ṣādāh' (Ex. 21:13), or אָרַב, ''ārab,' reveals the narrator's sensitivity to literary style. First, there is the matter of prepositions. In those passages where ''āmar' should be translated "to eye" or "to lie in wait," a לְ, 'l,' introduces the object, as in לְנַפְשִׁי, 'lᵉnapšî,' in the example from the Psalms (Ps. 3:3 and 11:1). But in our Genesis verse, אֶל, ''el,' not לְ, 'l,' introduces the object. Why the change? The answer to this question quite possibly lies in the narrator's effort to construct out of the following a complete parallelism of form:

וַיֹּאמֶר קַיִן אֶל הֶבֶל אָחִיו ... וַיָּקָם קַיִן אֶל הֶבֶל אָחִיו

wayyō'mer qayin 'el hebel 'āḥîw . . . wayyāqām
qayin 'el hebel 'āḥîw
And Cain lay in wait for Hebel, his brother
. . . and Cain rose up against Hebel, his brother. (Gen. 4:8)

Aside from the verbs, the words in the two phrases are identical. Significantly, in the second phrase, the narrator departed again from the norm by replacing עַל, "al," by the rarely used אֶל, "el," found only in I Sam. 22:13 and 24:7, when used with קוּם, "qûm," to express "to rise up against" someone. These two rare instances of אֶל, "el," substituted for ל, "l," and עַל, "al," strongly suggest that the narrator deliberately wanted to achieve a stylistic effect. To attribute *both* usages to the carelessness of the redactor would be to strain one's credulity.

82. M. Dahood, "Hebrew-Ugaritic Lexicography I," *Biblica* 44 (1963), 296.

83. R. Gordis, "Commentary On The Text Of Lamentations," in *The Seventy-Fifth Anniversary Of The Jewish Quarterly Review* (Philadelphia: The Jewish Quarterly Review, 1967), p. 282.

84. Gen. 4:5, Chicago.

85. Sarna, p. 30.

86. *Ibid.*, p. 31.

87. Gen. 37:29f.

88. Daube, *Biblical Law*, p. 13.

89. Cassuto, 1:218.

90. Eitan, p. 57.

91. E. A. Speiser, "An Angelic Curse: Exodus 14:20," in *Oriental and Biblical Studies* (Philadelphia: University of Pennsylvania Press, 1967), p. 107.

92. *Ibid.*

93. *Ibid.*, p. 111.

94. Num. 16:32.

95. Num. 16:30.

96. *BDB*, p. 805.

97. The narrator probably used פֶּה, "peh," instead of פֶּתַח, "petaḥ," in this particular instance to personify the earth as swallowing the blood of Abel.

98. *BDB*, p. 473. The Chicago Bible also translated the word as "though."

99. *BDB*, p. 713.

100. *BDB*, p. 678.

101. *BDB*, p. 470.

102. H. A. Hoffner, Jr., "Second Millennium Antecedents To The Hebrew OB," *JBL* 86 (1967), 394.

103. *Ibid.*, 393.

104. *Ibid.*, 394.

105. *Ibid.*

106. *Ibid.*, 395.

107. KUB XV 31 obv ii 26, *Ibid.*, 390.

108. KUB X 63 obv 28, *Ibid.*, 391.

109. Odyssey XI 34–43, *Ibid.*, 392.

NOTES TO CHAPTER 7

1. Gen. 4:11 and Num. 16:30.
2. Cassuto, 1:220.
3. *Ibid.*
4. *BDB*, p. 631.
5. Speiser, *Genesis*, p. 31 (literal translation).
6. *BDB*, p. 626.
7. To regard Cain's spasticity as a manifestation of divine anger would go counter to common understanding of God's justice. Yet, within the context of biblical thought it conceivably could be argued that this condition was meant as a punishment. The head, hands, and legs could be punished if the hypothesis is correct that "the limbs and organs of a person were often thought of as, up to a point, forces in their own right" (D. Daube, "Direct and Indirect Causation in Biblical Law," *VT* 11 (1961), 255). This theory possibly is supported by an example from Deuteronomy in the case of a corpse found in the open countryside. Once it was determined which of the surrounding towns was nearest the corpse, the elders of that town had to undergo an elaborate ritual of purification that ended with the following declaration of innocence: "Our hands did not shed this blood, nor did our eyes see it done" (Deut. 21:7, NJPS). Here, hands and eyes seem to be considered forces in their own right. Applying this theory to the crime of Cain, the limbs and organs could be held culpable because the head, with its sense of sight, observed and planned, and the hands, calm and steady, wielded the weapon and later poured out the sacrificial blood to the אֲדָמָה, ''ădāmāh.'

The role of Noah as the second Adam is made even more apparent, observed Sarah Lynch, my editor, in a private communication, by comparing the crime of Ham with the crime of Cain. Both are symbolically the same, for both were guilty of stealing the 'nepeš' in their overpowering desire to become the 'ṣelem,' the agent of God, and both were frustrated in reaching their goal: Cain, by God's preventative measure and Ham, by Noah's cursing of Canaan.

8. Onians, p. 238.
9. *Ibid.*, p. 121.
10. *Ibid.*
11. *Ibid.*, p. 108.
12. *Ibid.*, p. 111.
13. *Ibid.*, p. 123.
14. *Ibid.*, p. 125.
15. *Ibid.*
16. *Ibid.*, p. 232.
17. *Ibid.*, p. 233.
18. *Ibid.*, p. 130.
19. Aeschylus, *The Suppliant Women* (London: George Allen and Unwin Ltd., 1930), p. 49.
20. Onians, p. 234.
21. H. P. Smith, *The Book of Samuel—The International Critical Commentary*, (Edinburgh: T. and T. Clark, 1st. ed., 1899, 1961), p. 281.
22. Equally as convincing as these Scriptual references is the evidence from the Hebrew language itself. This relationship between the head and limbs of the body

and the transmission of the life-seed is expressed in the words גֻּלְגֹּלֶת, 'gulggōlet,' "skull," and קָדְקֹד,'qādqōd,' "head, crown of head." Stemming from the root גלל, 'gll' (*BDB*, p. 164 and Palache, p. 19), are 'gulggōlet,' "skull" (*BDB*, p. 166), גַּלְגַּל, 'galggal,' "bowl, jar" (Palache, p. 19 and Dahood, "Hebrew-Ugaritic Lexicography II," *Biblica* 45 (1964), 399), and גֻּלָּה, 'gullāh,' "basin, bowl" (*BDB*, p. 165). The Akkadian 'gulgullu,' "skull," also denoting a "container shaped like a human skull" (Dahood, *Biblica* 45:399), reflects in a single word this relationship between "skull" and "jar" or "container." From the root כדד, 'kdd,' come כַּד, 'kad,' "jar," and כָּדוֹד, 'kidôd,' "child, son" (*Ibid.*, 46:327). Schematically, the etymological equation looks like this:

'gulggōlet,' "skull"—'galggal,' "jar"

'kad,' "jar"—'kidôd,' "child"

On one side there is a connection between "skull" and "jar"; on the other, a connection between "jar" and "child." With "jar" as the common meeting point, "skull" and "child" reveal a hitherto unsuspected relationship.

This theory linking the head with generativity is corroborated further by the relationship between 'qādqōd,' "head," and 'kidôd,' "child." Their roots, כדד, 'kdd,' and קדד, 'qdd,' are identical in sound, differing only in their initial consonants, which can be interchangeable in some cases (Gesenius-Kautzsch, p. 38). Thus, etymologically 'kidôd' and 'qādqōd,' "head," are related to each other in Hebrew thought.

Even within the same word there is evidence of this relationship:

ראש, 'rō'š,' "head"
רוש, 'rûš,' "to be abundant" (G. D. Driver, "Studies in the Vocabulary of the Old Testament," *JTS* 31:278). Alike in root structure (*Ibid.*), 'rō'š,' "head," the agent for abundant progeny, equals 'rûš,' the resulting abundance of children.

23. *BDB*, p. 283.
24. *BDB*, p. 282.
25. Dahood, *Biblica* 44:295; and Jastrow, p. 75.
26. Jastrow, p. 110.
27. M. Tsevat, "Some Biblical Notes," *HUCA* 24 (1952–53), p. 110; and M. Delcor, "Two Special Meanings Of The Word יָד In Biblical Hebrew," *JSS* 12 (1967), 234–235. Although Delcor would be inclined to derive יָד, 'yād,' "phallus," from a special Semitic root 'yd' or 'wd,' "to love" (p. 239), he does list as analogies to the use of the word "hand" for "phallus" such biblical Hebrew euphemisms as "feet," "flesh," "instrument," "wing" or "pinion," and "finger" in rabbinical Hebrew (p. 237). In addition he cites the Ugaritic 'yd,' "hand," as possibly having been used as a euphemism for the Ugaritic 'yd,' "phallus" (pp. 238–239).
28. von Rad, p. 103.
29. Cassuto, 1:222.
30. *Ibid.*
31. Also, Chicago and Speiser's *Genesis*.
32. I. Efros, J. Kaufman, B. Silk, *English-Hebrew Dictionary* (Tel-Aviv: Dvir Publishing Co., 1947), p. 620.

33. Jastrow, p. 1049.
34. *BDB*, p. 730.
35. Palache, p. 53.
36. Gen. 4:7.
37. *BDB*, p. 670.
38. Cassuto, 1:222.
39. *Ibid.*, p. 223.
40. Gen. 4:16.
41. Dahood, *Psalms 51–100*, p. 253.
42. *ANET*, p. 196.
43. *Ibid.*

NOTES TO CHAPTER 8

1. Cassuto, 2:5.
2. For a detailed examination of similarities and differences, cf. Heidel, pp. 260–269 and Cassuto, 2:16–23. The hypothesis that the Mesopotamian Flood story and *Gilgamesh Epic* might well have been the model for the biblical Deluge story is strengthened by the discovery of cuneiform fragments of the story at Megiddo and Ugarit. M. E. L. Mallowan, "Noah's Flood Reconsidered," *Iraq* 26 (1964), 62, n. 3.
3. L. Woolley, *Excavations at Ur* (London: Ernest Benn Ltd., 1954), p. 35.
4. L. Woolley, "Stories Of The Creation And The Flood," *PEQ* 88 (1956), 18.
5. Woolley, *Excavations at Ur*, p. 36.
6. Mallowan, who worked at Ur of the Chaldees from 1925 to 1930, asserts that the Mesopotamian Flood was not to be regarded as a world-wide, or even country-wide, catastrophe, no matter how deep the impression it made upon the minds of contemporaries. M. E. L. Mallowan, "Mesopotamia," in *Archeology and O. T. Study*, D. W. Thomas, ed. (Oxford: Oxford University Press, 1967), p. 91. Consequently its legends are not necessarily related to the flood stories found in other parts of the world. Mallowan, *Iraq* 26 (1964), 63.
7. J. Bright, "Has Archeology Found Evidence Of The Flood?" in *The Biblical Archeologist Reader I* (Anchor: Garden City, New York: Doubleday and Co., 1961), p. 37.
8. A. Parrot, *The Flood And Noah's Ark* (London: SCM Press Ltd., 1955), p. 52. In Mallowan's opinion, the presence or absence of flood-traces depends entirely on the topography of each individual city. *Iraq* 26:77, n. 43.
9. L. Cottrell, *The Land of Shinar* (London: Souvenir Press, 1965), p. 133.
10. Mallowan, *Iraq* 26:81.
11. Heidel, p. 240.
12. *Ibid.*
13. Sarna, p. 48.
14. Cassuto, 2:77.
15. *Ibid.*, p. 88.
16. Thomas Mann, *Joseph and His Brothers* (New York: Alfred A. Knopf, 1945), p. 29.
17. Thera, the ancient name of the island, has been officially revived; it is derived from Theras, the leader of the Dorian colonists who occupied the island in the

Geometric period. The alternative name Santorin (Santorini) dates back to the Venetian occupation after the Fourth Crusade. J. V. Luce, *Lost Atlantis* (New York: McGraw-Hill Book Co., 1969), p. 213.

18. J. Mavor, Jr., *Voyage To Atlantis* (New York: G. P. Putnam's Sons, 1969), p. 31; A. G. Galanopoulos and E. Bacon, *Atlantis* (Indianapolis: The Bobbs-Merrill Co., 1969), pp. 133–134. In addition to Mavor's authoritative report on the technical aspects of deepwater sounding and its application to the waters of Thera and the east Mediterranean, the reader will find in *Atlantis* the thesis, based on geophysical data, for locating the Ancient Metropolis of Atlantis at Thera (Santorin) and the Royal City of Atlantis in Crete. J. V. Luce in *Lost Atlantis* (p. 204) identifies the city and island of Atlantis with Knossos and Crete, arguing that "lost Atlantis" as a historical rather than a geographical concept meant the destruction of Crete, the Minoan heartland. Nicholas Platon, while presenting additional archeological data linking Plato's Atlantis with Crete, concludes that the principal center of Atlantis bears less resemblance to Knossos than to Phaistos in the south of Crete. *ZAKROS—The Discovery of a Lost Palace of Ancient Crete* (New York: Charles Scribner's Sons, 1971), pp. 312–320.

19. Galanopoulos and Bacon, pp. 125–128, 131.

20. S. Marinatos, "The Volcanic Destruction of Minoan Crete," *Antiquity* 13 (1939), 430 and 438.

21. Mavor, p. 67.

22. A petrified skull of a monkey, unearthed on the island of Thera, is thus far the only evidence of a living creature that perished in the catastrophe following the eruption. A. N. Poulianos, "The Discovery of the First Known Victim of Thera's Bronze Age Eruption," *Archeology* 25 (1972), 229–230.

23. Mavor, p. 99.

24. Galanopoulos and Bacon, p. 116.

25. Mavor, p. 98.

26. *Ibid.*

27. *Ibid.*, p. 62.

28. *Ibid.*, p. 64.

29. E. Engle, *Earthquake!* (New York: The John Day Co., 1966), p. 79.

30. Euripides, *Hippolytus,* 1198–1212, as quoted by J. V. Luce, p. 146.

31. W. Sullivan, *New York Times,* February 16, 1969.

32. "The Eruption of Krakatoa and Subsequent Phenomena," *Report of the Krakatoa Committee of the Royal Society* (London: Trübner and Co., 1888), p. 26.

33. *Ibid.*, p. 26.

34. Mavor, p. 52.

35. *Ibid.*, p. 61.

36. R. Graves, *The Greek Myths,* 1:139. Luce, pp. 202–203, writes: "The historical basis for the Deucalion story is probably to be sought in Boeotia, where the Copaic Lake certainly inundated some settlements in the second millennium. The inundation could have been brought on by excessive rainfall, and by the blockage of natural and artificial outlets by earthquakes, and both these events could be synchronous with stages in the Thera eruption." Also, cf. Galanopoulos and Bacon, p. 192.

37. Cassuto, 2:67.

38. *Ibid.*, p. 66. Tur-Sinai agrees with Cassuto in that he relates יָבָל, 'yābāl,' יוּבָל, 'yûbāl,' and יַבּוֹל, 'yibbôl,' all derivatives of יָבַל, 'yābal,' to מַבּוּל, 'mabbûl' in *The Book of Job* (Jerusalem: Kiryath Sepher Ltd., 1957), p. 241.

39. Isa. 30:25, 44:4.

40. *BDB*, p. 385.

41. *Ibid.*, p. 164.

42. *Ibid.*, p. 990.

43. *Ibid.*, p. 991.

44. A tablet found at ancient Ugarit describes how a seismic wave smashed into the Syrian coast in the second millennium B.C.E.; and another tablet tells of another seismic wave that levelled the port of Ugarit around 1370 B.C.E. Galanopoulos and Bacon, p. 192.

45. To translate יָם, 'yām,' as "sea" or "west" would be to no advantage; no new information would be added, for a seismic wave naturally would come from the sea, which at the same time is in the west.

46. Gaster, p. 114.

47. M. K. Wakeman, "The Biblical Earth Monster in the Cosmogonic Combat Myth," *JBL* 88 (1969), 314–316.

48. Cassuto, 1:36, 50.

49. Wakeman, p. 317.

50. Mavor, p. 64.

51. Mavor, in a private communication.

52. Mavor, p. 66.

53. Mavor, in a private communication.

54. Verse 13 (NJPS) begins: "I have set My bow in the clouds. . . ."

55. G. Thomas and M. M. Witts, *The Day The World Ended* (New York: Stein and Day, 1969), p. 104.

56. *Ibid.*, p. 116.

57. *Ibid.*

58. *Ibid.*, p. 276.

59. From a conversation with Dr. Mavor.

60. Gen. 9:15.

61. H. Wexler, "Radiation Balance Of The Earth As A Factor In Climatic Change," in *Climatic Change* (Cambridge, Mass.: Harvard University Press, 1965), p. 95.

62. *Ibid.*, p. 102.

63. *Ibid.*, p. 103.

64. R. C. Sutcliffe, *Weather and Climate* (New York: W. W. Norton and Co., 1966), p. 168. That climate can be altered in a relatively brief period of time by increased atmospheric dust is shown to be a possibility in a study of the effects of a huge but weak dust storm that hit Phoenix, Arizona on the evening of July 29, 1972. The data suggests that "the likely effect of increasing the dust content of the atmosphere would be to produce a warming trend at the earth's surface." S. B. Idso, "Thermal Radiation from a Tropospheric Dust Suspension," *Nature* 241 (1973), 449.

65. R. Carpenter, *Discontinuity in Greek Civilization* (Cambridge, England: Cambridge University Press, 1966), p. 18.

66. *Ibid.*, p. 60.

67. *Ibid.*, pp. 60–61.

68. Mavor, p. 181. This possibility is supported by Leon Pomerance, who makes a strong case for changing the date of the Thera eruption and collapse to 1200 B.C.E. in "The Final Collapse of Santorini (Thera)," *Studies In Mediterranean Archeology* (Göteborg: Paul Aströms Forlag, 1970), XXVI. I am grateful to Dr. Mavor for bringing this paper to my attention.

69. R. J. Lifton, "On Death And Death Symbolism: The Hiroshima Disaster," *Psychiatry* 27 (1964), 203.

70. *Ibid.,* p. 204.

71. R. J. Lifton, *Death In Life* (New York: Random House, 1967), p. 68.

72. *Ibid.,* p. 22.

73. *Ibid.,* pp. 22–23.

NOTES TO THE APPENDIX

1. Speiser, *Genesis,* p. 36.

2. Rashi, the medieval rabbinical exegete, admits the possibility of this interpretation when he makes it a point to specify that Cain, not Enoch, was the builder (*Pentateuch and Rashi's Commentary,* p. 19). Driven by vanity, Cain wanted to immortalize his name by building cities as monuments to himself (Ginzberg, 1:115).

Cassuto rejects Rashi's interpretation and understands the text to designate Enoch as the city-builder:

Cain knew his wife, and she conceived and bore Enoch, who became a city-builder; and he called the name of the city after the name of his son, Enoch. (Cassuto, 1:228)

3. *BDB,* p. 747.

4. Gen. 49:11.

5. F. Zimmermann, "קִיר,עִיר And Related Forms," in *The Seventy-Fifth Anniversary Volume Of The Jewish Quarterly Review* (Philadelphia: The Jewish Quarterly Review, 1967), p. 592.

6. *BDB,* p. 124.

7. W. F. Albright, *History, Archeology and Christian Humanism* (New York: McGraw-Hill Book Co., 1964), p. 151.

8. H. Te Velde, *Seth, God of Confusion* (Leiden: E. J. Brill, 1967), p. 14.

9. Lev. 11 and Deut. 14.

10. M. H. Gottstein, "After Thought and the Syntax of Relative Clauses in Biblical Hebrew," *JBL* 68 (1949), 37.

11. *BDB,* p. 335.

12. Cassuto, 1:231.

13. Gen. 34:2.

14. Num. 13:6.

15. II Sam. 10:2.

16. S. Rin, "Ugaritic-Old Testament Affinities," *BZ* 11 (1967), 179.

17. Cassuto, 1:232.

18. *Ibid.,* p. 232.

19. *BDB,* p. 562.

20. *Ibid.*

21. *Ibid.,* p. 383.

22. Cassuto, 1:233 and Speiser, *Genesis,* p. 36.

23. *BDB,* p. 607.

24. *Ibid.,* p. 982.

25. L. Koehler, "Problems in the Study of the Language of the Old Testament," *JSS* 1 (1956), 20.

26. *Ibid.*

27. Ex. 21:23–25.

28. Cassuto, 1:243.

29. *Ibid.,* p. 233.

30. *Ibid.*

31. *BDB,* p. 568.

32. *Ibid.,* p. 557.

33. W. L. Moran, "The Hebrew Language in its Northwest Semitic Background," in *The Bible and the Ancient Near East* (Garden City: Doubleday and Co., Anchor, 1965), p. 68.

34. Cassuto, 1:234.

35. *BDB,* p. 723.

36. *Ibid.,* p. 852.

37. von Rad, p. 107.

38. *BDB,* p. 384.

39. R. North, "The Cain Music," *JBL* 83 (1964), 380.

40. *Ibid.,* p. 379.

41. Cassuto, 1:238.

42. W. F. Albright, *Archeology and the Religion of Israel* (Baltimore: The Johns Hopkins Press, 1946), p. 98 as quoted by R. North, p. 380.

43. *Ibid.,* 381.

44. Cassuto, 1:196.

45. *Ibid.,* p. 201. Cassuto presents an extended list of examples to justify this rendition and conclusion.

46. According to midrashic interpretation, Seth was born after the generation of Lamech. L. Ginzberg, *The Legends of the Jews,* 1:120–121.

47. *BDB,* p. 60.

48. G. R. Driver, *Canaanite Myths and Legends* (Edingburgh: T. and T. Clark, 1956), p. 135.

49. S. Rin, p. 180.

50. Cassuto, *Genesis,* 1:198 f.

51. Gordon 76, iii, 6 f. as cited in P. Katz, "The Meaning of the root קנה." *JSS* 3–5 (1952–54), 128.

52. *BDB,* p. 467.

53. Gen. 42:11, 19, 31, 33, 34.

54. Cassuto, *Genesis,* 1:280.

55. *BDB,* p. 921.

56. R. H. Pfeiffer, *History of New Testament* (New York: Harper and Bros., 1949), p. 75.

57. To cite just a few examples: Dahood, *Psalms 1–50,* p. 301; von Rad, pp. 69–70; E. Jacobs, p. 307.

58. Dahood, *Psalms 1–50,* p. 301.

59. J. Muilenberg, "Usages of Particle כי in the Old Testament," *HUCA* 32 (1961), 143; and Dahood, *Psalms 1–50,* p. 301.

60. Dahood, *Psalms 1–50,* p. 223.

61. *BDB*, p. 535.

62. Cassuto, 1:233.

63. *Ibid.*, p. 255.

64. Gen. 49:3–4. The Deuteronomic law (Deut. 21:15–17) abrogating the power of the father to choose arbitrarily a first-born from among his sons in no way invalidates this theory, for it was promulgated to prevent the bulk of an estate from being transferred to another son on the basis of favoritism; here the moral issue probably would not be a factor.

65. I. Mendelsohn, "On The Preferential Status Of The Eldest Son," *BASOR* 156 (1959), 40.

66. Cassuto, 1:272.

GLOSSARY

AKKADIAN (ACCADIAN). Defined nowadays as the North-East branch of the ancient Semitic family of languages, this Mesopotamian cuneiform system is called after the city of Akkad, the center of the Akkadian kingdom, which flowered briefly under Sargon around the middle of the second millennium B.C.E. From Sargon's time on, southern Mesopotamia was known as Sumer and Akkad, with Sumer designating the more Sumerian south and Akkad the more Semitic north. Long after the Akkadian dynasty was displaced, Akkadian survived as an international written language until the sixth century B.C.E.

ASSYRIA. Geographically, Assyria occupied a small district in northern Mesopotamia, bounded by the Tigris valley on the west, the mountains of Armenia and Kurdistan on the north and east, and the Lower Zab on the south. Historically, however, it had firmly established its foothold on the shores of the Mediterranean by 850 B.C.E., its domain extending over the entire Fertile Crescent, from the Persian Gulf to the Egyptian border. After the death of Ashurbanipal (629 B.C.E.?), the Assyrian empire began to shrink steadily until a coalition of the Chaldeans of the Persian Gulf area and the Medes, living east of Assyria, brought the Assyrian empire to an end when its forces overran the capital city of Nineveh in 612 B.C.E.

BABYLONIA. The first period of Babylonian supremacy began with Hammurabi (1792-1750 B.C.E.) and lasted until 1600 B.C.E., when the Kassites assumed control after a Hittite invasion of the city. From then on, the delta region of Mesopotamia failed to produce any real center of power, although there was considerable maneuvering for leadership among a number of important cities. Babylon came under the yoke of the Assyrians in 744 B.C.E., remaining subservient until 626 B.C.E. when Nabopolassar, with the help of the Chaldeans, was crowned king of an independent Babylon. In 605, Nebuchadnezzar II extended his domain over most of the vast Assyrian empire; and in 586 he destroyed Jerusalem, carrying off into exile many of its leading people. After the death of Nebuchadnezzar in 561, the power of the Babylonians ebbed to the point where they were subdued by Cyrus of Persia in 539.

CANAAN. Greater Canaan, consisting of Palestine, western Syria, and Lebanon, was the focal point of the great powers of Egypt, Hatti, and Mesopotamia. Here the many political and cultural trends met—and often clashed. When the Hebrews established themselves in the hill country of Palestine in the second half of the second millennium, they adopted the script of the conquered Canaanites, adding later their own refinements.

156

DEUCALION. Upon the advice of his father Prometheus, Deucalion constructed an ark and thus survived the flood sent by Zeus to destroy an overbearing and violent mankind. Continuous rain caused the rivers and sea to rise so rapidly that the whole world was flooded except for a few mountain peaks. The ark floated for nine days and finally came to rest on Mt. Parnassus, or, according to other accounts, on Mt. Aetna, or Mt. Athos, or Mt. Othrup, where Deucalion disembarked with his wife Pyrrha and the pairs of male and female animals.

GILGAMESH EPIC. This beautiful poem, discovered in the palace library of the Assyrian king Ashurbanipal (seventh century B.C.E.) contains the best preserved and most extensive Babylonian account of the deluge. The eleventh of the twelve tablets relates how Ea thwarted the decision of his fellow gods to destroy all the inhabitants of the city of Shurippak by appearing to Utnapishtim in a dream and instructing him to build a vessel for himself, his family, and the various species of animal life. After being battered by a rainstorm lasting six days and nights, the ship grounded on Mt. Nisir, east of the Tigris. Thereupon, Utnapishtim sent out a dove, a swallow, and a raven to determine how much the waters had abated. When the raven did not return, Utnapishtim, with his family and the animals, left the ship.

HITTITES (HATTI). Coming from the interior of Europe or Asia, the Hittites extended their dominion over the whole of central Turkey during the second millennium. Their status as a world power was confirmed when around 1600 B.C.E. they marched to Babylon, thereby precipitating the collapse of Hammurabi's dynasty, and then prevented further Egyptian penetration into Syria. The kingdom of the Hittites finally crumbled, never to recover, around 1200 B.C.E. under the large-scale onslaught of migrating peoples from the northwest.

MASORETES. Jewish scholars, principally from the Palestinian school at Tiberius, established by the end of the ninth century the model for all copyists of the Bible, thus ensuring the accurate transmission of the standard Hebrew biblical text. This work has come to be known as the Masoretic text (MT). The Masoretes divided the biblical text into sections, paragraphs, and verses, added vowel signs beneath the Hebrew consonants to vocalize the text, established accents as musical notes for cantillation and as a guide for sentence division, and noted all inconsistent spellings, alternative readings, and other peculiarities in the text.

MESOPOTAMIA. The name given by the Greeks to the long wedge of land between the Tigris and Euphrates Rivers.

MIDRASH. The Hebrew term for "expounding" or "inquiry" became the post-biblical generic name for the form of exegetic exposition appended to biblical verses. As a major type of rabbinic literature, written and compiled from the second to about the twelfth century, Midrash often is characterized by highly imaginative embellishments of the scriptural text. The midrashic collection on Genesis is entitled *Bereshit Rabbah* (Genesis Rabbah).

MINOAN CIVILIZATION. A precursor of classical Greece, this ancient civilization flourished mainly on the island of Crete. Between 1950 and 1350 B.C.E. the Minoans had established trade relations with Sicily, Greece, Asia Minor, Egypt, Syria, and Phoenicia. The decipherment of the Minoan script (Linear A) reveals a close relationship with the West Semitic language spoken in Phoenicia.

MYCENAEANS. Founded by Greek-speaking peoples who entered mainland Greece sometime after 1900 B.C.E. from the Balkans or further east, the Mycenaean civilization flourished from about 1650 to about 1125 B.C.E. About 1400

B.C.E. the martial Mycenaeans, called Achaeans by Homer, became the rulers of Knossus, the capital of Crete, creating thereafter a joint Minoan-Mycenaean culture in Crete. Around 1100 B.C.E. the Mycenaeans fell before the Dorians, Greek-speaking invaders from the north.

NA'AMAN. The title of Adonis, the Syrian deity of vegetation, whose death was mourned particularly at the river Adonis.

RASHI. An acronym of Rabbi Solomon bar Isaac of France, 1040–1105, whose commentaries on the Bible and Talmud rank as the greatest in Jewish exegesis.

SUMERIA. From the northeast of Mesopotamia the non-Semitic Sumerians (ca. 3500 B.C.E.) pressed forward into the alluvial plain of southern Mesopotamia, where they established in the wealthy city-states of Ur, Uruk, Kish, Eridu, and Lagash the earliest civilization in the ancient Near East. Shortly after 3000 B.C.E. the Sumerians developed a system of writing from pictographs to create the world's first great written language and literature. This cuneiform script survived through temple schools long after it ceased to be a spoken language and was studied up to the third century B.C.E. With the establishment of the Akkadian kingdom around 2300 B.C.E., followed by the invasion of the Amorites (ca. 2000) from the Syro-Arabian desert, the Sumerians never reestablished their hegemony over Lower Mesopotamia.

TALMUD. A vast compilation of Jewish Oral Law with rabbinical elucidations, elaborations, and commentaries in contradistinction to the Scriptures or Written Law. Its two divisions are the Mishnah, the Hebrew text of the Oral Law, and the Gemara, the Aramaic commentary on the Mishnah. The Talmud records the discussions over a period of about eight centuries by the scholars working in the academies in Palestine and Babylonia. The Palestinian school produced the Talmud Yerushalmi around the fifth century, and the Babylonian school produced the Talmud Babli, the authoritative work, about the sixth century.

UGARIT. On the northern coastal area of Canaan, facing the northeastern point of what is now Cyprus, stood the Phoenician city of Ugarit, the cultural intermediary in the second millennium between Egypt, Mesopotamia, Asia Minor, and Crete. Excavations in Ras Shamra, a mound beneath which ancient Ugarit lies buried, reveal that about 1500 B.C.E. this city had begun to develop a simplified system of writing with letter symbols, thereby eliminating the need to learn the hundreds of hieroglyphs and cuneiform symbols. These thirty letters, following the same order of the later Hebrew alphabet, made it possible—at least in theory—for everyone to master the art of reading and writing.

ZOHAR. This "Bible" of kabbalists is composed of several literary units written by different people. The largest unit, the Zohar proper, is a mystical commentary on the Pentateuch, written in Aramaic by Moses de Leon, a Castilian kabbalist, who died in 1305.

Volcanic Terms

CALDERA. This Spanish term for "caldron" is a basin-shaped depression at the summit of a volcano, formed by the collapse of the empty magma chambers. Most calderas extend to more than a mile in diameter and reach depths of a thousand or more feet.

DUST, VOLCANIC. Very fine particles of less than one hundredth of an inch in diameter are ejected by a volcano and blown into the upper atmosphere, where they travel for months over thousands of miles.

MAGMA. This hot rock material in a liquid or semiliquid state is called "lava" when it emerges from a fissure or volcano.

PUMICE. A highly porous, glassy volcanic rock, formed from viscous magmas expanded by gas. Some varieties, light enough to float on water, have been known to drift thousands of miles before becoming waterlogged and sinking.

SEISMIC SEA WAVE. Known also by the Japanese word "tsunami," meaning "large waves in harbors," this ocean wave can be generated by a submarine landslide set off by faulting or a submarine volcanic eruption. Racing between three hundred and six hundred miles per hour and extending from sixty to one hundred and twenty miles, these sea waves slow down in the shallow coast waters, as they drag along the sea bottom, and then pile up to heights of forty feet or more as they crash ashore.

VOLCANO. A vent in the earth's surface through which hot melted rock, rock fragments, gases, and vapors are erupted.

BIBLIOGRAPHY

Ackroyd, P. R. "The Hebrew Root באש." *JTS*, N. S. 1–2 (1950–51), 31–36.
Aeschylus. *Eumenides*. The Loeb Classical Library, vol. 2. New York, 1930.
———. *The Suppliant Women*. London, 1930.
Albright, W. F. *Archeology and the Religion of Israel*. Baltimore, 1946.
———. *History, Archeology, and Christian Humanism*. New York, 1964.
———. "Northwest Semitic Names in a List of Egyptian Slaves from the Eighteenth Century B.C." *JAOS* 74 (1954), 222–233.
———. *Yahweh and the Gods of Canaan*. New York, 1969.
Allen, D. C. *The Legend of Noah*. Urbana, Illinois, 1963.
The Babylonian Talmud (English). 18 vols. London, 1935.
Bachelard, G. *The Psychoanalysis of Fire*. London, 1964.
Bailey, J. "Initiation And The Primal Woman In Gilgamesh And Genesis 2–3." *JBL* 89 (1970), 137–150.
Barr, J. *Comparative Philology And The Text Of The Old Testament*. Oxford, 1968.
Bassett, F. W. "Noah's Nakedness And The Curse Of Canaan—A Case Of Incest?" *VT* 21 (1971), 232–237.
Biggs, R. D. *ŠÀ. ZI. GA—Ancient Mesopotamian Potency Incantations*. Locust Valley, New York, 1967.
Blank, S. H. "The Curse, Blasphemy, the Spell, and the Oath." *HUCA* 23, pt. 1 (1950–51), 73–95.
Brichto, H. C. "The Problem Of 'Curse' In The Hebrew Bible." *JBL Monograph Series* 13 (1963).
Bright, J. "Has Archeology Found Evidence Of The Flood?" In *The Biblical Archeologist Reader I*. Garden City, New York, 1961.
Brown, F.; Driver, S. R.; and Briggs, C., eds. *A Hebrew and English Lexicon of the Old Testament*. Oxford, 1962.
Büchler, A. *Studies In Sin And Atonement*. New York, reprinted 1967.
Campbell, E. F., and Freedman, D. N., eds. *The Biblical Archeologist Reader II*. Garden City, New York, 1964.
Carpenter, R. *Discontinuity in Greek Civilization*. Cambridge, England, 1966.
Cassuto, U. *The Documentary Hypothesis*. Jerusalem, 1961.
———. *A Commentary on the Book of Genesis*. 2 vols. Jerusalem, 1964.
Castellino, G. R. "Genesis IV 7." *VT* 10 (1960), 442–445.
The Complete Bible. An American Translation. Translated by J. M. Powis Smith and E. J. Goodspeed. Chicago, 1949.
Cottrell, L. *The Land of Shinar*. London, 1965.

Dahood, M. "Hebrew-Ugaritic Lexicography I." *Biblica* 44 (1963), 289–303.
——. "The Phoenician Contribution To Biblical Wisdom Literature." In *The Role Of The Phoenicians In The Interaction Of Mediterranean Civilizations.* Beirut, 1968.
——. *Psalms 1–50.* Anchor Bible, vol. 16. Garden City, New York, 1966.
Dalglish, E. R. *Psalm Fifty-One In The Light Of Ancient Near Eastern Patternism.* Leiden, 1962.
Daube, D. "Direct And Indirect Causation In Biblical Law." *VT* 11 (1961), 246–269.
——. *Studies in Biblical Law.* Cambridge, England, 1947.
Delcor, M. "Two Special Meanings Of The Word יד In Biblical Hebrew." *JSS* 12 (1967), 230–240.
De Tolnay, C. *Michelangelo, The Sistine Ceiling.* Princeton, 1945.
Driver, G. R. "Theological And Philological Problems In The Old Testament." *JTS* 47 (1946), 156–166.
Efros, I.; Kaufman, J.; Silk, B. *English-Hebrew Dictionary.* Tel Aviv, 1947.
Ehrman, A. "A Note On עשי In Mic. 6:14." *JNES* 18 (1959), 156.
Eichrodt, N. *Man in the Old Testament.* Chicago, 1951.
Eissfeldt, O. *The Old Testament.* New York, 1965.
Eitan, I. *A Contribution To Biblical Lexicography.* New York, 1924.
Engle, E. *Earthquake!* New York, 1966.
"The Eruption of Krakatoa and Subsequent Phenomena." *Report of the Krakatoa Committee of the Royal Society.* London, 1888.
Fenichel, O. *The Collected Papers of Otto Fenichel.* New York, 1953.
Fensham, F. C. "Father and Son as Terminology for Treaty and Covenant." In *Near Eastern Studies In Honor Of William Foxwell Albright.* Baltimore, 1971.
Galanopoulos, A. G., and Bacon, E. *Atlantis.* Indianapolis, 1969.
Garnett, D. *Two By Two—A Story of Survival.* New York, 1964.
Gaster, T. *Thespis.* Garden City, New York, 1961.
Gerstenberger, E. "Covenant And Commandment." *JBL* 84 (1965), 38–51.
Gevirtz, S. "The Reprimand Of Reuben." *JNES* 30 (1971), 87–98.
Ginsberg, H. L. "Ugaritic Studies And The Bible." In *The Biblical Archeologist Reader II.* Garden City, New York, 1964.
——. "Lexicographical Notes." In *Supplements To Vetus Testamentum.* Leiden, 1967.
Ginzberg, L. *The Legends Of The Jews.* 7 vols. Philadelphia, 1909–1938.
Good, E. M. *Irony In The Old Testament.* Philadelphia, 1965.
Goodenough, E. R. *Jewish Symbols in the Greco-Roman Period.* 13 vols. New York, 1956.
Gordis, R. "Commentary On The Text Of Lamentations." In *The Seventy-Fifth Anniversary Of The Jewish Quarterly Review.* Philadelphia, 1967.
——. "The Knowledge Of Good And Evil In The Old Testament And The Qumran Scrolls." *JBL* 76 (1957), 123–138.
——. *The Song of Songs.* New York, 1954.
——. "Studies In The Relationship Of Biblical And Rabbinic Hebrew." In *Louis Ginzberg Jubilee Volume.* New York, 1945.
Gordon, C. H. "Fratriarchy in the Old Testament." *JBL* 54 (1935), 223–231.
——. *Ugaritic Literature.* Rome, 1949.

———— . *The Common Background of Greek and Hebrew Civilizations.* New York, 1965.

Gottstein, M. H. "After Thought and the Syntax of Relative Clauses in Biblical Hebrew." *JBL* 68 (1949), 35–47.

Graves, R. *The Greek Myths.* 2 vols. Baltimore, 1955.

Graves, R., and Patai, R. *Hebrew Myths.* Garden City, New York, 1964.

Greenfield, J. "Lexicographical Notes 1." *HUCA* 29 (1958), 203–228.

Greenstone, J. *Proverbs.* Philadelphia, 1950.

Grossman, R.; Sachs, H.; and Segal, M. H. *Compendius Hebrew-English Dictionary.* Tel-Aviv, 1947.

Guillaume, A. *Hebrew and Arabic Lexicography.* Leiden, 1965.

———— . "Paranomasia in the O. T." *JSS* 9 (1964), 282–290.

Heidel, A. *The Gilgamesh Epic and Old Testament Parallels.* 2nd ed. Chicago, 1963.

Herbert, D., and Pardossi, F. *Kilauea: Case History Of A Volcano.* New York, 1968. The glossary terms relating to volcanos were taken from this book.

Hoffner, H. A., Jr. "Birth and Name-Giving in Hittite Texts." *JNES* 27 (1968), 198–203.

———— . "Second Millennium Antecedents To The Hebrew Ob." *JBL* 86 (1967), 385–401.

———— . "Symbols For Masculinity And Femininity." *JBL* 85 (1966), 326–334.

The Holy Bible (RSV). New York, 1953.

The Holy Scriptures (JPS). Philadelphia, 1917.

Honeyman, A. M. "Merismus In Biblical Hebrew." *JBL* 71 (1952), 11–18.

Idso, S. B. "Thermal Radiation from a Tropospheric Dust Suspension." *Nature* 241 (1973), 448–449.

Jacob, E. *Theology Of The Old Testament.* New York, 1958.

Jastrow, M. *A Dictionary of the Targumim, the Talmud Babli and Yerushalmi, and the Midrashic Literature.* New York, 1950.

Jung, C. G. *Symbols of Transformation.* New York, 1956.

Katz, P. "The Meaning of the Root קנה." *JJS* 3–4 (1952–54), 126–131.

Kautzsch, E. *Gesenius' Hebrew Grammar.* Oxford, 1949.

Kitchen, K. A. *Ancient Orient and Old Testament.* Chicago, 1968.

Koehler, L. *O. T. Theology.* London, 1957.

———— . "Problems in the Study of the Language of the Old Testament." *JSS* 1 (1956), 3–24.

Koehler, L., and Baumgartner, W. *Lexicon In Veteris Testamenti Libros.* Leiden, 1948–1953, 1958.

Kosmala, H. "The Term *Geber* in the Old Testament and in the Scrolls." In *Supplements To Vetus Testamentum.* Leiden, 1969.

Kraeling, E. G. "The Significance And Origin of Gen. 6:1–4." *JNES* 6 (1947), 193–208.

Lifton, R. J. *Death In Life.* New York, 1967.

———— . "On Death And Death Symbolism: The Hiroshima Disaster." *Psychiatry* 27 (1964), 191–210.

Luce, J. V. *Lost Atlantis.* New York, 1969.

Mallowan, M. E. L. "Noah's Flood Reconsidered." *Iraq* 26 (1964), 62–82.

Mann, T. *Joseph and His Brothers.* New York, 1945.

Marinatos, S. "The Volcanic Destruction of Minoan Crete." *Antiquity* 13 (1939), 425–439.

McCarthy, D. J. *Treaty And Covenant.* Rome, 1963.

McKenzie, J. L. *Myths and Realities.* Milwaukee, 1963.

Mendelsohn, I. "On The Preferential Status Of The Eldest Son." *BASOR* 156 (1959), 38–40.

Mendenhall, G. E. *Law And Covenant In Israel And The Ancient Near East.* Pittsburgh, 1955.

Midrash Rabbah. English trans. 10 vols. London, 1939.

Milgrom, J. "A Prolegomenon to Leviticus 17:11." *JBL* 90 (1971), 149–156.

Miller, J. M. "In the 'Image' and 'Likeness' of God." *JBL* 91 (1972), 284–304.

Morgenstern, J. "The Mythical Background of Psalm 82." *HUCA* 14 (1939), 29–126.

Muilenberg, J. "Usages of Particle כי in the Old Testament." *HUCA* 32 (1961), 135–160.

Neiman, D. "The Date and Circumstances of the Curse of Canaan." In *Biblical Motifs.* Cambridge, Mass., 1966.

New English Bible. New York, 1970.

North, R. "The Cain Music." *JBL* 83 (1964), 373–389.

Noth, M. *Leviticus.* London, 1965.

Odets, C. "The Flowering Peach." In *The Best Plays of 1954–1955.* New York, 1955.

Onians, R. B. *The Origins of European Thought.* Cambridge, England, 1954.

Palache, J. L. *Semantic Notes On The Hebrew Lexicon.* Leiden, 1959.

Parrot, A. *The Flood And Noah's Ark.* London, 1955.

Patai, R. "Hebrew Installation Rites." *HUCA* 20 (1947), 143–225.

———. *Man and Temple.* London, 1947.

Pedersen, J. *Israel: Its Life and Culture.* 4 vols. London, 1964.

Pentateuch and Rashi's Commentary. New York, n. d.

Platon, N. *ZAKROS—The Discovery of a Lost Palace in Ancient Crete.* New York, 1971.

Pomerance, L. "The Final Collapse of Santorini (Thera)." In *Studies In Mediterranean Archeology.* Göteborg, 1970.

Pope, M. H. "The Word שחת in Job 9:31." *JBL* 83 (1964), 269–278.

Poulianos, A. N. "The Discovery of the First Known Victim of Thera's Bronze Age Eruption." *Archeology* 25 (1972), 229–230.

Pritchard, J., ed. *Ancient Near Eastern Texts Relating to the Old Testament.* 2d ed. Princeton, 1955.

Rad, G. von. *Genesis.* Philadelphia, 1961.

Rin, S. "Ugaritic-Old Testament Affinities." *BZ* 7 (1963), 22–33.

———. "Ugaritic-Old Testament Affinities." *BZ* 11 (1967), 174–192.

Robertson, E. "The Urim and Tummim; What Were They?" *VT* 14 (1964), 67–74.

Saggs, H. W. F. "The Branch To The Nose." *JTS*, N. S. 11 (1960), 318–329.

Sarna, N. M. *Understanding Genesis.* New York, 1966.

Seligman, P. "Some Notes on the Collective Significance of Circumcision and Allied Practices." *JAP* 10 (1965), 5–21.

Simpson, C. A. "Exegesis of Genesis." In *The Interpreter's Bible.* New York, 1952.

Skinner, J. *A Critical and Exegetical Commentary on Genesis.* New York, 1910.

Smith, H. P. *The Book of Samuel.* 1899. Reprint. Edinburgh, 1961.

Speiser, E. A. "An Angelic 'Curse': Exodus 14:20." *JAOS* 80 (1960), 198–200.
———. *Genesis*. Anchor Bible, vol. 1. Garden City, New York, 1964.
———. "YDWN, Gen. 6." *JBL* 75 (1956), 126–129.
Stern, H. S. "The Knowledge of Good and Evil." *VT* 8 (1958), 405–417.
Sutcliffe, R. C. *Weather and Climate*. New York, 1966.
Te Velde, H. *Seth, God of Confusion*. Leiden, 1967.
Thomas, D. W. ed. *Archeology and O. T. Study*. Oxford, 1967.
Thomas, G., and Witts, M. M. *The Day The World Ended*. New York, 1969.
The Targums of Onkelos and Jonathan Ben Uzziel on the Pentateuch. English trans. 1862. Reprint. New York, 1968.
The Torah (NJPS). Philadelphia, 1962.
Torczyner, H. (Tur-Sinai). "Semel Ha-qin'ah Ha-maqneh." *JBL* 65 (1946) 293–302.
Tsevat, M. "Some Biblical Notes." *HUCA* 24 (1952–53), 107–114.
Tur-Sinai, N. H. *The Book of Job*. Jerusalem, 1957.
Twain, M. *Letters From The Earth*. Greenwich, Conn., 1963.
Vermes, G. "The Torah Is A Light." *VT* 8 (1958), 436–438.
Wakeman, M. K. "The Biblical Earth Monster in the Cosmogomic Combat Myth." *JBL* 88 (1969), 313–320.
Webster's New International Dictionary of the English Language. Springfield, Mass., 1913.
Weinfeld, M. "Traces of Assyrian Treaty Formulae in Deuteronomy." *Biblica* 46 (1965), 417–427.
Wexler, H. "Radiation Balance Of The Earth As A Factor In Climatic Change." In *Climate Control*. Cambridge, Mass., 1965.
Wiener, N. *God and Golem, Inc.* Cambridge, Mass., 1966.
Woolley, L. *Excavations at Ur*. London, 1954.
———. "Stories Of The Creation And The Flood." *PEQ* 88 (1956), 14–21.
Zimmermann, F. "עִיר. קִיר and Related Forms." In *The Seventy-Fifth Anniversary Volume Of The Jewish Quarterly Review*. Philadelphia, 1967.
The Zohar. English trans. 5 vols. London, 1956.

INDEX OF BIBLICAL CITATIONS

INDEX OF PRINCIPAL HEBREW WORDS

169

INDEX OF SUBJECTS

172